Inspir

Women
Every Day

One-year devotional
by women for women

CWR

The readings in this compilation were originally published 2005, 2008 by CWR as bimonthly Bible-reading notes, *Inspiring Women Every Day*, as January/February, March/April, May/June, July/August, October, November/December 2005 and May 2008.

First published in this format 2011 by CWR, Waverley Abbey House, Waverley Lane, Farnham, Surrey GU9 8EP, UK. Registered Charity No. 294387. Registered Limited Company No. 1990308.

For a list of National Distributors visit CWR's website: www.cwr.org.uk

Unless otherwise indicated, all Scripture references are from the Holy Bible: New International Version (NIV), copyright © 1973, 1978, 1984 by the International Bible Society.

Other versions used: CEV: Contemporary English Version c 1995 by American Bible Society

TLB: *The Living Bible*, © 1971, 1994, Tyndale House Publishers

The Message: Scripture taken from *The Message*. Copyright © 1993, 1994, 1995, 1996, 2000, 2001, 2002. Used by permission of NavPress Publishing Group.

Concept development, editing, design and production by CWR

Cover image: Getty Images/amanaimagesRF

Printed in Finland by Bookwell

ISBN: 978-1-85345-620-6

Contents

Having spent long periods of time overseas with young children, separated from family and friends, I came to rely more on God's Word than perhaps I ever had before. My thirst for teaching, fellowship and the Bible was acute and God, being God, certainly provided endless ways and opportunities for that thirst to be quenched. Through reading the living Word of God each day, my faith grew and my trust in God's never-ending, unconditional love deepened: I was truly sustained by the Bread of Life.

What a joy it is, therefore, for me now to be introducing readers all around the world to this special collection of readings and meditations, written by twelve wonderful women of God. I know that whatever your circumstances – whether surrounded by countless friends and family and gasping for a moment's peace and quiet, or in a somewhat solitary situation longing for fellowship and assurance – these words will sustain you, strengthen you and deepen your knowledge of God's love for you.

One of those 'key passages' for me was Proverbs 3:1–8; do take a few moments to read it. I pray you will experience God making your paths straight as you learn to trust Him with your whole heart.

Lynette

Lynette Brooks
Director of Publishing

God's long
view

Rosemary Green

Rosemary Green is the wife of a supposedly retired Anglican clergyman, mother of four and grandmother of 14. She enjoys trying to bring the Bible to life in a culture that is largely biblically illiterate. She also loves seeing God at work in changing people's lives, and used to do a lot of pastoral counselling. Her book *God's Catalyst* was written to help pastors use the Bible and prayer sensitively and wisely. Nowadays she spends more time helping in her fairly small local church in whatever way she can.

WEEKEND

God's long view

For reflection: Colossians 3:1–17

D o you make New Year's resolutions? Or don't you dare, afraid you will break them by January 3?

I have a suggestion. Instead of saying, 'This is what I plan to do,' ask, 'What do I want God to do in me?' That puts a whole new light on the possibility of success! I love Philippians 2:12–13, where Paul wrote, 'work out your salvation with fear and trembling, for it is God who works in you to will and to act according to his good purpose'. That does not mean that I have to work to earn my salvation, nor do I just sit back and wait for Him to do it all. No, I work out the fruit of my salvation by co-operating with God's work in me.

We can go one better. If it is God who works in me to *will* and to *act* in ways that please Him, my question becomes 'Lord, what do You want to do in me?' That has even more chance of fulfilment! If I let Him set the goal *and* give the power – well, that seems to be a recipe for success!

Take time to reflect on Colossians 3:1–17, and the implications of the 'new self' in verse 10.

A dysfunctional **family**

Joseph, famous for his technicolour dreamcoat, is our topic this month. His family background is a sad one. Rivalry was the name of the game. It started with his parents. His father, Jacob, cheated his twin Esau out of their dying father's special blessing, so he had to flee from his furious brother. Jacob travelled to his uncle Laban's home where he fell in love with his beautiful cousin Rachel. (Does this sound like a fairy story? No, it's true, 40 centuries ago!) He worked for seven years as his uncle's shepherd to win his bride, but the cheater was cheated; Jacob found himself married to the plain older sister before he could marry the beautiful Rachel.

Worse was to follow. Leah bore Jacob four sons, while Rachel was barren. This added to the rivalry and tension in the home. In desperation, Rachel offered her personal maid to sleep with Jacob, and two boys were born, which Rachel claimed as her own. (Surrogate motherhood is nothing new.) Leah copied, with her own maid. Two more boys, Leah's 'sons'. Then Leah herself conceived again, and two more boys and a girl arrived.

Those eleven children grew up in an atmosphere of disharmony, with the seeds of discontent sown in the next generation. The best foundation for a child's birth is the love between the parents, overflowing in the conception of a baby who is wanted for himself or herself, who is loved without strings, who can grow up in a climate of love and harmony. How different it was in Jacob's family! Cheating, suspicion, jealousy, no peace and little love. How could Jacob's offspring develop happily in such a climate?

Genesis 29:31–30:13

'When Rachel saw that she was not bearing Jacob any children, she became jealous of her sister.' (30:1)

For prayer and reflection

Think of one family you know with broken relationships; pray for that family, and for emotional stability for the children.

The pain of **infertility**

Genesis 30:17–24

'[Rachel] became pregnant and gave birth to a son and said, "God has taken away my disgrace." ' (v.23)

Recently I was with a couple who had just celebrated their sixteenth wedding anniversary. They had almost given up hope of having a child – but now Eric is over a year old! What a joy he is to them! I think of other couples who have conceived against all apparent odds, after many years of barrenness, but also of those who have endured years of fruitless IVF treatment or who have experienced the sadness of successive miscarriages.

This may be your own grief, or it may be that of others you know. Many readers can sympathise with Rachel, Jacob's favourite wife, as she watched her sister bearing one child after another, yet stayed infertile herself. The misery of her barrenness was exacerbated by her sister's taunts, as well as by the public disgrace in a culture where a woman's role in society was to bear children.

Then at last – a son! But instead of undiluted joy over her child we sense that she was more concerned with herself than with her son. 'God has taken away my disgrace,' she said. Joseph's name even means, 'May he add'. Not content with one child, she immediately wanted more to satisfy her own needs. It is easy to load our personal ambitions onto our children for our own sakes. We all want them to do well, but we should not pressurise them to follow in our successful footsteps, nor to compensate for our own failures. I did this with my own daughters. 'Succeed where I succeeded' in playing the piano. 'Make up for my disappointments as a Girl Guide by getting numerous badges.' That attitude may obstruct them from developing in the way that God wants for them.

For prayer and reflection

Lord, please give the comfort of Your love and Your presence to any who are struggling with the pain of infertility, and wisdom to all who are parents.

Family **favouritism**

We have four children, all adults now. We love them all – but when they were young they were rarely all nice at the same time! Four children, each one different in character and temperament, each one needing slightly different treatment. How easily that can lead to the charge of 'It's not fair!' How parents need heavenly wisdom!

Israel (Jacob's new God-given name) was certainly short of wisdom. He was blatant in his favouritism for the 17-year-old Joseph, older son of his favourite wife Rachel, who had died giving birth to Benjamin, the youngest (Gen. 35:18). The 'richly ornamented robe' was a mark of status and leisure. Who is going to do a dirty, practical job with long, wide sleeves that obstruct work and are easily soiled? It is not surprising that jealousy and hatred reared their ugly heads among Joseph's half-brothers.

Joseph felt their antagonism. So when he went with them to guard the sheep, he watched carefully – not just the sheep, but his brothers; not to learn the job, but to tell tales to his father.

What an unhappy family! The warning is clear, not only for parents, but also for anyone who is a leader at work, in church or in leisure activities. The Bible is uncompromising about God's attitude to favouritism. God Himself 'shows no partiality and accepts no bribes' (Deut. 10:17). He expects the same of us. 'Do not show partiality to the poor or favouritism to the great' (Lev. 19:15) and to church leaders he says, 'Do nothing out of favouritism' (1 Tim. 5:21).

Genesis 37:1–4

'... Israel loved Joseph more than any of his other sons ... he made a richly ornamented robe for him.' (v.3)

For prayer and reflection

Lord, please help me to love even the people I don't like, and to treat everyone fairly and with justice.

Spiritual **gifts misused**

Genesis 37:5–11

'Joseph had a dream, and when he told it to his brothers, they hated him all the more.' (v.5)

Dreams can have many sources. They may be the expression of inner turmoil, of hidden fears or unconscious hopes. Joseph's dreams were not just the wishful thinking of a spoilt young man, but God-given (as with another Joseph nearly 2,000 years later). The trouble was that Joseph had neither the wisdom nor the humility to know how to handle the situation. Instead of keeping it to himself, encouraged that one day his brothers would no longer boss him around, he bragged to them about his dream. 'My sheaf stood upright while your sheaves bowed down to mine.' Of course they were infuriated. No one knew that the dream would be fulfilled 20 years later, in a very different situation.

Joseph's next dream had a different image but a similar meaning, and it included his parents. Would Joseph keep quiet this time? Not a bit of it! He boasted to his father as well as his brothers. 'Stupid lad!' is what I feel about him. Of course his father rebuked him, not seeing that Joseph's behaviour was the fruit of his own folly.

We all need wisdom to learn how to handle any spiritual gifts God may give us. For instance, I sometimes have a 'hunch' about another person, and I am not sure whether its source is my observation, my experience, divine insight, or a combination of them all. What do I do? Do I talk about my flash of insight? Do I act on it? Do I chew it over quietly (like Jacob, who 'kept the matter in mind')? I must first ask God for wisdom for the next step. The insight may be given to guide my prayers for that person, not to talk about it. Joseph blundered in arrogantly, without stopping to think.

For prayer and reflection

Lord, please refrain me from acting impulsively or stupidly. Help me to listen to You.

Little sins **become big sins**

Joseph's half brothers were a selfish, callous group, united in their hatred of their father's pet. At home, under their father's eye, they kept quiet. Now, out in the country, no one could watch. (How does our own behaviour change when there are no observers?) The jealousy that ate away in their hearts erupted when they identified the distinctive colourful robe as Joseph approached. 'Now's our chance to get rid of him!' We can see how revenge, murderous intent, greed and deceit all grew from that root of jealousy.

It reminds me of a story our children loved when they were young. An African family found an orphan leopard cub and kept it as a pet. 'Isn't it sweet?' they said. They played with it, had rides on its back as it grew. 'Little leopards become big leopards, and big leopards kill,' their father often warned them. They saw no danger. 'He's our friend!' But one day the boy scratched himself in the jungle. The friendly animal went to lick his wounds. He tasted blood; the killer instinct took over, and the father was killed saving his child.

Our 'small' sins can be like that. We try to ignore them, but isolated incidents easily become normal, and bad habits grow. I think with shame of the first time I hit my two-year-old son in anger. 'I must never do that again,' I thought. But, sadly, my anger and violence became chronic. Over 20 years the 'private' sins ('Don't tell Daddy') became more public. I am deeply grateful (though I wasn't at the time) for the friends who finally confronted me, and enabled me to repent of the anger and to allow God's Spirit to destroy its roots.

Genesis 37:12–28

'Come now, let's kill him … and say that a ferocious animal devoured him.' (vv.19–20)

For prayer and reflection

Reflect on Jesus' words: 'There is nothing outside a person that by going in can defile, but the things that come out are what defile.' (Mark 7:15, NRSV)

WEEKEND

Dreams – and obedience

For reflection: Matthew 1:18–25; 2:9–15

There is another well-known Joseph in the Bible. He, too, had significant dreams. At Christmas we hear the familiar stories of Jesus' birth. Without Joseph's readiness to listen to God in his dreams, things might have worked out very differently for Jesus in His earliest days on earth.

Joseph was in a dilemma. His fiancée was pregnant, and he knew he wasn't the father. What was the most honourable thing to do? As he dreamt, an angel brought an astonishing message. Joseph was clearly a man of faith, for when he woke, he did as the angel had told him. Faith and obedience go hand in hand.

Another astonishing situation came several months later. Visitors from the East, probably astrologers, brought rich presents for the baby. What was happening? Joseph dreamt again. 'Go to Egypt.' Obedience meant another huge step of faith, with a 250-mile journey through barren countryside into the unknown. But Joseph again did what he was told. So did the wise men, when God spoke to them, too, in a dream.

They all listened to God, and they obeyed. Do we?

Responsibility and integrity

What an unusual situation! Here was a youth from another country, bought as a slave from foreign travelling merchants, put to work as an underling for a captain of Pharaoh's guard. Yet within a few years the slave was given full responsibility for running his master's household and his estate. Why was Joseph elevated so quickly? One hint comes in verse 6: 'He [Potiphar] did not concern himself with anything except the food he ate.' So long as Potiphar had his creature comforts he was happy to be relieved of any household responsibilities! But the main reason was that 'the LORD was with Joseph and he prospered' (v.2).

Whether Potiphar recognised that God had a hand in Joseph's success, we don't know. But he saw in the young man (still in his early twenties) a man of integrity, whom he could trust implicitly, under whose hand everything prospered. So he was willing to hand over all the financial and organisational reins.

The spoilt youth had to grow up fast. Two major factors influenced Joseph in the fast learning curve of his development. First, the shock of his brothers' attack and the journey to Egypt with the Midianite traders must have shaken him to the core. Such events can leave us traumatised, disabled, giving up hope. Or they can be used – as with Joseph – to bring new purpose, with a resolve to make the most of adverse circumstances. At the same time, it must have been good to be released from the jealousy and bickering of the family home.

I wonder if Joseph was aware of this new freedom that gave him the chance to develop in integrity and responsibility.

Genesis 39:1–6

'Potiphar put him in charge of his household, and he entrusted to his care everything he owned.' (v.4)

For prayer and reflection

Lord, I pray that when I am in the middle of traumatic times I will not lose hope. Please use the tough circumstances for my good, to change me in truth and integrity.

Integrity v. seduction

Genesis 39:7–20

'… though she spoke to Joseph day after day, he refused to go to bed with her or even to be with her.' (v.10)

Imagine the scenario! The handsome young bachelor steward, the absentee, gluttonous boss and his rich, bored wife. It was a recipe for disaster.

Joseph might have thought that he had come through his earlier troubles to a place of security in his new life. He had already proved his integrity in his work. Now it was his integrity in his personal ethics and his obedience to God that were being tested. He passed the test in his steady refusal to succumb to the woman's relentless enticement.

As we think about the relevance of this incident to our own lives, we could focus on the utterly up-to-date need for sexual purity in an age when promiscuity is the norm for many. But the challenge is wider than that, as we consider our ability to resist temptation of any sort – whether our particular weakness is eating chocolate, wasting time playing computer games, lavishing money on supposed 'bargains' in the sales, or anything else.

But Joseph, too, had his weak spot. His old arrogance was still alive. 'No-one is greater in this house than I am.' He was soon to be reminded of his master's superior authority. His character had developed enormously since he was his father's pet, but humility was still lacking, and God had not finished with him in his school of discipline. Potiphar quickly jumped to the wrong conclusion about the guilty party. In Egypt there was summary justice for slaves, no right of appeal for unfair dismissal. Into prison he went. Potiphar's status was high, in charge of the jail that housed the king's prisoners. But it was back to the bottom for Joseph.

For prayer and reflection

'… among you there must not be even a hint of sexual immorality, or of any kind of impurity, or of greed …'
(Eph. 5:3)

Unjust punctuation

'… the LORD was with Joseph and gave him success in whatever he did.' (v.23)

ow would you feel if you were in Joseph's shoes? Everything had been going so well, and now *bump*! Everything was stripped away: his job, his home, his comfort, his responsibilities, his status. It might have helped him if he could have read Peter's advice to Christian slaves, written 2,000 years later. There is nothing special in being patient and submissive when you receive a beating you deserve, Peter says (1 Pet. 2:18–20). 'But if you suffer for doing good and you endure it, this is commendable before God.' That is when Christian character shows. Peter goes on to point to Jesus' example. 'When they hurled their insults at him, he did not retaliate; when he suffered, he made no threats. Instead, he entrusted himself to him who judges justly.' (1 Pet. 2:23).

I first read those words when, as a 20-year-old student, a fairly new Christian, my testimony against my mother for her careless driving was instrumental in her being summoned to court. She was scared of the possible outcome, so it is not surprising that she was furious with me. During the six weeks between the summons arriving and the court appearance, I didn't just hold on to that verse. I (metaphorically) tied it round my waist with a secure knot, so that it held me firm. 'Jesus, please help me to keep quiet and not answer back, whatever she says.'

Joseph behaved like that, for 'the LORD was with him'. His behaviour quickly won the respect of the prison warder. His experience of responsibility in Potiphar's house stood him in good stead now. God was in control, working out His purposes for Joseph in unexpected ways.

Father, when I feel that I am getting a raw deal in life, please help me to trust Your sovereignty and to behave in a way that pleases You.

God and **dreams**

Genesis 40:1–15

'Then Joseph said
to them, "Do not
interpretations
belong to God?
Tell me your
dreams." ' (v.8)

We don't know how long Joseph was in prison. He had already earned the jailer's respect when 'some time later' (v.1) Pharaoh's butler and baker offended the king, were imprisoned, and assigned to his care. He then had 'some time' (v.4) to earn their trust before each had a vivid dream. Years earlier Joseph's dreams about his family (37:5–11) had led him into trouble. But he still trusted God about dreams, and was willing to put his faith on the line before these pagan men. 'Interpretations belong to God.'

The butler was happy about his dream, and he was quick to describe it. Joseph was very clear; the servant would soon be reinstated, and Joseph asked for a word to be put in Pharaoh's ear to gain his release. I like the polite way he put his request, without naming Potiphar and his wife or speaking of their lies and injustice. He embodies words that struck our home group recently. '... the Lord's servant must not quarrel; instead, he must be kind to everyone, able to teach, not resentful' (2 Tim. 2:24).

**For prayer and
reflection**

Do we understand from this that all dreams are God-given prophecies? Certainly not. Years ago, one of our church leaders turned all her dreams and her supposed prophetic words towards me. I was in a mess, and I needed ministry; but I did not need the abuse that this became. (As I remember this time, I am glad to find that I am no longer resentful about it. Forgiveness has cleansed the memory.) Most dreams come from our subconscious, and whenever we remember even part of a dream we can pray about it, and ask God if there is anything He wants to show us through the dream.

**Lord, I pray that
I may be open to
receiving Your
message (however
it comes),
obedient in my
response, and
gentle in passing
it on to someone
else.**

Out of sight, out of mind

Emboldened by hearing the good interpretation for the butler, the baker risked describing his frightening dream. But his fears were realised: 'No favours for you; in three days you'll be hanged.' Joseph's message was blunt. He told it as it was, but could he have been gentler? (How do you pass on bad news?) Both predictions were fulfilled at Pharaoh's birthday celebrations three days later.

I guess the butler rejoiced to be back in favour, back in his job, back with his family. But Joseph, with his request to be mentioned to Pharaoh and his hope of an early release, was forgotten. We can be quick to judge him for his 'forgettery': but before we do, think how easily we break our own promises. 'I'll phone you.' (Rosemary, you promised six months ago to phone Carol in America.) 'We'll fix a date for coffee.' (Rosemary, when are you going to contact Elizabeth?) But where I fall down most is on my promise to pray. 'Out of sight, out of mind' is too often true. (How different from St Paul! See Ephesians 3:15–16.) I like to pray straightaway, with the person concerned, rather than promise to pray later. I know my weak spot! A mixture of discipline and spontaneity can help and here are some hints. A regular prayer list is useful – and a ten-day cycle may overcome the possible staleness of 'It's Monday, so ... ' Try to pray as soon as you read a letter or email, or straight after a phone call. Keep a few letters or Post-it® notes in your Bible. And the scores of Christmas letters that are speed-read when they arrive go into a folder, to be read and prayed through during the year, a few each day.

Genesis 40:1–23

'He restored the chief cupbearer to his position … The chief cupbearer, however, did not remember Joseph; he forgot him.' (vv.21,23)

For prayer and reflection

Lord, please help me to remember the warning of the butler's forgettery, and to show my love for my friends by praying for them more regularly.

WEEKEND

God's loving discipline

For reflection: Hebrews 12:1–12

For most of us life has its ups and downs. Joseph's life was a constant roller-coaster; father's favourite, brothers' assaults, sold in slavery, household manager, summarily imprisoned, jailer's right hand man. In it all, he continued to trust God, but I doubt if he could easily make sense of the switchback of experience.

Hebrews 12:1–12 shows us God's perspective on Joseph's life. 'God disciplines us for our good, that we may share in his holiness.' The sovereign God uses events in our lives (specially the tough ones) to refine our characters. Two hard situations brought some of the most important changes ever in my own life. My husband's meningitis was God's opportunity to revive me after a long period of spiritual barrenness; and the painful breakdown of a close friendship enabled Him to spring clean a deep cesspool of anger. God the patient sculptor was using His chisel to make me more like Him.

Reflect on your own life, and the ways that God, our loving Father, has disciplined, trained and moulded you for good.

Free at last

Joseph waited – and waited – and waited for news of his release to come from the palace. Two years passed. Still silence. Then one night, Pharaoh had two vivid dreams. None of his many advisers could offer any clue about their meaning. The butler's memory was prodded at last. 'Joseph! I quite forgot about him! I *am* sorry!' It was an opportune moment for him to tell Pharaoh about Joseph, who was summoned to the palace, and quickly smartened himself up for the royal audience.

We don't know what went on in Joseph's mind and emotions during those two years. He enjoyed a status above the other prisoners, but he was still in prison. He could have harboured a huge grudge, refuelled by the butler's failure to get him freed. But his readiness to acknowledge to Pharaoh the source of his skill in interpreting dreams shows that he kept fresh with God. That is something we cannot do if we hang on to bitterness, which can destroy us like a cancer, growing secretly before its symptoms are evident.

I used to know very little about forgiveness. I would mumble the line in the Lord's Prayer about 'forgive us our trespasses, as we forgive ...' *Did* God forgive me? I wasn't sure. The butler, realising his guilt, needed to know he was forgiven. The reality of God's forgiveness came home to me when a friend showed me Isaiah 43:25: 'I, even I, am he who blots out your transgressions, for my own sake, and remembers your sins no more.' He blots out; He forgets. Wow! That took the weight of my very real guilt. And that truth has a partner. God forgives us, so we must forgive others. Joseph knew that, and lived it.

Genesis 41:1–16

'Then the chief cupbearer said to Pharaoh, "Today I am reminded of my shortcomings."' (v.9)

For prayer and reflection

Meditate on 'forgive whatever grievances you may have against one another. Forgive, as the Lord forgave you' (Col. 3:13). Lord, please help me with that inclusive word 'whatever'.

From **prison to power**

**Genesis
41:32–49,53–55**

'Since God has
made all this
known to you,
there is no-one so
discerning and
wise as you.' (v.39)

Joseph's conviction that God would show him what Pharaoh's dreams meant (v.16) was amply rewarded. It was very clear: seven years of abundant harvests followed by seven years of famine. God added a gift of wisdom to the gift of interpretation, and Joseph gave Pharaoh a definite plan for storing the reserves during the plentiful years, to prepare for the famine. Pharaoh was quick to recognise the young man's wisdom and its source. 'Can we find anyone like this man, one in whom is the spirit of God?'

I pray that my character, life and speech may so reflect Jesus that others might say the same of me. When we allow God's Spirit full reign in our lives He gradually changes us to make us more like Jesus. That change can be scary. I may not like the person I am now, but I have to choose between the familiar (but less good) and the unknown (but better). Spiritual surgery can be traumatic but fruitful!

As he became Prime Minister, Chancellor of the Exchequer and Minister of Agriculture all rolled into one, the change in Joseph's lifestyle was dramatic. Fine clothes, subservient only to Pharaoh, the king's signet ring (a mark of power for stamping official documents), obeisance from the people, and a new wife and two sons (whose names reflected the changes in his life). God's hand was in all this. It was not only for Joseph's personal advancement, but God entrusted him with the good of the people of Egypt and of the surrounding nations, to save them from starvation. As we continue to read his story we will have a chance to assess how far his inner change matched his success in power and responsibility.

For prayer and reflection

Father when You give me new responsibilities, I pray that I may allow Your Spirit full sway in my character and in my actions.

Old **wounds reopened**

Everything was going according to plan. Enormous quantities of grain had been stored, enough to feed the hungry Egyptians, with surplus to sell abroad. Joseph must have felt pretty satisfied with the way he was running the national economy. Then he had a shock. His brothers, whom he had not seen for over 20 years, arrived to buy food. He recognised them at once; not surprisingly they had no clue that this important 'Egyptian' in his finery was the teenage brother whom they had assaulted and sold into slavery.

Joseph was shaken as he remembered his early dreams and all that had happened. Why do you think he did not tell them immediately who he was? I think there was still pain in those memories, despite the success that God had given him since. With that pain came anger, and a desire for revenge. His attack on them would not be physical, but mental and emotional. People say, 'Time heals'. But time by itself does not heal. A wound can heal on the surface, leaving infection inside.

I was over 40 when I remembered an incident with my mother when I was six – a shopping excursion for clothes, when she offered me choice and then over-ruled it. I had long outgrown those clothes, but when I remembered the event, I was absolutely furious! There were probably many times when the child had felt unheard and squashed. All my hidden feelings of resentment burst out. It took six months of repeated prayers to forgive her before I could think of those clothes without anger. At last the wound was clean. We don't need to be afraid of asking God to reveal any hidden sore spots that He wants to heal.

Genesis 41:56–42:17

'Although Joseph recognised his brothers, they did not recognise him … [He] said to them, "You are spies!" ' (42:8–9)

For prayer and reflection

Father, I don't want to live with hidden anger. Please help me to forgive those who have hurt me, as Jesus and Stephen did even as they were dying.

Guilt rears its ugly head

Genesis 42:18–28

'… they turned to each other trembling and said, "What is this that God has done to us?" ' (v.28)

Joseph longed to see his 'little brother' Benjamin again (now in his twenties). His harsh attitude continued, but his softer side was emerging, as he worked towards awakening their guilt and, ultimately, towards reconciliation for the whole family.

His approach was clever. His first threat was, 'Just one of you can go home and collect the brother you claim you have, while the rest stay here in prison.' After they had spent three days in captivity, he modified this. 'Only one of you need stay, while the rest go back to feed your hungry families', but he insisted that next time they return with Benjamin. They must have breathed a sigh of relief at this measure of let-up, and Joseph was deeply moved as he listened in on their supposedly private conversation. I doubt if they had ever spoken to one another of the guilt they felt over their treatment of Joseph. Now they were jolted into admitting it.

I didn't think I would ever talk to my elderly mother about the shopping incident. (To say 'I forgive you' can be a backhanded way of saying 'I hope you realise …'.) But many years later the conversation turned that way. Her immediate reply was 'I've always regretted that. You would have looked sweet in the yellow coat' (the one I had wanted). She had been sitting on guilt for nearly 50 years! It was important that it came out in the open, so that I could assure her of my – and God's – forgiveness.

Joseph was generous. They left to go home with their donkeys laden, and their payment returned. When they found the silver in their sacks, that very generosity enhanced their guilt and stirred up their fear.

For prayer and reflection

Father, thank You that when we confess our sins, You are faithful and just to forgive us our sins and to cleanse us from all unrighteousness. (1 John 1:9)

Testing, testing, testing

**Genesis
43:15–34**

'… the men were
frightened when
they were taken to
his house.' (v.18)

The gap in our readings tells us about the men's return home, about Jacob's determination to hold on to Benjamin, and about each man finding his silver returned in his sack. When the food ran out, Jacob finally let Benjamin go to Egypt with them. They took double payment, with gifts of nuts and spices, leaving their distraught father alone.

Their arrival in Egypt was perplexing. They were taken to the governor's home! Fearing the same treatment they had given Joseph decades earlier, they protested their innocence about the silver to the steward. He told them, 'God gave it to you. I've got your payment.' Then Joseph came, checked up on Benjamin, disappeared again (to weep in private) and finally returned. The meal was served, with Benjamin's plate piled five times as high as anyone else's!

Did Joseph need to hide his real identity for so long? I'm not sure. While he was pretending to test the genuineness of their story he was actually testing their characters. Perhaps he was even testing himself, shocked by his own tears and emotions, unsure how he – and they – would react when he declared who he was. We are all complex people, and we often have mixed motives for our own behaviour. We never need to be afraid to ask God's Spirit to shine His searchlight into our soul to reveal the flaws. Uncomfortable it may be, but He wants to heal and strengthen us.

God's testing is always for our good and for our growth. 'No discipline seems pleasant at the time, but painful. Later on, however, it produces a harvest of righteousness and peace for those who have been trained by it' (Heb. 12:11).

**For prayer and
reflection**

**Father, I pray that
I may be open
to be examined
by You. I do not
want my own
complexities to be
a source of pain to
other people.**

WEEKEND

No need for retribution

For reflection: Romans 12:17–21

As we look at the way Joseph treated his family of half-brothers it is hard to discern his motives and what was going on in his mind. Did he enjoy seeing them squirm? Was he trying to break their spirit? Was he looking for signs of repentance? Was he trying to pave a way for reconciliation?

How might I have behaved if I had been in Joseph's shoes? I remember a time of intense anger against some friends whom I felt had betrayed and rejected me. I wanted reconciliation, yet at the same time I wanted to throw a brick through their window! We can have intense, opposing feelings simultaneously.

I learnt an important lesson at that time. Read again Romans 12:19, where Paul quotes: "'It is mine to avenge: I will repay,' says the Lord' (from Deut. 32:35). The word 'revenge' does not need to be in our vocabulary. If I think I have been wronged, I can trust God, the righteous Judge, to act with faultless justice and mercy. I can drop my anger. I have no need to act – except for good.

Lord, help me to pray with love for those who hurt me.

I'm **your brother!**

A t last! After another devious scheme to scare his brothers, to test their integrity and to ensure that Benjamin stayed with him, Joseph was ready to tell them who he was. Whatever his mixed emotions and motives may have been, one thing was absolutely clear to him. God was in ultimate control of his life in all its ups and downs. He says it three times: 'God sent me here to save lives.' He may not have been quite so sure of that when he was languishing in prison! But now he could see how God's good purposes had been worked out in bringing him to his position of influence.

I remember becoming sure that God is sovereign. During a turbulent time in my life I was speed-reading the book of Job (with intermittent understanding!). Then I came to Job 42:2. It was one of those rare moments when God takes His metaphorical highlighting pen: 'I know that you can do all things; no plan of yours can be thwarted.' To change the image, He hammered a huge stake of His reliability into the ground. I saw that there is no point in trusting a God who can be wrong even 2% of the time. He has to be a 100% God (even 110%!).

That doesn't mean to say that in this spoilt world He plans all the bad things that happen. When we see good coming out of a bad situation we don't have to say, 'Well, it wasn't really bad after all', or 'God planned that'. But God is a Redeemer, who can actually make use of wrong situations and weave them into His good purposes. That turbulent time of mine was largely of my own making. But God used it for transformation, for spring cleaning my life.

Genesis 45:1–18

'So then, it was not you who sent me here, but God.'
(v.8)

For prayer and reflection

Look back at your life and see how God has been in control, even when you could not recognise it at the time.

Father's journey, **father's joy**

**Genesis
45:25–46:7,
28–34**

'Do not be afraid
to go down to
Egypt, for I will
make you into a
great nation there.'
(46:3)

When Pharaoh heard the news about Joseph's family, he ordered for generous provisions to be sent to Canaan, and two-wheeled oxcarts to bring back all the families. The old man Jacob could hardly believe the news that his long-lost son was still alive, until he saw the carts, hard evidence to back their story. So he agreed to travel to Egypt, with all his dependants.

Today's readings contain two family traits seen in both Jacob and Joseph's lives, traits of spirituality and scheming that we might not expect to run concurrently. First, spirituality. When Jacob reached Beersheba, a place where others had met with God, he stopped to offer sacrifices. There God spoke to him directly, not for the first time in his life. He reassured Jacob that this journey would be good in every way, and in keeping with the promises made to Jacob's grandfather Abraham when He first called him to go to the land of Canaan (Gen. 12:2). Jacob, for all his weaknesses, was a spiritual man, as was his son Joseph.

But both were schemers, at times devious in their plans. Joseph chose five of his brothers as spokesmen (including, maybe, Reuben, Judah, Simeon and Benjamin). Then he armed them with words to say to Pharaoh (46:33–34). 'Tell them that you are shepherds; then you will get the best pasture lands.' Shepherds were anathema to the Egyptians, who would soon move away! Do you call this planning devious scheming or worldly (or heavenly) wisdom? It leads me to ask myself, before God, whether I am always as transparent and straightforward as I could be in all my plans, my words and my actions.

For prayer and reflection

What family characteristics, for good or ill, have you inherited? Which traits do you want to strengthen, which to lose?

Comfort and **security**

W hat a turnaround for Jacob and his sons from their situation a year earlier! Then, Jacob still mourned the loss of his son, and they all feared starvation. Now they had benefited from the king's generosity; one of their family was Prime Minister; they had property, grazing for their animals in the most fertile part of the country and ample food. They were comfortable and safe.

Genesis 47:1–12

'Pharaoh said to Joseph "… settle your father and your brothers in the best part of the land."' (vv.5–6)

Comfort and security are good for our physical wellbeing, and they usually bring relief from stress. But beware! They do not always enhance character or spirituality. Prosperous civilisations easily degenerate into decadence – the collapse of the Roman Empire is a notable example. For individuals, riches and comfort can slide into carelessness, slackness, thoughtlessness, idleness. Think of Joseph's former employer Potiphar and his wife, for example. Has your quality of character grown more in the easy or the tough times in your life? I remember a letter from a friend when, after an already long engagement, my marriage was to be postponed for a further year. She wrote 'This is the time when the iron enters into your soul.'

What about God's lessons for you? In my earliest years as a Christian I was excited by my new faith and its new opportunities, and I eagerly absorbed the rich teaching available. I grew like a plant in a hothouse. But it was later, in times of difficulty, that my roots went deeper, and God made the most lasting changes. I have referred to some of them in these notes.

Identify some of the ways He has changed you, both to encourage yourself, and to be ready to encourage others.

For prayer and reflection

Father, thank You for times when my life flows smoothly. But thank You even more for the rough patches You have used to teach me and change me.

Loyalty versus **compassion**

Genesis 47:13–26

'The land became Pharaoh's, and Joseph reduced the people to servitude, from one end of Egypt to the other.' (vv.20–21)

Joseph saw his family settled in the Nile delta, and then turned his full attention to his job of managing the land on his master's behalf. He was an opportunist, and he took full advantage of the famine to make Pharaoh even richer than he already was. We have to give Joseph Grade A for shrewdness, for business acumen and for loyalty to Pharaoh.

But, sadly, he appears totally lacking in compassion – Grade D. Look at the stages of deprivation for the Egyptians. First they spent all their money, then they gave their livestock to pay for food. In desperation they returned the following year. No money, no animals. So now they yielded not only their land but also their freedom, to become Pharaoh's slaves. They received grain to plant, seed which would not necessarily produce a crop in the drought. Even a fifth of that probably sparse crop was to be given back to the king, whose storehouses would be replenished. Joseph had the whip hand, and he showed no mercy.

Think of the saying 'Power corrupts; absolute power corrupts absolutely'. How far do you think that is true of Joseph? His honesty and his integrity appear unspoilt by his power. But it seems that his life experiences had made him a hard man (despite the tears we saw earlier). He was ruthless in his exercise of power.

It is good for us to stop and think of the situations in which we have power and authority over other people – at home, at work, in our church, even in our leisure interests. Are we hard and inflexible to those who are under us, or do we exercise our power with love and compassion, as well as with wisdom and justice?

For prayer and reflection

Lord, please fill me with Your love and wisdom. Help me to share that love with everyone, I meet, particularly those over whom I have any control.

Scars from the past

Jacob died with all his sons round him. He was treated like royalty, his body was carefully embalmed and – amazingly for a foreigner – there were two months of official mourning. Then, not only did Pharaoh accede to Joseph's request for leave to bury the body in the family tomb in Canaan, but many Egyptian dignitaries, as well as all the adults in Jacob's family, went too.

Back again in Egypt, Joseph's brothers were scared. Was Joseph's kindness to them only a front while their father was alive? They still found it hard to believe that Joseph would not take revenge. Their 20-year-old debris of guilt bred fear and mistrust. How often scars from the past blight our lives, whether it is the guilt of our own sins and failures or the effect on us of other people's mistakes. But God does not want us to live with the 'If onlys' of the past. While He cannot change the facts of past events, He can change the effects of those events. He forgives us. He wipes the slate clean (Isa. 43:25). He helps us to let go of any resentment against those who have wronged us (Col. 3:13). Those two directions of forgiveness clean the pus out of emotional wounds, and allow Him to heal us and change us. That was the difference between Joseph and the rest of his brothers. He was grieved at their continued mistrust, but he replied without anger, with assurance and kindness.

God still changes and heals people. I know how He has changed me deeply over many years, replacing diffidence with confidence and anger with love and patience (most of the time!). Can you look back and see how God has changed you?

Genesis 50:1–21

'What if Joseph holds a grudge against us and pays us back for all the wrongs we did to him?' (v.15)

For prayer and reflection

Father, thank You that You are a God who forgives us and changes us. Please continue Your work in me, however painful it may seem to be.

WEEKEND

An overview of Joseph's life

For reflection: Psalm 139

The following model of Joseph's life can be used for other character studies in the Bible.

Background: a sad family history of jealousy and disharmony, a poor atmosphere for a child's development.

Early life: a spoilt brat with spiritual gifts but no wisdom.

God's training: in a hard school: assault by his brothers, slavery, unjust imprisonment. Through it he grew in wisdom, integrity and patience.

Relationship with God: spiritual gifts showed early. Later he learnt to trust God's sovereignty and to forgive.

Main work: his leadership in Egypt, wise, shrewd and tough, enabled many people to survive the famine. Through it God was preserving Abraham's descendants.

Later years: were spent in peaceful obscurity as a family man.

Other Bible references: David told of God's faithfulness (Psa. 105:16–25); Stephen of the Israelites' rejection of God's servants (Acts 7:9–16); in Hebrews we read about faith in action (11:22). All cite Joseph as an example in their different slants on Israelite history.

Lessons to learn: God's sovereign hand in Joseph's life is outstanding, but each day's reading has brought us a new lesson. Which have been most relevant for you?

As you reflect on Psalm 139, thank God that He has His hand on your life.

Man of **faith**

**Genesis
50:22–26**

'... God will surely
... take you up
out of this land
to the land he
promised on oath
to Abraham, Isaac
and Jacob.' (v.24)

When I had the privilege of visiting the Holy Land in 1959, we were shown the immense tomb in Hebron where Abraham and his descendants (including Jacob) were said to be buried. Nearby was a separate tomb. 'That's Joseph's tomb. He came late!'

Joseph's dying words to his brothers expressed two convictions: that the Israelites would return from Egypt to the promised land of Canaan and that his bones would be buried in the family grave. Over four centuries later his expectations were fulfilled (Exod. 12:40). The Israelites went to Egypt as a family of 70 (Gen. 46:27); they left as a nation of over a million (Exod. 12:37), an unwieldy group for the journey but strong to conquer and colonise Canaan.

Joseph had no idea how long it would be before it all came about. It is intriguing to find him in the New Testament among a long list of men of faith. 'By faith Joseph, when his end was near, spoke about the exodus of the Israelites from Egypt and gave instructions about his bones' (Heb. 11:22). The man who could look back and see how God had been faithful in his own life, despite its many setbacks, could trust Him to fulfil His promises to the family who would become a nation and inherit a land.

We often think that faith is deficient if it doesn't see instant success, instant answers. That is not true. Faith may be in for a long haul. Perhaps, of all the lessons we have learnt from different incidents in Joseph's life, this is the most important. Our faith rests on an utterly trustworthy God who is all wise, all seeing, beyond time, whose big picture is not confined by our small perspectives.

For prayer and reflection

Father, I pray that You will enlarge my vision of Your all-encompassing faithfulness. May that affect the way I pray for myself and for others.

Daughters
of the King

Christine Orme

Chris Orme is an Anglican lay reader and works with her
husband, a non-stipendiary minister as part of the team in a
south Reading parish. They have four adult daughters and five
small grandchildren. Chris is a teacher by profession but having
been deafened 25 years ago, now tutors one-to-one from
home. She has many interests waiting to be fully pursued when/
if she retires but apart from the family, what she enjoys most is
writing for *Inspiring Women Every Day*.

Daughters of the King

Exodus 15:1–11,
19–21

'Then Miriam the prophetess ... took a tambourine ... and all the women followed her ... dancing.' (v.20)

For the rest of this week we shall look at four biblical prophetesses. Today's, Miriam, was Moses' sister, and other references to her roles as prophetess and leader appear in Numbers 12 and Micah 6. In this incident, the Israelites, fleeing from Egypt, have just experienced the miraculous crossing of the Red Sea and seen the pursuing Egyptian army destroyed. Naturally they are jubilant and praise God. Most of this chapter is Moses' song, but verses 20–21 describe how Miriam leads the women in worshipping God with singing and dancing.

In doing this, Miriam was fulfilling one of the functions of a prophet (we shall consider some of a prophet's other functions, too, this week) which was that of interpreting an historical event, to reveal God's hand in it and to emphasise to the people of Israel that God is sovereign and rules over history. Miriam's song has a slightly different emphasis from that of Moses. In verse 1, Moses says, '*I* will sing to the LORD' but Miriam's version is a command: '*Sing* to the LORD'. By her words and actions she urges the women to 'tell forth' God's greatness ('he is highly exalted') and His mighty acts ('The horse and its rider he has hurled into the sea').

The women respond. Picture the wonderful spectacle of a throng of women singing and beating their tambourines as an expression of their joy, and dancing their relief and gratitude to the God who has delivered them from slavery in Egypt. In this way the dance itself becomes prophetic – a 'telling forth' of what God has done.

Our lives of worship in the world can also be prophetic, 'telling forth' to those around us the greatness of our God. What a challenge.

For prayer and reflection

'Read by everybody ... you are a letter from Christ ... written not with ink but with the Spirit of the living God' (2 Cor. 3:2–3). Thank You, Lord.

Deborah – a **mother-figure**

Judges describes the period immediately after the Israelites entered the promised land following their wilderness wanderings. It's a dismal, repeated cycle of the Israelites rejecting God, enemy-oppression, the Israelites returning to God in despair and God raising up 'judges' to rescue them. Besides being a prophetess, Deborah, the only woman among these judges, was by any estimate remarkable. Her 'song' was written much earlier than the rest of the book; the prose version of her story is in Judges 4.

Deborah demonstrates another prophetic function – that of directing leaders and national affairs, a role which sat easily with that of judge. As our story opens, the Israelites are being terrorised by Jabin, a Caananite king, and his army under Sisera. Deborah orders Barak, an Israelite commander, to gather 10,000 men to oppose Sisera, promising (4:7) that God will give him victory. Motivated either by fear or by respect for Deborah, Barak refuses to act unless she accompanies him. She agrees, Israel's enemies are routed and Deborah's reputation enhanced.

What was Deborah's secret? The clue may be in that phrase 'mother in Israel'. By rejecting God's leadership the Israelites left themselves rudderless until God raised up Deborah. As well as settling disputes (4:5), we see from her conversations with Barak that she brought womanly qualities to her role, nurturing and directing Israel as mothers nurture and direct children. She was a trusted mother-figure – so her prophetic messages were heeded.

What does this say to us? That what we *are* is heard more loudly than what we *say*! We may have 'words from God' but they will be well received only if our lives reveal Jesus.

Judges 5:1–12, 20–27

'Village life in Israel ceased, ceased until I, Deborah, arose, arose a mother in Israel.' (v.7)

For prayer and reflection

'... **they took note that these men had been with Jesus' (Acts 4.13). Lord, may this be true of me today. Amen.**

Huldah – **God's mouthpiece**

'Because … you humbled yourself … and wept … I have heard you, declares the LORD.' (v.19)

The depressing catalogue of Judah's kings who 'did evil in the eyes of the LORD', is relieved only by Hezekiah and his great-grandson, the boy-king Josiah. In the 300 years since its dedication, Solomon's temple – built to honour the one true God – had been neglected, defiled by idolatrous Caananite worship, and its treasures stolen or sold. These were outward signs of national moral and spiritual decay and Josiah embarked on thoroughgoing religious reforms. He collected money for the repair of the temple (vv.4–7) and while those repairs were in progress, the high priest found (v.9) 'the Book of the Law' – probably Deuteronomy – which was read to the king.

Appalled at the extent of the nation's disobedience, Josiah sends a delegation to 'enquire of the LORD'. The high-ranking group goes, not to Jeremiah or Zephaniah, both well-known prophets, but to the prophetess Huldah, on whose authority the book was acknowledged as God's word to Israel. Huldah outlines God's anger and the disaster to come on this place and its people, because of their disobedience. She thus fulfils another prophetic role – warning of God's judgment, often with exhortations to repent and seek God's mercy. In Huldah's message there is mercy only for Josiah, because on hearing God's word he had spontaneously repented (vv.11,19).

Huldah spoke the truth as God had revealed it to her, apparently without regard for her own safety – prophets were not always well-treated if people took exception to their words! She did not 'water down' the message because of the status of those consulting her. She was clearly a woman of integrity and we can see why God used her as His mouthpiece.

'I have not hesitated to proclaim to you the whole will of God' (Acts 20:27). Lord, give me that same integrity in speaking of You. Amen.

Anna – **bridging the gap**

S everal women feature in Luke's account of the conception and birth of Jesus, but Anna is the only prophetess. She thus stands between the Old Testament prophetesses and Philip's four daughters (Acts 21:9), whose prophesying was an early manifestation of the spiritual gift of prophecy bestowed on the Church at Pentecost and discussed by Paul in 1 Corinthians 14.

Luke tells us that Anna was from the tribe of Asher, a northern tribe. This makes her the only person with family origins recorded in the New Testament who was not from Judah, Levi or Benjamin. She was old, but age had lessened neither her devotion to God nor the outward expression of that devotion. Her waking hours were spent in prayer and fasting. Living in God's 'house' and tuned in to Him, Anna recognised, as Simeon had done a little earlier (vv.25–35), that this baby in His mother's arms was the One who would bring 'redemption of Jerusalem', but, whereas Simeon's words to Mary were private, Anna 'went public'.

There were still those in Israel who believed God's promises of a deliverer and redeemer and who, like Simeon, were patiently waiting for Him to appear, even living as they did in an enemy-occupied country. Naturally, Anna knew these like-minded people and told all of them about this child whom the Holy Spirit had revealed to her. The spiritual gift of prophecy always encourages its hearers and glorifies Jesus – and Anna's words to those who were faithfully watching and waiting, did just that. Prophecy is a gift – but gifts can be cultivated or neglected. Anna clearly cultivated hers by being constantly in the Lord's presence and by the spiritual disciplines of fasting and prayer.

Luke 2:21–24, 36–39

'She never left the temple but worshipped night and day, fasting and praying.' (v.37)

For prayer and reflection

'For the testimony of Jesus is the spirit of prophecy' (Rev. 19:10). Reflect on these words today.

WEEKEND

Our God reigns!

For reflection: Isaiah 55:8–13
'"My thoughts are not your thoughts,
neither are your ways my ways," declares the LORD' (v.8).

God's thoughts and ways are different from ours! This opening verse of this passage of Isaiah 55 challenges us to trust the God who often works in ways entirely opposite to what we expect or would like. They also encourage us to realise that as we trust Him we shall see His purposes fulfilled and know the joy and peace (v.12) that only He can give. We may even experience His replacing of fruitless, useless things with ones that are beautiful and useful (v.13). God's promises will be made good as surely as season follows season (vv.10–11). Nothing can defeat His purposes.

Spend some time this weekend looking 'little and often' at these verses. Ask God to speak to you through them, especially if there are areas in your life at present where you can't understand what He is doing.

Next week we shall consider five women who were used by God to help bring about His purposes. As 'God's go-betweens', they were in the right place at the right time, apparently by accident – but God's ways are higher than ours!

The **watchful** sister

Moses' sister (possibly Miriam but she is not named and Moses could have had another sister) was *in the right place at the right time*! We are not told her age, but she was clearly too young to be employed as a slave like the adult Israelites and also too young to arouse suspicion or comment as she stood by the riverside. However, she was old enough to be left watching to see what happened to the baby brother that Jochebed, their mother (6:20), had left in the waterproofed basket in the reeds to avoid Pharaoh's cruel edict. She was also brave enough to approach no less a personage than the daughter of the Pharaoh, and quick-witted enough to use her initiative in offering to find a Hebrew wet-nurse for the baby.

We can imagine her rushing back to her mother to tell her that Pharaoh's daughter had found their baby – and wanted a nurse! So, by God's amazing overruling, Moses was restored to his family for a number of years (babies in that culture were not weaned until they were at least three or four years old), years in which no doubt he was taught about Israel's God, whom He would later serve so dramatically.

This intriguing little episode, like so many in the Bible, reminds us of God's sovereignty – the fact that God is in control not only of major world events but also of the details of our lives. Seemingly insignificant happenings or people become part of a chain in which God's purposes are worked out. Moses' sister here acted either instinctively or in obedience to Jochebed.

Either way, she was used by God to ensure that Moses grew up safely, to be used in his turn to deliver God's people from slavery.

Exodus 2:1–10

'Then his sister asked ... "Shall I go and get one of the Hebrew women to nurse the baby for you?"' (v.7)

For prayer and reflection

Lord, wherever I find myself today, help me to stay in touch with You so that I can be used in the working out of Your purposes. Amen.

Abigail **the peacemaker**

**1 Samuel
25:14–33**

'As she came riding … into a mountain ravine, there were David and his men descending towards her … ' (v.20)

At the time of this episode David was on the run from King Saul, who was determined to kill him. A band of outlaws had attached themselves to David and it appears that they made themselves useful by protecting local farmers' livestock from marauding gangs. Nabal, a wealthy local landowner, plans a sheep-shearing feast and David asks that his (600!) men be included as a reward for their efforts. Although Nabal's own men confirm the truth of David's claim (vv.14–16) Nabal boorishly refuses (v.11).

David's terse reaction is, 'Put on your swords!' and two thirds of his band go with him, intent on revenge. There would have been a massacre, as David himself confesses (v.34), had it not been for Abigail, Nabal's wife. She was clearly a complete contrast to her husband, listening to the servants (v.17) and acting decisively, rapidly collecting enough food for the whole of David's band before setting off to meet David himself.

Abigail too, was *in the right place at the right time* – and again we see God's hand at work, for the timing of her encounter with David is remarked upon (vv.21–22). Her gracious humility, her womanly tactic of assuming that David will behave honourably (when actually he is furiously bent on revenge!) and her words of blessing for him, all have the desired effect. He calms down as rapidly as he had become angry, acknowledges her role as peacemaker, and blesses her for 'keeping me from bloodshed' (v.33). Abigail solved this problem in a way that glorified God but sacrificed none of her personality or femininity. She acted in good faith, using her initiative and God overruled and blessed her efforts. If you don't know the end of the story, read the rest of the chapter!

For prayer and reflection

Pray for places where peace is desperately needed, and for opportunities to promote peace.

A slave-girl **speaks out**

I f you had been snatched from your home and family and forced into service as a slave in a foreign country, wouldn't you be at least angry and resentful? Would you naturally feel concern for the welfare of your master and mistress? The prophet Jeremiah instructed the Jews who had been taken into exile to 'seek the peace ... of the city' to which they had been taken (Jer. 29:7) and here we see someone acting on that principle centuries earlier.

The story of Naaman's healing is well-known but we focus today on the young Israelite who was 'God's go-between'. We know only that she was a slave serving the wife of Naaman, an illustrious army commander – the very man, in fact, who had led the slave-raid! Naaman had leprosy, an incurable skin disease. On a human level, it might have been satisfying to know that the man who had taken so many of God's people captive should himself be suffering now.

Instead, this girl feels compassion for Naaman and, displaying remarkable initiative for a slave, suggests he visits 'the prophet' (Elisha), who could heal him. Her suggestion was acted on at the highest level – a letter from the king of Aram to the king of Israel – which indicates that she was trusted enough to be taken seriously. Not only was she *in the right place at the right time* for God to use her, but the fact that her word was believed suggests that she had proved trustworthy and reliable. She glorified God both in her daily work and in her attitude to her enemies, seeking the welfare of those who had no natural claim on her compassion.

Our usefulness to God depends on right attitudes of heart as well as on being where He wants us to be.

2 Kings 5:1–19a

'If only my master would see the prophet who is in Samaria! He would cure him of his leprosy.' (v.3)

For prayer and reflection

'Love your enemies and pray for those who persecute you' (Matt. 5:44). Lord, I can't do this on my own – please help me today! Amen.

Esther – **a woman of destiny**

Esther 4:1–5:3

'And who knows but that you have come to royal position for such a time as this?' (v.14b)

Lord, give me the insight to see things from Your perspective, not mine, and the grace to obey You even when my reputation or standing may be at risk. Amen.

The book of Esther is set at a time when the Persian empire extended over much of the Middle East, including the promised land, from which most Jews had been taken into exile in 597 BC.

The Persian king dismisses his queen, Vashti, for insubordination and Esther, an orphan Jewess, is eventually chosen as the new queen. Her relative and guardian, Mordecai, refuses to bow down to Haman, a highcourt official. In revenge, Haman devises a plan to destroy the Jews throughout the empire and confiscate their property.

Mordecai's distress at the news is reported to Esther, who sends someone to discover what is going on. Mordecai sends the messenger back to ask Esther to plead with the king for her people. Persian kings were absolute rulers and Esther replies that to approach the king uninvited would be risking her life. However, Mordecai points out that her position as queen will not exempt her from destruction with the rest of the Jews and that maybe she has become queen 'for such a time as this'. Esther takes this to heart, rising to the challenge: she asks all the Jews in the capital to fast (and presumably pray) for three days and nights. She and her maids do the same. Then she will 'go to the king, even though it is against the law. And if I perish, I perish' (v.16).

Esther was another of God's go-betweens, *in the right place at the right time*, but needed a reminder that God had put her there! To her credit, she put the welfare of her people before her personal safety – and God honoured her actions and her faith. Haman received his come-uppance, Mordecai was honoured and the Jews were saved.

Is God calling you to be an Esther?

An unlikely **go-between**

WEEK 6 FRI

This is an astonishing story on many counts! Jesus disregards several taboos in striking up a conversation with a lone woman. Moreover, this woman is not only a Samaritan, and 'Jews do not associate with Samaritans' (v.9) but one whom Jesus knows to be a social outcast. She had been divorced five times (although this was not necessarily her fault as men could divorce their wives, while women couldn't divorce their husbands) and was now living with someone to whom she was not married. No wonder His disciples were surprised (v.27) – 'surprised' is doubtless an understatement.

But Jesus' candid discussion with this woman and His acceptance of her have amazing results. Leaving her water jar she goes back into town where she summons her acquaintances to come and see the remarkable man she has encountered at the well. Presumably no respectable woman would speak to her so she must have spoken to 'women of ill-repute' and to the men of the town, who respond to her invitation and come to hear Him. Many of them believed and 'urged him to stay with them', and Jesus does so. This is truly incredible! Jews avoided Samaria and Samaritans like the plague, but Jesus, a Jewish rabbi, not only spoke to them, but stayed as their guest – and 'many more became believers' (v.41).

In God's overruling, the men of Samaria heard the good news from the Saviour Himself. And the catalyst? The woman at the well, *in the right place at the right time,* although she didn't know it. How else could they have been reached? Samaritan men would never have initiated a conversation with a Jew, but the woman's excitement was obviously infectious and they had to see for themselves.

John 4:4–15, 27–30, 39–42

'Come, see a man who told me everything I ever did. Could this be the Christ?' (vv.28–29)

For prayer and reflection

Lord, may my faith in and enthusiasm for You be as infectious as the Samaritan woman's was. Amen.

43

WEEKEND

God's makeover

For reflection: Isaiah 61:1–3
'… beauty instead of ashes … gladness instead of mourning … praise instead of a spirit of despair' (v.3)

I t's difficult to open a women's magazine these days without finding someone or something (a house, a garden) getting a 'makeover'. Such makeovers, impressive as they may sometimes be, only change the outward appearance of the subject.

These lovely verses describe 'God's makeover' – the wonderful positives He offers for the negatives in our lives (v.3) once He has healed us and set us free from our dark prison (v.1). And God's makeovers are not superficial – they change us from the inside out!

Take some time this weekend to think about the vivid pictures Isaiah uses here to describe what God wants to do for us and ask Him to do for you what you most need.

Luke tells us that this is the passage that Jesus read in the synagogue of his hometown, Nazareth, before astounding, and then antagonising, His listeners when He claimed to be the Messianic fulfilment of them. Next week we shall be looking at five unnamed women whose healing encounters with the Lord demonstrate how He put these verses into practice.

Restored to service

R ejected in His hometown of Nazareth, Jesus went to Capernaum, home of Andrew and Peter. In *their* synagogue His authority is recognised and respected after a dramatic confrontation with a demon-possessed man. From this public, high-profile encounter, Jesus goes home with Peter, whose mother-in-law is dangerously ill with a high fever. Perhaps emboldened by what has taken place in the synagogue, her family ask Jesus to help. Of course He did – Jesus made no distinction between public and private ministry. His compassion was the same for everyone – old or young, male or female. He 'rebuked' the fever as He had rebuked the demon – and the fever left her as the demon had left the man in the synagogue.

I love the reaction of Peter's mother-in-law. There was no, 'Well, I feel a bit better, but I'll take things easy for a day or two to make sure I'm really fit.' Nor did she bask in the spotlight of attention as 'the woman Jesus healed'. Not a bit of it. Instead 'she got up at once ... to wait on them'. Her gratitude to Jesus expressed itself in immediate, practical service – and they were all probably soon run off their feet because once the Sabbath was over crowds more sick people arrived seeking healing (v.40).

We too are 'saved to serve'. The epistle of James reminds us that 'faith by itself, if it is not accompanied by action, is dead' (James 2:17). I think there are two points from this story for us to take with us into our day. Firstly, we can bring anyone and any situation to Jesus, asking Him to intervene, and secondly, our appreciation of what He has done in our own lives is best expressed in loving service to others.

Luke 4:31–44

'... he... rebuked the fever, and it left her. She got up at once and began to wait on them.' (v.39)

For prayer and reflection

Lord, thank You for all that You have done so far in my life. Help me to live out my gratitude in loving service. Amen.

Renewed in hope

Luke 7:11–17

'When the Lord saw her, his heart went out to her and he said, "Don't cry."' (v.13)

O nly Luke records this wonderful story, which demonstrates again Jesus' concern for women and the marginalised. Here, the object of Jesus' compassion is a widow bereaved of her only son. The vulnerability of such widows is underlined by the Old Testament emphasis (especially in the Law of Moses and in the prophetic books) on caring for them. In a society where there was no social security and none of the benefits we associate with a 'welfare state', widows relied on their children to provide for them in old age.

Most of us can probably identify with this unnamed woman, devastated by grief and facing destitution with no son to provide for her. She must have felt utterly hopeless and empty as she followed the bier. Jesus, whose own mother was probably widowed by this time, is deeply moved by the woman's plight and speaks just two simple words to her: 'Don't cry.'

Then in another taboo-breaking gesture (touching a bier made one ritually unclean) He halts the procession and orders the corpse to get up! The young man does so, the crowd goes wild and Jesus 'gave him back to his mother'. In so doing He also restored her joy and her hope for the future.

For prayer and reflection

Jesus saw the hopelessness in that woman's life. His compassion was expressed in words of comfort and in an action that totally transformed the situation. Perhaps you are facing some situation that seems utterly hopeless or that fills you with dread or panic. Jesus is the same today as He was in the story we have just considered; He longs to comfort you and to change that situation – or your perception of it. Will you give Him access to the deepest fears and griefs of your heart?

'"I know the plans I have for you," declares the Lord, "... plans to give you hope and a future"' (Jer. 29:11). Lord, help me hold on to this promise today.

Reinstated into the community

Luke 8:40–48

'Daughter, your faith has healed you. Go in peace.' (v.48)

The anonymous woman in today's reading probably had some kind of chronic menstrual problem. She would have been anaemic, lacking in energy and, in addition, ritually 'unclean' (Lev. 15:25–28), contaminating everything with which she came into contact and transferring her ceremonial uncleanness to anyone who touched her.

Interestingly, Luke, a doctor, omits a detail which Mark adds – that she had spent everything she had on doctors, who had been unable to cure her, so she was poverty-stricken too. Had she planned to touch Jesus' clothes (Matt. 9:20) or was it something she did on the spur of the moment, thinking that in the crush, He wouldn't notice?

Nothing escapes Jesus. Just as she was healed instantly so He knew immediately that someone had touched Him, and asked who it was. Brave, but 'trembling' and embarrassed, she bears public witness to her healing. We can imagine her, crouched fearfully at Jesus' feet, wondering what He would say – she had, after all, made Him, too, ritually unclean. Jesus speaks to her tenderly, calling her 'Daughter' – the word is used nowhere else – and reassuring her. There is not a whisper of rebuke, just a commendation of her faith which has brought about her healing. His 'Go in peace' (the *shalom* wholeness only He can bring) reinstates her as a member of the faith community: her days as a social and religious outcast are over.

I love this story! It encourages us to 'reach out' to Jesus about situations that seem to be impossible or without remedy, or issues that drain us of energy and joy. However poor or pitiful our faith may seem to us, Jesus will respond with that gentle reassurance, 'Daughter … Go in peace.'

For prayer and reflection

Bring to God today anything that you feel completely helpless about; ask Him to intervene and to give you His shalom peace.

Raised **to life**

Luke 8:40–56

'Don't be afraid;
just believe, and
she will be healed.'
(v.50)

Today's story is 'interrupted' by yesterday's, just as in reality Jesus' journey was interrupted (v.42) by the healing of the woman with the haemorrhage. In verse 42 the girl is described as 'dying', but in verse 49, 'while Jesus was still speaking' (to the woman who had been healed) news comes that she is dead. There are other links: Jairus' daughter was about 12 and the just-healed woman had been ill for that length of time.

Jairus was 'ruler of the synagogue' (a bit like a churchwarden) so a man of some standing in the community. He must have been aware, at this stage of Jesus' ministry, of the controversy surrounding Jesus, so it must have been costly for him to fall at Jesus' feet to plead publicly with Him on behalf of his only child. Picture his increasing desperation and frustration as Jesus is delayed by the woman in the crowd, till he hears the words he has been dreading: 'Don't bother ... your daughter is dead.'

Jesus hears those words too, and reassures him. He goes home with Jairus, ejects the professional mourners, takes the girl by the hand (making Himself ritually unclean again by touching a corpse) and addresses her directly and tenderly, telling her to get up. To her parents' amazement she does so and Jesus, ever-practical, suggests they give her something to eat.

There is so much for us here! Often we get anxious when problems don't get sorted out in our timescale. We forget that God's timetable and priorities are different, that He is even more concerned than we are for those we bring to Him in prayer. We get frustrated, fearful and our faith wobbles. Jesus says to us, as to Jairus, 'Don't be afraid; only believe ...'

For prayer and reflection

Lord, I feel frustrated about ... Help me to 'let go' of the people and needs I bring to You in prayer and to trust Your timescale and Your love.

Released from bondage

nother Sabbath, another synagogue, another unnamed woman, another confrontation! This poor woman had suffered for 18 years from what Luke describes as a 'spirit of weakness', so that she was bent double. She may have had some physical condition where her vertebrae had fused, but it is also possible, as Tom Wright points out in *Luke for Everyone*, that this was a psychological condition, resulting perhaps from years of abuse. Jesus saw her, had compassion on her, called her to Him and, laying hands on her, announced her release.

Instead of joining in the general rejoicing, the synagogue ruler objects violently because Jesus had healed her *on the Sabbath*! The petty laws and regulations that had accumulated over the years were more important to him than this amazing display of God's grace and power! Jesus exposes the double standards – if it's all right to give animals a drink on the Sabbath, how much *more* all right is it to set people free from things that have held them for years?

Perhaps, reading this, you realise that you need release from something that has you in its grip as surely as that woman was bent double. Jesus can call you, touch you and release you. Ask Him. If, however, by God's grace, nothing has that kind of hold over you, don't be like the ruler of that synagogue. It's so easy to refuse to acknowledge God's work because it's not in *our* church or denomination, or not according to *our* rules or *our* understanding! Such attitudes can only hinder the growth of God's kingdom, which Jesus describes so simply and vividly in the closing verses of today's reading.

Are you like the woman? Or the synagogue ruler?

Luke 13:10–20

'When Jesus saw her, he called her forward and said to her, "Woman, you are set free ..."' (v.12)

For prayer and reflection

'Let the Son of God enfold you ... Let Him have the things that hold you, and His Spirit, like a dove, will descend upon your life and make you whole.'
John Wimber

49

WEEKEND

What's in a name?

For reflection: Isaiah 43:1–7
'… called by my name … created for my glory …' (v.7).

Parents usually give a lot of time and thought to naming their children. Our names are so important to us, aren't they? We are pleased if someone remembers our name and upset if it's spelt wrongly. Our identities are inextricably bound up with our names – and God knows them!

Read and reflect on today's passage, inserting your own first name after the 'yous' in verses 1, 2, 4 and 5 and taking the words as an assurance from God to you personally. He knows you (*insert your name*) by name; you belong to Him; nothing can separate you from His loving care.

And there's more too! We also have God's name – because He is our Father and we were created for His glory! Take these thoughts into your weekend and meditate on them.

Until the end of the month we shall be looking at seven very different women named in Acts and the epistles, who were among the first to be called by Christ's name – 'Christians' – and who in varying ways demonstrated that they were created for His glory.

Rhoda – **a young doorkeeper**

Herod increased the pressure on the young Church in Jerusalem. He had James beheaded and Peter imprisoned. Imagine the effect on the Christians. All they could do was support each other and pray – so they gathered in the home of Mary, mother of John Mark and aunt of Barnabas. Mary was probably wealthy, her house enclosed by a protective wall and with an outer gate. (The upper room, setting for the Last Supper, may also have been here.)

Whilst they are praying – and in answer to their prayers – Peter is miraculously released from prison. Arriving at the house he knocks on the outer gate. Enter Rhoda. She is described as a 'girl' so was quite young, probably a slave and almost certainly a Christian, for in times of intense persecution, no Christian household could risk allowing an unbeliever to man the gate. Her joyful reaction to hearing Peter's voice indicates that she knew him and recognised the answer to prayer that he represented! She was not believed at first – but eventually Peter gained admission to show them he was alive before 'disappearing' again – for their safety and his.

Rhoda has the briefest of mentions, but she witnesses to the fact that in Christ, 'there is neither ... slave nor free' (Gal. 3:28). This was truly revolutionary thinking! Rhoda was young, female and a slave, all lowly categories – but in Christ she was the equal of her employer and trusted to keep the door. Perhaps she would rather have been in the prayer-meeting. But her faithfulness to duty was rewarded by being the first witness of Peter's miraculous deliverance! Whatever our 'station in life', in Christ we are daughters of the King. Rejoice in that today!

Acts 12:1–19

'When she recognised Peter's voice, she was so overjoyed she ran back without opening ...' (v.14)

For prayer and reflection

Lord, keep me faithful today in whatever You've called me to.

Tabitha – **helping hands**

Acts 9:32–42

'… there was a disciple named Tabitha … who was always doing good and helping the poor.' (v.36)

I ronically, we might never have heard of Tabitha if she hadn't died! But because she was raised to life through Peter's prayers, we have a record of the distress her death caused to those she had blessed in so many ways when she was alive. She was 'always doing good and helping the poor'. What a lovely epitaph! In particular, it seems, she helped widows. Tabitha helped them in practical ways, as Peter realised when he was taken to see her body (v.39).

Most of us can help in a crisis, but some people 'spread the fragrance' of Christ everywhere (2 Cor. 2:14) by giving themselves totally and ungrudgingly to others. Often they are women whose gifts, like Tabitha's, are practical – they sew, bake, clean, baby-sit, garden – for people who can't do these things for themselves. They rarely hold official positions in the church and may even go unnoticed because they 'do good by stealth'. Yet these are often the very people who sow the seed of the gospel in people's lives, by doing, not by preaching. They live out Jesus' teaching in ways that those who have never opened a Bible can understand. Jesus 'went around doing good' (Acts 10:38) and Tabitha followed His example.

Unfortunately, for too long Tabitha's kind of service was perceived as the only legitimate way for women to exercise ministry. But, as we shall see over the next week, early Christian women did not just man the first-century equivalents of teapots and sewing machines! On the contrary, their gifts and ministries covered a very broad spectrum. So be encouraged! God can use your gifts to further His kingdom.

For prayer and reflection

'My talents, gifts and graces Lord, into thy blessed hands receive; and let me live to preach thy word and let me to thy glory live.' (Charles Wesley)

Lois and Eunice – **educators**

WEEK 8 WED

Once again we piece together a jigsaw of references to form a picture of two godly women who were instrumental in bringing to faith Timothy, a young man from Lystra. Timothy joined Paul on his second missionary journey and was deeply loved by the apostle, who referred to him as a son. He became a teacher and leader in the Early Church, and in these few verses we see the importance of his early upbringing.

We learn that Timothy's mother Eunice was Jewish, and that his grandmother Lois was also a Jewish Christian. Paul commends their 'sincere faith' – one that was obviously from the heart and worked out in their daily lives, not just lip-service to their religion. It is often said that 'God has no grandchildren', that we all need to make our own commitment to Christ, even if we have been brought up in a Christian family, but there is something very special about families where succeeding generations are taught the Scriptures from early childhood – not just theoretically but practically, as Bible principles are lived out by family members. Those of us in that position are truly privileged, for as Paul reminds Timothy, knowledge of God's Word is key to the working out of God's purposes for us.

We know nothing of Timothy's Greek father, but his mother and grandmother took seriously their responsibility to teach this little boy God's Word. They were sowing the seeds for Timothy's future ministry. As parents, godparents, grandparents, teachers or friends we cannot control the lives of the young people entrusted to us – but if we ground them in God's Word, pray for them and set them an example of 'sincere faith' we equip them to fulfil God's purposes.

**Acts 16:1–2;
2 Timothy 1:1–7;
3:14–17**

'... your sincere faith, which first lived in your grandmother Lois and in your mother Eunice ...'
(2 Tim. 1:5)

For prayer and reflection

Lord, may my faith be 'sincere'; help me narrow the gap between what I believe and the way I live, so that I'm a good role model for younger Christians.

Lydia – open heart, open home

Acts 16:6–15

'… Lydia … a worshipper of God. The Lord opened her heart to respond to Paul's message.' (v.14)

These verses describe how the gospel came to Europe – and how Paul's first convert there was a woman! On his second missionary journey Paul had a vision of a man from Macedonia asking him to visit. In response, Paul and his companions travel to Philippi in modern Greece.

On the Sabbath, because there was no synagogue, they made their way to the river and its 'place of prayer'. They spoke to the women gathered there and one in particular responded – Lydia. She was probably well-educated and wealthy as she is described as 'a seller of purple cloth', which was much sought-after. Thyatira, her native town (in modern Turkey), was well-known for its dyeing industry, the purple dye being extracted from shellfish. God had already been at work in her life for she is described as 'a worshipper of God'; she may have become a Jewish convert in Thyatira, which had a large Jewish population. As she listens to Paul preaching about Jesus 'God opened her heart' and she believed in Him. Obviously an influential woman, either single or a widow, she headed a household and all her dependants were baptised with her.

With humility as well as open-heartedness, she invites the itinerant preachers to stay with her, and it is likely that her home became the meeting place of the Philippian church, the recipients of Paul's 'letter to the Philippians', whom he held in such high regard. He commended their generosity and hospitality – traits which we see here in Lydia and which, as one of its leaders, she must have modelled and fostered in others.

Open-heartedness towards God can and should result in open-handedness towards others.

For prayer and reflection

Lord, make me, too, a worshipper whose heart is open to hear and receive from You, and generous – open-handed and open-hearted – towards those I encounter today.

Phoebe – a servant heart

**Romans
15:23–16:5**

P hoebe appears before the list of people to whom Paul sends greetings in the church in Rome. She is thought to have been the person entrusted with delivering the letter to the Romans, written by Paul in or around Corinth.

'… our sister Phoebe, a servant of the church … has been a great help to many people …' (16:1–2)

Although this is the only reference to Phoebe in the New Testament, scholars have managed nevertheless to deduce quite a lot about her from the points made! It was customary at that time for those unknown to a particular congregation to carry a letter giving their credentials – in the light of the persecution the young Church suffered we can understand the need for this. Here Paul warmly commends Phoebe to them as his 'sister' in Christ, asking them to welcome her 'in the Lord' and give her any help she may need. This suggests that besides being the bearer of the letter Phoebe was on a specific errand, perhaps to raise support and get official permission for Paul's proposed trip to Spain (visiting the church in Rome on the way) which he mentions in chapter 15.

To have travelled independently like this Phoebe must have been a woman of wealth and status, yet she is described as a 'servant' (literally 'deacon') of the Cenchrean church. We know from Acts 6 that deacons undertook rather humdrum practical jobs, so Phoebe, despite her social standing, was prepared to serve her fellow-believers. Paul also comments that she has 'been a great help to many people' including him; the Greek word he uses is 'benefactor', which further underlines Phoebe's status and wealth and highlights her willingness to share her wealth to bless many who were doubtless her social inferiors according to the prevailing culture.

Are we ready humbly to serve others?

For prayer and reflection

Lord, give me a heart like Phoebe's – ready and willing to serve You in other people, however humble the task.

WEEKEND

Faith in action

For reflection: Isaiah 58:6–12
'You will be like a well-watered garden, like a spring whose waters never fail' (v.11).

In this weekend's reading God speaks to the people of Isaiah's day about what the epistle of James later called 'true religion' (James 1:27), ie faith which makes an impact on those around us. The women we have considered this week demonstrated their faith in Christ in immensely practical ways, by putting into practice many of the principles outlined here – feeding the hungry, clothing the naked, fighting oppression and injustice (including gossip! – v.9), and rebuilding communities. God's desire has always been to see His people's faith expressed in action as well as in 'going to church'.

Ponder these verses this weekend, and be encouraged by the promises in them. Here God's response to our faith in action is conveyed in images of light (vv.8,10) – we shan't be in the dark. As we reach out to others He promises help and guidance whenever and wherever we ask for it (vv.9,11), and as verse 11 describes, we shall be refreshed and thus empowered to share God's refreshment with those in need.

Priscilla – **teacher-tentmaker**

P riscilla was quite a woman! Ejected from Rome on the orders of the emperor Claudius because they were Jewish, she and her husband Aquila went to Corinth. All Jews had a trade and theirs was tentmaking, so they could 'set up shop' anywhere. Paul, also a tentmaker, stayed with them in Corinth for 18 months before sailing to Syria, accompanied by this married couple who had become his friends and whom he left in Ephesus whilst he continued travelling, evangelising and teaching.

Hearing Apollos preach in the synagogue at Ephesus, they realised that the young man's zeal was not matched by his knowledge of the gospel. Instead of confronting and correcting him publicly, they graciously and diplomatically invited him to their home and whilst he enjoyed their hospitality they filled him in on the teaching about Jesus that he had missed. His lessons learned, Apollos became a notable teacher, mentioned by Paul in 1 Corinthians 1.

Other references to Priscilla and Aquila in the final chapters of Romans and 2 Timothy mention a church that met in their home (they had by this time returned to Rome), the fact that they had risked their lives for Paul and that 'all' the Gentile churches were grateful for them.

From these scattered verses we have a picture of a woman probably of higher social standing than her husband (indicated by the fact that she is often mentioned first) who may even have written Hebrews and who was prepared, for the sake of the gospel, to work hard, to pay her way, to live a nomadic existence, to teach those needing instruction, to open her home for the church to meet and to risk her life to support Paul. What a testimonial – and what a challenge to us!

Acts 18:1–4, 18–19,24–28; Romans 16:3–5

'Priscilla and Aquila … invited him to their home and explained to him the way of God more adequately.' (Acts 18:26)

For prayer and reflection

Lord, thank You for Priscilla's example; help me to use my gifts and possessions in the service of the gospel as willingly as she obviously did.

Journey through the Temple

Anne Le Tissier

Anne is a Guernsey girl but left the island in 1996 when her husband began training for Baptist ministry. She now lives and works between two homes in the West Midlands and Worcestershire, writing primarily for Christian women, although she is also keen to expand her boundaries and reach out to unbelievers through fiction. Anne enjoys long country walks, playing and listening to music, a good film, a good read, gardening, cooking, trying out new activities and relaxing with family or close friends. She also has a fabulous daughter and son-in-law.

Journey through the Temple

1 Corinthians
3:9–17

'Don't you know
that you yourselves
are God's temple
and that God's
Spirit lives in you?'
(v.16)

For prayer and
reflection

**Lord, please flood
my heart with
Your Holy Spirit
and bring new life
to Your temple,
Your house of
prayer.**

What jumps to mind when you read the word, 'temple'? Temples come in all sorts of shapes, sizes and colours to serve a wide variety of gods. Paul, however, would have been referring to one in particular – the Temple of God in Jerusalem. His heritage had instilled into him the reverence and significance of this awesome building. It was of paramount importance to God's people for it was the site God chose where He would dwell among men.

Today, we can lose the significance of the Temple in our New Testament, 'Westernised', Gentile Christianity, passing it off as interesting history, but irrelevant for modern worship. Nevertheless, both Jesus and Paul referred to it in post-resurrection terms and I believe it still has much to teach us, nearly 2,000 years after the Romans ransacked and destroyed it.

The Temple housed all manner of activities which were in full swing long before Jesus stepped into its courts, but it was never called a house of teaching or a house of singing; of markets, priests, cleansing, tithes, festivals and so on. Although these activities were intrinsic to temple ministry and service, they were intended to simply focus the attention on the core function of the Temple, the *raison d'être* of God's house – to be a temple for sacrifices and a house of prayer (2 Chron. 7:12; Isa. 56:7). Paul teaches that we are now temples of God's Holy Spirit which, by definition, infers that we are His house of prayer. Prayer is not just something we do, but prayer is what we are.

Through Jesus, God's Spirit comes to dwell amongst His people in a temple of flesh and bone. As we revisit our bricks and mortar predecessor this month, let us ask God to revive His New Testament house of prayer.

Journey **to the Temple**

Psalm 84:1–12

'Blessed are those whose strength is in you, who have set their hearts on pilgrimage.' (v.5)

As pilgrims travelled to Herod's Temple, excitement buzzed amongst their chattering groups, speculating who might be the first to glimpse God's house. It dominated Mount Moriah on a platform covering some 14 hectares, looming above the city, possibly reaching 45 metres at its highest point.

Encased in gleaming marble, the imposing landmark was famed for its magnificent splendour which awakened the soul to God's power and might, His majesty and holiness. Picture it in your mind's eye – proud and regal, glinting in the sun, a protective refuge from the shadows of night. Indeed, this holy house for the King of kings demanded superior timber, untainted stone, pure gold, exquisite gems and finest linen.

How do we feel in our approach to God in prayer? Are we struck by the sense of awe that His splendour evokes?

The anticipation of drawing close to the Temple put a spring in the pilgrims' steps with their rousing songs of praise. Likewise, when our eyes focus on where we are heading, the soul cannot help but overflow with joyful praise and adoration. This King, our God, delights to hear an exalting cry of approach that magnifies His name above all other names in our hearts.

Perhaps, though, you have been struggling to praise God. Remember that no matter how barren the wilderness of our journey, His glory awaits us daily on the horizon. Downcast eyes see the dirt and dust, the stony path, the withered tree and fading flower, but eyes lifted up can focus and feast on the promise of His awesome presence.

Call out to Him in faith, a defiant cry against desolate feelings. Bring songs and shouts of jubilation in praise of His wonderful name, for a sacrifice of praise brings peace beyond our understanding.

For prayer and reflection

Pause and allow the delight of drawing near to God to fill your heart with expectation.

'Enter his gates
with thanksgiving
and his courts with
praise …' (v.4)

Enter His courts with thanks

Moving on, we find ourselves in Jerusalem, climbing its tiers in approach of the Temple courts. It might be hot and dusty but it is well worth the uphill effort. It is essential to focus on our goal, otherwise the tiring, mundane trudge can easily dissuade us from the path and tempt us to seek solace with someone or something other than God.

Tiredness and busyness may tempt us to take a short cut or race ahead quickly to the Holy Place, but either way we would forget to bring our thank offerings. Pause for breath, therefore, as we enter through a gate into the Court of the Gentiles (the Great Outer Court).

If we are expecting hushed reverence, we may be surprised by the bustle of worshippers, the cries of market traders, the flapping doves and bleating lambs. As Jesus overturned the tables of the moneychangers in this court, the disciples remembered that it was written: 'Zeal for your house will consume me' (John 2:15–17). The provisions were necessary for sacrifice, but the ethos of worship was obscured by profit-making activities in pursuit of selfish gain. Are there such things in our lives – objects, situations or relationships that feed personal gratification in place of filling God's house with prayer?

Jesus is just as zealous for the New Testament temple in our lives but we need not be discouraged when He turns over the tables. Moreover, we can thank Him for His passion to sanctify us into God's holy house of prayer, and give Him the free reign necessary to re-establish His Lordship.

Take time to sit amongst these grand porches and colonnades. Contemplate and give thanks for the goodness of the Lord in this court of thanksgiving.

For prayer and reflection

Give thanks to God for all that He has done for you, for everything He has provided for you and for His unconditional love for you.

Be strong and **do the work**

As you sat among the marble pillars yesterday, I wonder if you felt somewhat overawed by the size of this immense structure. Remember, it was not built overnight! Furthermore, God started to build His temple in your life from the moment you were conceived – hewn, as it were, from the quarry of your parents' gene pool. It was handed back to its true owner at the time of your Christian conversion and will require constant maintenance until the day you are called home to heaven. Are you prepared to roll up your sleeves and commit to this endeavour?

The Spirit put into David's mind all the detailed plans for the Temple (vv.11–12). God had a specific plan for the design and function of His house and still has today – who are we to question His choice of physical appearance, family circumstances, talents and so on?

Although David had it on his heart to build a temple, he was a man of war, so the task fell to his son Solomon (vv.2–3,6). Before we walk through this house of prayer, let us consider whether we are at peace with God, with our family, neighbours, colleagues, friends and everyone in our church fellowship. Jesus said that we are first to be reconciled to anyone with whom we have broken relationship before we offer our gift at the Temple altar (Matt. 5:23–24).

Finally, our personal devotion to God will influence the preservation and productivity of His temple (1 Chron. 28:9–10). Are we serving Him with wholehearted devotion and a willing mind? Consider now, for the Lord has chosen us to build a sanctuary, so 'be strong and do the work'.

1 Chronicles 28:9–21

'Consider now, for the Lord has chosen you to build a temple as a sanctuary.' (v.10)

For prayer and reflection

Do not be afraid or discouraged by the size of this task, for when we follow God's plan, He will not forsake us but will see it through to completion.

WEEKEND

The Temple: Scene 1

For reflection: Leviticus 23:33–43; John 7:37–52

A lush parade of leafy branches rippled across the Temple courts as the priests poured out waters of Siloam upon the great altar. Flutes harmonised with rapturous praise as the Feast of Tabernacles reached its concluding ceremonies: 'Give thanks to the LORD, for he is good; his love endures for ever' (Psa. 118:29). With great gusto the amassed worshippers celebrated God's faithfulness in the wilderness, gave thanks for the recent harvest and prayed for future rainfall. They rejoiced with anticipation for the day of God's salvation when His Spirit would pour out upon His people (Isa. 12:3; Joel 2:28).

And then He appeared – Jesus, disrupting the service with His commanding voice: 'If anyone is thirsty, let him come to me and drink' (John 7:37). Sadly, the anticipation of their lips did not tally with their hearts – they were not expecting such an immediate answer. How mixed and muddled was their response!

Are you thirsty? Do you recognise God's coming to you, or is previous experience and personal expectation blinding you to His presence? Drink afresh of His Spirit, renew the power and vitality of His living temple, and quench the thirst of your soul.

The **temple guard**

od's house of prayer required a system of walls, gates, guards and doorkeepers to preserve its sanctity. Numerous rabbinical laws, supervised by the Levitical temple guard, strictly regulated who might pass through each gate. Without this, anyone unclean could have walked right into the Most Holy Place.

Pilgrims pronounced Levitically clean could enter the outer Court of the Gentiles. Depending on their state of cleanness, Israelite men and women then passed through the Beautiful Gate into the Court of the Women where men could then enter through the Nicanor Gate into the Court of Israel. This was a narrow strip, separated from the Court of the Priests by a low fence.

Priests ministering before the Lord could enter the Holy Place, and the high priest, just once a year, into the Most Holy Place.

Only Jesus can make our lives clean in God's sight but we still have a responsibility to uphold our sanctification by what we allow to enter through our eyes and ears. Scripture reminds us: 'If I had cherished sin in my heart, the Lord would not have listened' (Psa. 66:18), '... be clear minded and self-controlled so that you can pray' (1 Pet. 4:7).

Are we filling our lives with treasure or trash? It requires a constant watch on the gates of our lives in a world that too easily compromises God's standard of living. What do we wittingly or unwittingly bring into the sanctuary that defiles it?

The heart is the Most Holy Place of our lives, outside of which is the Holy Place of our soul. Our mind bombards this consecrated house of prayer with its numerous gateways to the world, so let us remember to keep them well maintained and supervised.

---

1 Chronicles 9:22–27; 26:12–19

'They and their descendants were in charge of guarding the gates of the house of the LORD ...' (9:23)

For prayer and reflection

'... whatever is true ... noble ... right ... pure ... lovely ... admirable ... excellent or praiseworthy – think about such things' (Phil. 4:8).

The 'Word' for the courts

John 1:1–14

'The Word became flesh and made his dwelling among us.' (v.14)

At the dedication of Solomon's Temple, the cloud of God's glory had so filled the sanctuary that the priests were unable to perform their tasks (2 Chron. 5:14). Herod's larger Temple with its great outer court was even more lavish than its predecessor, but the ark of the covenant, the cherubim and the cloud of God's presence in the Most Holy Place had long since disappeared.

Enter Jesus, moving through the courts in the power and glory of God – mingling with the crowds, debating with the rabbis, teaching the disciples and joining the pilgrims in worship. Fully man, yet fully God, He paved the way for Jew and Gentile to enter God's holy presence. He fulfilled Old Testament prophecy and ignited the New.

Until we make a personal commitment, the Bible is merely a collection of 66 books of historical writings. However, as Jesus the Word makes His dwelling in our living temples, we engage with His Spirit and the written Word becomes alive to us: 'For the word of God is living and active. Sharper than any double-edged sword ...' (Heb. 4:12).

Priests, rabbis and pilgrims read, taught and discussed the Scriptures in the Temple's vast porches and precincts. What is happening in His house of prayer today? Are we engaging with the living Word, reading it, chewing it over and asking the Spirit to breathe life into the words that fill our minds and hearts? The Word of God is flawless and penetrates the depth of our being, preparing us for sweet communion with Jesus. It teaches the heart, comforts the soul, disciplines the flesh, guides the will and offers a sure hope for the future. It is a treasure chest of power and a wonderful tool in prayer – good reasons to keep it close at hand!

For prayer and reflection

Dear Lord, 'Open my eyes that I may see wonderful things in your law.' (Psa. 119:18)

The **Temple treasury**

'They all gave out of their wealth; but she, out of her poverty, put in everything …' (v.44)

Continuing on our journey we pass through the Beautiful Gate in the eastern wall and into the Court of the Women – women took their place in galleries above the simple colonnade at its perimeter. For the men, it was far more than a mere thoroughfare into the Court of Israel. Within Herod's Temple it not only housed the infamous treasury but provided chambers where healed lepers washed themselves and Nazarites made preparations before presenting their offerings to the priest. Similar rooms were used to store oil and wine for the drink offerings and wood for the bronze altar.

Come aside with me between the pillars to find thirteen trumpet-shaped boxes, each allocated for a specific monetary offering – nine obligatory and four voluntary. Here Jesus taught the throngs of worshippers (John 8:20), and here too He taught His disciples concerning the widow's humble offering.

Jesus was deeply moved as He observed her complete devotion, untainted by the lure of wealth. How we spend both our money and our time reflects the depth of our commitment. God is not necessarily expecting us to give away every last penny of our salary or spend 12 hours a day in prayer, but He looks beyond the outward façade, observing the motives of our hearts.

As we are each a unique house of prayer, God will reveal how He wants to use our time and resources. Are we therefore willing to hand everything back to His Lordship, or do we still hold on to those few hours each week when we can do 'our' thing, or those additional savings in the bank to pay for 'our' future. God is completely trustworthy, the most secure investment we could ever make!

For prayer and reflection

We say and sing that we submit to His Lordship – but do we truly give Him everything? 'Why do you call me, "Lord, Lord," and do not do what I say?' (Luke 6:46)

Encouragement for your day

Psalm 121:1–8

'The LORD will watch over your coming and going both now and for evermore' (v.8)

Fifteen semi-circular marble steps lead up from the Court of the Women to the Gate of Nicanor, each one drawing us closer to God's presence in the sanctuary beyond. Some believe they represented the Psalms of Ascent sung by pilgrims travelling to the Temple, so we too could use them for our own approach.

Step 1 (Psa. 120): Call to God if you are in distress and know that He will answer you.

Step 2 (Psa. 121): Take comfort, for He constantly watches over your life.

Step 3 (Psa. 122): Rejoice with others when you join together for worship.

Step 4 (Psa. 123): Draw near to Him with a humble spirit.

Step 5 (Psa. 124): Praise Him, for He alone is your help and protection.

Step 6 (Psa. 125): He is completely trustworthy, seek security in Him alone.

Step 7 (Psa. 126): Thank Him for releasing you from captivity to sin.

Step 8 (Psa. 127): Consider, is your life built upon personal dreams or God's purposes.

Step 9 (Psa. 128): Revere His ways and you will find peace.

Step 10 (Psa. 129): Trust Him to bring you through times of difficulty or persecution.

For prayer and reflection

Step 11 (Psa. 130): Confess your sins and receive His unfailing forgiveness.

Step 12 (Psa. 131): Accept His ways though you may not understand them.

How might these steps apply to your personal circumstances and approach to God in prayer?

Step 13 (Psa. 132): Offer yourself afresh as a dwelling for His Holy Spirit.

Step 14 (Psa. 133): Be united and reconciled to everyone.

Step 15 (Psa. 134): Be prepared to minister to Him, by day or by night.

Dressed **for service**

Walking through the Gate of Nicanor we arrive in the Court of Israel, adjacent with, but separated by a low fence and a few steps from the Court of the Priests. Within the perimeter walls of these courts were chambers, meeting rooms and living quarters used by the priests – and in one of these they kept their vestments.

The priestly robes distinguished the tribe of Levi for service in the Lord's Temple. Those belonging to the high priest were far more ornate than the simple tunics of the priests, but all were made of fine linen and rich yarn to bring them 'dignity and honour' in ministry. They reminded the Israelites that priests were set apart for God, inciting respect for the priestly service performed on their behalf, in addition to their teaching and instruction of the Law.

Solomon dedicating the Temple, and pilgrims singing the Psalms of Ascent, prayed for the priests to be clothed with salvation and righteousness (2 Chron. 6:41; Psa. 132:9,16). These prayers proved prophetic and found their fulfilment in Christ. Jesus is the High Priest of the new covenant in which we are God's royal priesthood (Heb. 6:20; 1 Pet. 2:9). He clothes us with garments of salvation and robes of righteousness (Isa. 61:10) – not through our own effort, but in His perfect atoning blood. But what do people see when they look at us? Do the attitudes with which we adorn ourselves bring dignity and honour to the Holy One whom we serve, or have we tarnished our robes with selfishness and pride?

'Therefore, as God's chosen people ... clothe yourselves with compassion, kindness, humility, gentleness and patience ... Forgive as the Lord forgave you. And ... put on love, which binds them all together in perfect unity' (Col. 3:12–14).

Exodus 28:1–5, 40–43

'Make tunics, sashes and headbands for Aaron's sons, to give them dignity and honour.' (v.40)

For prayer and reflection

Place a discreet note somewhere as a reminder each morning to pause, and ask Jesus to clothe you in His righteousness and humility.

WEEKEND

The Temple: Scene 2

For reflection: John 8:1–11

Cold eyes bored through her soul – accusing her sin, mocking her shame, leering at her half-naked body. With trembling fingers she tightened the inadequate shawl around her bare shoulders. Crouching in the midst of the throng, however, her judge never looked at her. Yesterday's conclusion to the Feast ensured a larger than usual crowd in the Temple courts, but she found solace in His distracted contemplations, her only means of escape from brazen scrutiny.

Jesus arose and the court fell silent. Wielding His judgment like a double-edged sword He slashed their stony hearts, then returned to His squat.

Neighbouring feet shuffled away, disappearing within the porticoes, leaving the two of them alone as He then stood before her. His loving discipline unlocked her tears as she fell at His feet. Her sins did not deserve such mercy, yet this man had chosen to save her life – how could she ever express the depth of her gratitude?

What do you feel in this Temple scene? Naked shame? Undeserved mercy? Inexpressible gratitude? Take time to be alone with Jesus – His conviction is pure, His forgiveness unfailing and His love overwhelming. All He seeks in return is your sincere devotion.

The altar **of sacrifice**

I n the Court of the Priests, the great bronze altar – a square of 14.5 metres – sat in front of the sanctuary guarding against desecration of God's holy dwelling place. Countless animal and bird sacrifices were offered upon it for the forgiveness of sins, the resultant pungent smoke arising as a pleasing aroma to the Lord.

God's holiness abhors sin so we cannot enter His presence without an atoning sacrifice for our stained lives. Jesus was the perfect sacrificial Lamb, offering His life upon the altar of a wooden cross. We are appalled by the cruel torture He endured and the agonising death – but challenged, too, for Jesus commanded all His disciples to carry a cross if they were to follow Him (Luke 14:27).

Jesus paid the ultimate price to grant us access into God's presence but there remains an altar that still seeks to burn a daily sacrifice as a pleasing aroma to God. Most of us won't have to face the abominable wooden cross but our altar is still costly. As Christ's disciples we are called to sacrifice our personal choice in submission to the will of God. Jesus made that choice in Gethsemane and asks us to do likewise.

All our decisions must be under His Lordship as we nail them daily to the altar of choice – how we spend time and money, how we serve God in the home, church and workplace. God no longer seeks the aroma of roasting meat but He relishes the sacrifice of a broken and contrite heart.

The outward visible sacrifice in the Temple was prerequisite to preparing the inner core of prayer. Similarly, as we confess our sin and realign our choices to the Lord's will, we too prepare our hearts for that intimate place of prayer.

Romans 12:1–2

'… offer your bodies as living sacrifices, holy and pleasing to God …' (v.1)

For prayer and reflection

Pray through Psalm 51.

The Sea of cast metal

Hebrews 10:19–25

'… to cleanse us from a guilty conscience and having our bodies washed with pure water.' (v.22)

Between the altar and the porch of the sanctuary, placed towards the south, was the immense Sea, or laver, made of cast iron and holding about 66 kilolitres of water. Approximately 4 metres in diameter and 2 metres high, it sat on 12 bronze bulls with a rim shaped like a lily blossom. Its position enabled the priests to wash themselves for consecration before touching any sacred vessel in their temple ministries.

The Temple had to be holy because it housed a holy God. Holiness relates to extreme purity, perfectly manifested in God. We too are called to be a holy temple but we cannot make ourselves holy through our own efforts – only through Jesus Christ: 'And so Jesus also suffered outside the city gate to make the people holy through his own blood' (Heb. 13:12). We are, however, instructed to live a holy life (1 Thess. 4:7), which prevents us behaving too liberally and taking our sanctification for granted.

The priests consecrated themselves for service as they washed in the Sea, thereby dedicating themselves formally to the worship and service of God. So how do we consecrate ourselves if Jesus alone can make us holy?

Paul instructs us to live by the Spirit so that we will not gratify the desires of our sinful nature (Gal. 5:16). We are holy in God's sight because of what Jesus did but we also try to live holy lives, consecrating ourselves for divine service as we respond to the Spirit's convictions within. Each day we have a choice to make: will we offer our lives to the pursuit of self-gratification, or offer them in slavery to righteousness leading to holiness (Rom. 6:19)?

Pause at the Sea and determine to consecrate the day to dedicated and holy service (2 Cor. 7:1).

For prayer and reflection

In which areas of your life do you struggle to make the right sacrifice of choice? Talk to the Lord about it.

The **call to prayer**

**2 Chronicles
2:1–4; 13:10–12**

Worshippers came to the Temple throughout the day but there were set times for priests to minister to the Lord on their behalf within the Holy Place.

'Every morning and evening they present burnt offerings and fragrant incense to the LORD.' (13:11)

At the morning and evening sacrifice, a signal for prayer interrupted all other activity. It is thought they used an organ-like instrument called the *magrephah* whose persistent tones, filtering throughout the busy courts, were impossible to ignore. Whatever they used, however, it was loud enough to refocus the attention onto the core function of the Temple – that of prayer.

God still longs for us to minister to Him, but if we find it difficult to make time, perhaps we too could benefit from a *magrephah* – a call to prayer. We can pray at any time, no matter what we are doing, but it is the quiet space with Jesus that develops intimacy and depth of relationship. When couples or close friends become too busy to spend time together, communication may break down and they can start to feel out of touch with each other. It is no different with the Lord who calls for us daily.

Our Creator knows best what will really grab our attention and supersede the noisy distraction of busy lives. Perhaps we might ask Him to show us our personal *magrephah*. It may be an alarm clock, a set period of the day, the front door closing as children leave for school, the daily walk with the dog and so on.

In considering what it might be, it's helpful to know whether it sounds at the same or different times, whether we recognise its tone and persistence and whether it overrides the volume of daily activity.

As we establish and respond to our *magrephah*, we develop the fundamental purpose of our innermost being, to be a house of prayer.

For prayer and reflection

Lord, teach me daily to hear and to heed Your call upon my busy life, to just spend time with You.

The **place of prayer**

Psalm 27:1–14

'… to gaze upon the beauty of the LORD and to seek him in his temple.' (v.4)

As the officiating priest and his assistants disappeared inside the sanctuary, everyone else knew where they should be. Whether standing on the steps leading up to the porch or restricted to one of the courts, each person knew his or her familiar place of prayer.

As we approach the Holy Place of the New Testament temple – the quieting of the soul to minister to the Lord with reverent worship and prayer – where is that place which subdues activity to focus on the Lord?

Through Jesus, of course, we have the freedom to pray at any time of day or night. Sometimes, however, our spirit is willing but our weak flesh gets easily distracted from spending quality time with Him, and instead of that quiet space, we find ourselves living and praying 'on the run'. We can survive a little while like this, but it helps develop our relationship with the Lord to have a special and familiar place that draws us into worship.

Where is that place of prayer? As our *magrephah* sounds, where do we go? Perhaps it is the lounge, the kitchen, the bedroom, the study, a certain chair or a particular window? Or maybe it's being outside on the beach, in the woods, the park or beside the riverbank? Is our place of prayer quiet when we want to come to it? Is it suitably warm and comfortable without sending us off to sleep? Can we ignore the telephone and doorbell? If it is somewhere outside, where can we go when it rains?

Wherever it is, God is always waiting for us, and the more we use our habitual place of prayer, the more our hearts will naturally open and flow with praise and adoration as its familiarity compels us to worship.

For prayer and reflection

Dedicate afresh that special place where you meet with the Lord in private. If you are able, commit yourself to going there more often.

Shut doors, **open doors**

Thuis is a classic example of the changing face of commitment exhibited by the kings of Israel. Ahaz shut the doors of the Temple, but hot on his heels we find Hezekiah reopening them.

To be honest, 'The Chronicles of Anne's Commitment' would not be so very different, albeit more subtle. Sadly, there have been times when I have shut down prayer, intentionally or otherwise. Perhaps some of us have to face that question today – have we closed the doors of the Holy Place and put out the lamps? Has the once fragrant air turned musty and cold? When Ahaz began to offer sacrifices to other gods it was not long before the Temple doors were closed. What or who is our first love? Are we giving too much attention and credence to someone or something in preference to God?

The subsequent effect of Hezekiah's actions rippled across the nation. As the doors opened, the priests and Levites were consecrated for service, the city officials brought sacrificial offerings, the people of Israel demolished their false altars, resurrecting the festivals ordained by the Lord (chapters 29–31), and religious leaders, government heads and the population at large recommitted themselves to God. Surely we need look no further for encouragement today to reopen the doors of God's house of prayer!

Paul urged Timothy to 'first of all' pray, intercede and give thanks (1 Tim. 2:1), he instructed the Colossians to 'devote' themselves to prayer (Col. 4:2) and told the Thessalonians to 'pray continually' (1 Thess. 5:17). Nothing could be sweeter than our communion with God, to that alone should we be 'devoted' – earnest, untiring and steadfast, unperturbed by circumstance in our pursuit of seeking God's heart 'continually'.

**2 Chronicles
28:24–29:7**

'… he opened the doors of the temple of the LORD and repaired them.'
(29:3)

For prayer and reflection

Ask the Holy Spirit to swing wide the doors of your heart once again and consecrate your life with a continual spirit of prayer.

WEEKEND

The Temple: Scene 3

For reflection: Mark 11:1–11; Luke 19:41–44; John 12:17–19

Jesus shivered in the cool spring air as early evening shadows consumed the Temple courts. The multitude of jubilant pilgrims had finally dispersed, but their cries of *Hosanna* scourged His soul – *Oh save!* He came in peace but they saw war. Had anyone noticed His tears amidst their tumultuous exaltations? Certainly He came to save them, but not from the Romans – rather from themselves.

Hero today, heretic by Friday. Those attracted by sensational miracles would soon bay for His blood. Others stirred up with rebellious hysteria would bemoan their missed opportunity.

He looked around. Moneychangers and traders counted their profits – tomorrow would be a different story. Priests completed their daily service – within days they would spit in His face. Wearily moving through the courts and colonnades He lamented the destruction their hardened hearts evoked – if only they had known what would bring them peace.

Do we only see what we want to see? Are we enticed by sensationalism? Are we expecting Jesus to do something He will not do? Are we using God's temple for our own business and profit? Has our relationship with God stiffened into a mechanical adherence to faith?

The **Holy Place**

Today, we shall follow the priest up the steps of the sanctuary, through the porch and into the Holy Place. This awesome haven was entirely overlaid in intricately carved gold. Daylight squeezed through narrow clerestory windows, scattering golden reflections into the mellow lamplight. Even the furnishings and vessels were overlaid in gold, including the altar of incense, situated in front of the Most Holy Place.

Left alone, the officiating priest waited reverently, in readiness for burning incense, the most honourable service in their daily ministry. Silence.

The courts were hushed as priests and people bowed before the Holy Place, spreading their hands in prayer.

Hebrews 5:7 tells us that Jesus' prayers were heard because of His reverent submission. He surely had the rightful position to be unrestrained in approaching God, and yet we learn that His reverent submission was fundamental to His prayer life. We enjoy a comfortable approach to our loving Lord and friend, but this place reminds us that He is still to be revered as Almighty God. It is good to pause quietly here, and minister to the Lord, allowing the beauty of the Holy Place to focus our hearts onto the glory of God – coming not for what we can get, but to touch His heart with worship.

As incense was sprinkled upon the golden altar, it filled the Holy Place with fragrant smoke. The people began to pray, their words encased by the rising cloud entering the Most Holy Place through openings above the veil, which in turn brought a sweet fragrance to the Lord.

It takes self-discipline to still our busy souls before God, but as we do so, we can say with David, 'May my prayer be set before you like incense; may the lifting up of my hands be like the evening sacrifice' (Psa. 141:2).

Ecclesiastes 5:1–3

'Guard your steps when you go to the house of God.' (v.1)

For prayer and reflection

'Be still, and know that I am God' (Psa. 46:10).

The **Most Holy Place**

Matthew 6:6–13

'But when you pray, go into your room, close the door and pray to your Father, who is unseen.' (v.6)

For prayer and reflection

God waits for you to draw up close to Him. What does He want to say to you in this private place of prayer? What is your response?

nce a year, on the Day of Atonement, the high priest entered the inner room of the sanctuary – the Most Holy Place. It lay veiled from view behind an exquisite curtain of blue, purple and crimson yarn and fine linen.

Unlike the Holy Place, this golden room was dark, but for the glowing coals in the high priest's censor. Originally housing the ark of the covenant, it was here that God dwelt, seated above the cherubim. The high priest sprinkled incense over the burnt coals until the room was filled with smoke, and then he prayed alone with God, in that dim, private place.

Jesus still calls us into that quiet, solitary place where we might touch the heart of God. He set us an example by frequently taking Himself off to be alone with His heavenly Father. When Jesus breathed His last, the curtain was torn in two, both illustrating and confirming that God's presence was no longer restricted to the annual visit of the high priest.

All kinds of things will constantly shout for our time and try to interrupt us. Amidst the distractions, however, the still, quiet voice of God will continue to call until we take ourselves beyond the curtain, into the Most Holy Place of our hearts, and stop with Him a while.

God's heart beats in the secret place of our lives. It throbs with a love that yearns for intimate communion with us. He opened the way but how often do we come? No other relationship or activity can ever quench the thirst of a parched soul or nourish the hungry spirit. Spending time here with God, in prayer, will satisfy and fulfil us beyond our wildest expectations – for that is what we are, God's house of prayer.

Lamplight and shewbread

Withdrawing from the sanctuary, we pass by some furnishings in the Holy Place that we overlooked earlier. The seven-branched golden candlestick was decorated with flowers and buds and weighed at least 30 kilograms. The gold table of shewbread was refreshed each Sabbath with 12 new loaves of bread, and laid with offerings of grain, new wine and oil amidst a host of golden utensils, consecrated for ministry.

The light and the offerings were a constant reminder of Israel's complete dependence upon God, *Jehovah Jireh*, their provider of both physical and spiritual sustenance. Sadly, however, we read many accounts of the Israelites turning to other gods and activities to satisfy their needs and we are at no less of a risk today.

Emerging from our secret place of prayer, it is helpful to pause a few moments to look upon these furnishings. Are we going to keep in step with the Lord on our way out, leaning upon Him to resource us for life, work and service, or will we turn our backs and dash out of the door?

Jesus, light of the world, inhabits His people – humility opens the windows of the soul to let Him shine. Jesus, bread of life, feeds His children – complete trust and dependence unlocks the power of heaven to do His work.

How will He choose to express Himself through the body He made us, the personality He gave us and the talents He entrusted to us? Could we be so Christ-dependent that people would only see and hear and experience Jesus in His living, breathing, walking, talking, laughing, crying temple? It is certainly a goal worth pursuing, but will only develop as we spend time with Him in the sanctuary and remain utterly dependent upon Him for our activities throughout the day.

2 Corinthians 3:15–4:11

'… this all-surpassing power is from God and not from us.' (4:7)

For prayer and reflection

Without You, Lord, I can do nothing.

Priestly **service**

. . . .
1 Peter 2:1–9
. . . .

'… you … are being built into a spiritual house to be a holy priesthood …' (v.5)

The tribe of Levi was chosen to minister in the tabernacle and subsequently the Temple. Their duties were as numerous as they were varied. In addition to offering sacrifices and burning incense, they prayed for the people and taught the Law; they trimmed the wicks and refilled the oil-lamps, cleaned the sanctuary and took care of the courts and side rooms. They prepared unleavened wafers, flour, wine, oil and grain for the offerings; they de-wormed wood for the altar, looked after the priestly robes and ministered as singers, musicians, gatekeepers, guards, officers, judges and treasurers.

We are a 'royal priesthood' (1 Pet. 2:9). Our body is a temple of God's Holy Spirit and our actions perform His priestly duties. The Holy Spirit desires to be master over our time and efforts and, as God reveals His purpose, we simply need to dovetail into His will. Just as numerous duties were distributed among the priests and Levites, so we have been gifted to fulfil certain tasks. Although they were many in number, they didn't try and do someone else's job or tread on each other's toes in the process – they knew their calling and quietly and reverently got on with it.

For prayer and reflection

Aaron's sons began doing things their own way and it was the death of them (Lev. 10)! Are we trying to tailor God's will to suit our personal desires?

We are each created for unique tasks that God prepared in advance for us to do (Eph. 2:10), and so we offer our hands, feet, minds and hearts to minister within His house of prayer. Every dedicated act of service is esteemed equally in His sight, from cleaning the church to preaching the Word, from raising children to leading a government.

Jesus said, 'I have come down from heaven not to do my will but to do the will of him who sent me' (John 6:38). Let us follow His example.

The **curtain parts**

Mark 15:21–41

'... Jesus breathed his last. The curtain of the temple was torn in two from top to bottom.' (vv.37–38)

I wonder how you reflect on the crucifixion. Wherever you are, and whomever you are with, take a moment to pause in the Holy Place. Picture in your mind's eye the expanse of blue, purple and crimson yarn and fine linen, with cherubim worked into it, separating you from the Most Holy Place of God's presence.

It is the time of the evening sacrifice – three o'clock in the afternoon. As the paschal lamb is slain on the altar, so Jesus breathes His last on the cross: 'It is finished' (John 19:30).

Before your very eyes a snag appears in the top of the curtain and without further warning, as if pulled by invisible hands, it tears straight down the middle. For the first time in many years light penetrates the mysteries of the inmost sanctuary, its golden interior beckoning you to walk through the gaping curtain.

Jesus grants access to God's presence by a new and living way through the curtain that is His body (Heb. 10:19–20). The fullness of the Godhead dwelling in Jesus was veiled from view by His flesh, but in death His body was torn apart, so revealing the Father: 'Surely he was the Son of God!' (Matt. 27:54). With His own divine hand, God desecrated the holiness of His Temple to prepare and make way for the new.

Physical and spiritual life moves through its seasons (Eccl. 3:1–8). Standing here with remnants of crimson yarn at your feet, and a pool of blood at the foot of the cross, what season in your life is God bringing to an end? What does He want to bring to life in you over the coming days?

For prayer and reflection

Take and use my life Lord – it is all I can offer as a meagre token of humble gratitude for the suffering You endured on that black and bloody day.

WEEKEND

The Temple: Scene 4

For reflection: Matthew 27:62–28:15

So much for forethought! How they rued the day that fraudster 'Jesus' came to town. On pain of death the eminent Roman guard would not have fallen asleep, and even if they had, any attempt to steal the body would certainly have awoken them – the stone was huge.

Robes billowing as furrowed brows unmasked their anguish, the chief priests and elders gave their response to this latest news. There was no other way – money, substantial quantities of it, was the only language these heathens understood. And so the story circulated that the disciples had stolen His body.

Hallelujah, Jesus is alive! If, like me, you have been ridiculed and grieved by loved ones who shun His name, then be encouraged. Bribery failed to silence the truth and neither should emotional blackmail or peer pressure have a hold on your testimony.

Your witness may be with words or with actions (1 Thess. 4:11–12; 1 Pet. 3:1–2,15; Rev. 12:11).

Reflect on these scriptures, asking the Spirit to guide you as you reach out with His love – 'And surely I am with you always, to the very end of the age' (Matt. 28:20).

Golden **glory**

**2 Chronicles
2:5–18**

'The temple I am
going to build will
be great …' (v.5)

A s we walk through the Temple in our mind's
eye we can indulge the imagination with
its overwhelming splendour. God looked
favourably upon the wealth Solomon invested in
its décor and filled His house with the glory of His
presence. It served a purpose for its period – inspiring
the Israelites to revere God's majesty, setting them
apart from surrounding nations who looked on in
admiration, and preparing them to meet their Messiah
who would make the ultimate sacrifice.

The architecture and décor were indeed beautiful,
but its intrinsic feature was the God who dwelt at its
centre. While its purpose was to be a house of prayer
and sacrifice, its construction arose from a spirit of
holiness, quintessential of the holy God whom it
served. Sadly, people became more enamoured with
its elegance and religious rites than with the One whom
it housed. Although the building and its contents were
extremely valuable in monetary terms, its priceless
quality was determined by God's presence. The fact
that His glory had departed from His house in Herod's
day, was overshadowed by the beauty and religiosity
predominating their minds.

What are we known for? What is our reputation with
other people – and with God? From where do we get
our value and sense of self-worth? Is it from looking
good, earning a good salary, achieving promotion or
recognition, mothering a model family, keeping a tidy
home, preaching a cracking sermon, singing beautiful
solos? If God were to leave the temple of our bodies,
how long would it take us to notice?

We are called to build a temple for the glory of God
but are we building in God's image or our own?

**For prayer and
reflection**

**Reflect: Whatever
we look like and
whatever we do,
our one pursuit is
that God would
be known through
our lives.**

Return and **rebuild**

Haggai 2:1–9

"'And in this place I will grant peace," declares the LORD Almighty.' (v.9)

After 70 long years serving in exile, only an elderly remnant could still remember the former glory of Solomon's Temple. The Babylonians ransacked it, stealing its treasures and destroying it with fire (2 Chron. 36:19–21), but with the advent of King Cyrus of Persia, the time came for God's people to return and rebuild His house of prayer.

Many of us still find ourselves in times of exile – feeling distanced from God's intimate presence in bondage to other people or circumstances. Looking back, we remember the days when we rejoiced at the touch of His Spirit, when we served with energy and enthusiasm and when other people were drawn to God because of our testimony and witness. What changed? What stripped His temple of treasure and eroded His house of prayer?

Personal sin is often the stumbling block, setting us on the path into exile, but also the bereavement of a loved one, relationship breakdown, job loss, financial hardship or long-term illness. Have these winds of adversity ravaged the temple and robbed you of the joy of ministering in God's house? Perhaps His temple lies shattered at His feet but He wants to rebuild it, one precious stone at a time.

For prayer and reflection

'Be strong ... I am with you' (Hag. 2:4); 'I will grant peace' (v.9); 'I will bless you' (v.19); 'I have chosen you' (v.23).

Scripture teaches us that He always starts with the altar. If you are in exile but wanting to return, the first offering you can sacrifice is your choice to allow Him onto the building site. You may feel painfully vulnerable, your open wounds still raw from recent attack. Trust Him to take the fragments of your life and remake them, not into what was before, but into something even better. God is with you and will help you to restore your life into His holy dwelling place.

... For **all nations**

O ur temple-tour is drawing to a close having taken us through the courts and the sanctuary that make up God's house of prayer.

Of prime concern is our regular approach to God with thanksgiving and praise, preparing our hearts for intimacy through confession and consecration, worshipping Him in the beauty of His holiness and seeking His face in the intimacy of the sanctuary. The priestly ministry brought sweetness and light to the Holy Place. Likewise, as we soak ourselves in prayerful ministry before the Lord, the radiance and fragrance of Jesus will fill His living temple. It doesn't stop with us though, for God built His temple to be a house of prayer and a witness for all nations (Isa. 56:7). His empowering through our devotions will enable us to offer so much more to people we meet in the courts of our lives.

As we exit the sanctuary, our private place of prayer, the demands of family, work, church and personal expectations could so easily take our focus off His intentions and send us tumbling down the steps into a dishevelled heap! As we learn to keep in step with the Spirit of God's house, however, we won't waste time on the things we are not supposed to be doing, and we will have time for the things that we were created and gifted for.

We have considered how we may be God's house of prayer, but prayer is not merely words, it is the deep communion with God in song, in silence, in service and in rest that pervades each hour of our day. Whether we are dancing with praise, flat on our face in worship, caring for our family or serving in our church or workplace, we shall fulfil God's purposes in being His house of prayer.

2 Corinthians 2:14–16

'... thanks be to God, who ... through us spreads everywhere the fragrance of the knowledge of him.' (v.14)

For prayer and reflection

Thank You, Lord, for helping me to consider how I may be Your house of prayer. May Your fragrance bear witness to everyone You bring my way.

Home **to heaven**

**Revelation
21:1–4,15–27**

'Now the dwelling
of God is with
men, and he will
live with them.'
(v.3)

We surely cannot conclude our look at the temple without taking a glimpse at the future. We have learnt about the past and considered how that applies to the present, but where is it all leading?

Before the end of time, God will judge the nations from His temple in heaven (Rev. 15:5–16:1). After judgment, however, heaven and earth will pass away to be replaced with a new heaven, a new earth and a new Jerusalem. The Garden of Eden had no need of a physical temple and nor will there be need of one in eternity – for the temple will be God dwelling with man: 'I did not see a temple in the city, because the Lord God Almighty and the Lamb are its temple' (Rev. 21:22).

Aside of our salvation, can we prepare ourselves for that day or are we merely in transit, serving the Lord in our bodily temple while we wait? Paul reminded Timothy that being generous and rich in good deeds will lay up treasure as a foundation of our eternal home (1 Tim. 6:18–19).

In material terms, however, there is nothing that we can save or buy to take with us: 'Naked I came from my mother's womb, and naked I shall depart' (Job 1:21). The holy place of our lives is not lined with material gold – savings, homes, furnishings, clothing and so on – that will fade away with the world. The gold of our temple is His priceless love overlaying the sanctuary of our heart – and that is our treasure for eternity. The more we nurture our relationship with God now, the greater the treasure we store for our future. Let us invest wisely!

**For prayer and
reflection**

**Home is where the
heart is. Where
does your heart
lie? 'For where
your treasure is,
there your heart
will be also.'
(Matt. 6:21)**

The Song
of Songs

Sandra Holt

Sandra Holt was formerly a computer programmer and lecturer
in IT. After 17 years of living in rural Aberdeenshire, she and
her husband now minister to a city church in Edinburgh. An
experienced spiritual director, she divides her time between
guiding people through *The Spiritual Exercises of Ignatius of
Loyola*, working with the Church of Scotland's candidate selection
process and writing. She is the author of three books: *Intimacy
Human and Divine*, *Listening to the Soul*, *Make Decisions that
Matter*, and is a columnist for *Woman Alive* magazine.

The Song of Songs

Ecclesiastes
3:1–8;
Song of Songs
1:1

'Solomon's Song of Songs.' (Songs 1:1)

The Song of Songs is aptly named. Not only does it claim to be the best of all songs, it is also unique and arguably the most enigmatic book of the Bible. No one is certain who wrote it, though it is attributed to Solomon and opinions vary on its interpretation. Some approach it as an allegory, others as drama or a series of love songs possibly sung at a Syrian wedding. Its place in the Hebrew Bible was defended in AD 90 by Rabbi Aqiba for whom the whole of God's revelation was summarised in its poetry. He told the Council of Jamnia that, 'In the entire world, there is nothing to equal the day on which the Song of Solomon was given to Israel'.

We would classify the Song as Wisdom Literature along with Proverbs, Job and Ecclesiastes. Just as Job explores the mystery of suffering, and Ecclesiastes the meaning of existence, so the Song of Songs explores the enigma of love.

Here is a poem celebrating love, beauty and intimacy. We will immerse ourselves in its lyrical verse and allow its simple, sensual passion to address our hearts as all true poetry does. This will be an emotional rather than an intellectual experience, but it will also be a spiritual one. We will encounter in its verses many themes found in our personal relationships and in the song of the Son; the gospel of Jesus Christ. These include the desire for and the consolation of intimacy, the pain of absence, the clouding of fellowship, the restoration of communion and the permanency of a love stronger than death. Exploring these themes will inspire a deep and unambiguous trust in the love God longs to share with each one of us.

For prayer and reflection

To love is to know and be known. Ask God to help you discover a new attraction to the Son as you get to know Him in the poetry of the Song.

WEEKEND
Poetry in motion

For reflection: 1 Corinthians 13:1–13
'Love does not delight in evil but rejoices with the truth.
It always protects, always trusts, always hopes,
always perseveres.' (vv.6–7)

Milton said that true poetry is 'simple, sensuous, and passionate'. Take time this weekend to enjoy the poetry of the Song. A poem's main task is to transfuse emotion rather than thought into the reader. Notice which verses and images move you. Perhaps some attract while others disturb. Allow yourself to experience both responses without immediately seeking either to understand why or fathom the meaning of the more obscure language. The poetry of the Song is a gift in itself. Welcome it as Elizabeth did the gift of a visit from her Lord's mother, when she felt her own child leap in the womb in recognition of the Saviour. Poetry ministers to our soul, moving us not just with images but with sounds.

If you have a copy, read aloud the poem 'Pied Beauty' by Gerard Manley Hopkins to experience both. Look for poetry in your day. Use 1 Corinthians 13 as a guide once you have enjoyed reading it aloud. Like the Song it does not mention God yet we know that it is God's love that never gives up, never stops reaching out to us, and never fails our searching souls.

A **spirituality of desire**

**Song of Songs
1:2–4**

'Take me away with you – let us hurry! Let the king bring me into his chambers.' (v.4)

Surprisingly, the first words in this poem are spoken by a female, as is 53 per cent of the Song's text. The essentially feminine tone and texture of her speeches suggests a female poet as author. This is entirely possible; both Deborah and Miriam sang victory songs and may have composed these. The Song invites us to hear God speak to us in a new way.

The woman takes the initiative, inviting the young man to intimacy and expressing her feelings without reserve or ambiguity. Immediately we are captivated by her honest emotion. She sings her lover's praises; 'the king' signifying the dignity and nobility she is delighted and proud to find in him. She rejoices in the admiration he attracts from every woman. Then, luxuriating in the memory of past encounters, she is gripped with a desperate desire. She wants her lover to run off with her so that they can be alone together in his private chamber. Who can blame her?

The Holy Spirit speaks through our desires, working differently with those that are God's will for us and those that are not. So we need to be honest about them. If we are not, it may be our relationship remains too formal – we are unsure how deep God's love for us goes. The beloved enjoys a relationship that has already deepened well beyond the tentative peck of acquaintance. Her unambivalent desire invites us to feel the heat of our own love for Christ and cast off the reserve that keeps us 'neither cold nor hot' (Rev. 3:15). So, confess your desires, hopes and fears as passionately as you feel them and let truth ignite your love.

For prayer and reflection

What delights you about God? What delights God about you? Both are pointers to God's greatest desires for your life in Christ.

Suddenly **feeling unsure**

Comparing oneself to others is usually a mistake; one advertisers like us to make. The woman is confident in her attractiveness until she compares herself to the 'daughters of Jerusalem'. They have protected their pale complexions from the ravages of the sun and, standing next to them, she feels suddenly unfashionable and uncertain of her ability to keep her lover. Working in the vineyards for her brothers has darkened and dried her skin and poignantly she realises too late that she has neglected her own 'vineyard' for so long that the damage is permanent. She turns to her lover for reassurance, pleading with him to tell her where he will be grazing his sheep so that she can join him there and leave these sophisticated beauties behind.

Peter felt the same anguished uncertainty looking into the eyes of Jesus: 'Go away from me, Lord; I am a sinful man!' (Luke 5:8). Jesus is the one Person with whom it is worth comparing ourselves, His life the only appropriate model for our own. No doubt we, like Peter, will feel humbled by the incomparable humanity we find perfected in Jesus' life as we read about it in the Gospels. But we can also be reassured – Jesus is not offended by either Peter's sinfulness or ours. When we are at our lowest ebb He reassures us that our companionship is precious to Him. As the friends of Jesus we can be confident not in our looks or our intellect or even in our deep faith, but in God's love for us. It is a love made tangible in the life of Jesus and in the invitation to discipleship He offers us, calling each of us out of the crowd to be our incomparable selves.

Song of Songs 1:5–8

'Do not stare at me because I am dark, because I am darkened by the sun.' (v.6)

For prayer and reflection

Tend the vineyard of your friendship with Jesus by spending time gazing at Him as we meet Him in the Gospels. Let Him gaze on you too.

A heart to **sing God's praise**

**Song of Songs
1:9–2.2**

'How beautiful you are, my darling! Oh, how beautiful! Your eyes are doves.' (v.15)

Love is something to sing about and the world is full of well-known songs that celebrate love. Now the gospel of Jesus Christ is the world's greatest love story: 'For God so loved the world that he gave his one and only Son, that whoever believes in him shall not perish but have eternal life' (John 3:16), so it is no surprise that Christianity, more than any other religion, uses song. There are many songs in the New Testament: The Magnificat, the angels' chorus, Simeon's *Nunc Dimittis* to the infant Jesus. Paul sang when he was chained in a prison cell and encouraged Christians to 'Speak to one another with psalms, hymns and spiritual songs. Sing and make music in your heart to the Lord, always giving thanks to God the Father for everything, in the name of our Lord Jesus Christ' (Eph. 5:19–20).

In these verses of the Song of Songs, the woman and man seem to pre-empt Paul's advice as they sing one another's praises. Modestly she calls herself 'a rose of Sharon, a lily of the valleys'. But he professes her 'a lily among thorns'. She reciprocates: he is handsome and charming. They delight in each other and in love that has surprised them with its joy.

When I am in a congregation that sings God's praises from the heart, the hairs on my neck tend to stand and I know that heaven doesn't get much closer. My heart continues to sing with gratitude long after worship has ended. When we sing, alone as Mary did or together with others, of God's love for the world and of our love for Christ that His compassion has surprised in us, we experience the gratitude that Paul tells us is the sign of true love.

For prayer and reflection

Christ is the expression of God's esteem for you. Make this your wakening thought and let your heart sing its grateful response all day long.

Constraining the consolation

W hen Peter, James and John see Jesus transfigured, they are profoundly moved. Peter wants to make the moment last: 'Master, it is good for us to be here. Let us put up three shelters – one for you, one for Moses and one for Elijah' (Luke 9:33). The Gospel comments: 'He did not know what he was saying.'

Sometimes when we experience God very close in prayer or at worship, we want to hold on to the experience in a way that has more to do with fantasy than reality. We may make decisions in this afterglow that seem inspired by the Holy Spirit but which are as mistaken as Peter's notion of a mountain retreat.

Today's passage is spoken by a woman who is 'faint with love', gripped by extreme emotion. She imagines herself lying in the arms of her lover letting him arouse her with his gentle caresses and searching kisses. Then just as things could get no steamier a brake is thrown. The woman, lost a moment ago in her daydreams, suddenly brings to mind those daughters of Jerusalem and pleads with them: 'Do not arouse or waken love until it so desires.' She longs for her relationship to be consummated but knows that the proper place for this is within a marriage that has not yet taken place. Now she wakens to the dangers of fantasy and the necessity for constraint.

If we are wise, like the woman in the Song, we too will learn to contain our consolation. It will help to recall that the standard or banner of Christ is love. An inspiration may seem delightful but until we can confirm Christ's banner hoisted over it we are wise to hold it lightly and be prepared to let it go.

Song of Songs 2:3–7

'He has taken me to the banquet hall, and his banner over me is love.' (v.4)

For prayer and reflection

Lord, in all I do and think and say, help me to seek the Giver rather than the gift until love is the only banner over my life.

Christ is risen indeed

**Song of Songs
2:8–14**

'See! The winter is past; the rains are over and gone. Flowers appear on the earth; the season of singing has come …'
(vv.11–12)

T he young man's joy is infectious as he leaps over the mountains; sure-footed as a stag, swift as a gazelle. He is impatient to share his good news with his beloved. Read these verses aloud and you begin to share in his joy. Now imagine Christ bounding out of the tomb and leaping over the hills to find His friends and tell them the good news of God's faithfulness. Take time to really feel something of the joy He felt on that Easter morning. Remember, Jesus actually died and though He surrendered His spirit into God's hands He also felt alone: 'My God, my God, why have you forsaken me?' (Mark 15:34).

Sometimes we too feel abandoned in those times of dark suffering we all experience. Christ's gospel invites us, not to whistle in the dark, but to share in the joy of the risen Christ. There's no need to pretend that the Christian faith makes life's hardships disappear. Pray instead for the grace to be glad because Christ is glad, to be confident in the future because the risen Christ is confident in the future. Ask God to give you a deep confidence and trust in Christ's eagerness to leap over mountains to come to you whatever the circumstances.

The joy expressed in the Song and experienced by Christ is the joy of resurrection; God's response to the darkest times we all face. It is clarity after confusion, light breaking on a dark situation, confidence after uncertainty; knowing the right path to take and finding the courage to take it. Then it does seem that flowers appear in our hearts – and singing too. God seems to say to us, 'Arise, come, my darling; my beautiful one, come with me.'

For prayer and reflection

What deaths, big and small can you identify in your experience? What form did resurrection take? Give thanks for each springtime in your life.

WEEKEND

Living flame of love

For reflection: Mark 12:28–34

'Love the Lord your God with all your heart and with all your soul and with all your mind and with all your strength.' (v.30)

John of the Cross (1542–91), poet, mystic, theologian and spiritual director, gave us insight into the dark night of the soul where love like fire rises ever upwards with the desire to be absorbed in God, its source. His entire life was a response to the greatest commandment: love God with your whole being. In his *Cantico espiritual*, an interpretation of the Song of Songs, God invites us to an intimate, passionate and transforming union with the Beloved.

For John, the living flame of love was ignited many times a day as he encountered God in the ordinary events of life. A beautiful landscape, an act of kindness, talking with a friend or meditating on a Gospel passage: all invited him to be aflame with God's love.

Take time to acknowledge and reflect on the invitations of love you have received in the past week. Respond in gratitude with the poet's words: 'How tenderly you make me love!' (*O Living Flame of Love!**)

* *The Poems of St John of the Cross*, translated by Willis Barnstone (New Directions Publishing Corp.).

Too good to be true?

'Catch for us the
foxes, the little
foxes that ruin the
vineyards ...' (v.15)

This one verse seems oddly out of place, interrupting the woman's thoughts and her flow of loving endearments. Commentators have seen no point to it, and one even places it in parenthesis. Reading aloud from verse 8 of chapter 2 to verse 17 missing out today's verse demonstrates how easily the little foxes are overlooked. However, a devotional approach to Scripture assumes that every verse that has stood the test of time is there for a reason. None can be overlooked in our task of listening for God's word to us.

The woman remembers how her lover came proclaiming his confident love for her and inviting her to a future together. But as she luxuriates in his love she becomes vaguely aware of some doubts that flit across her mind like shadows. Left unattended they will undermine the hope beating in her breast as they insinuate – isn't it all too good to be true? Can he really love someone like you that much? The questions seem reasonable enough, even sensible, but the woman is sufficiently self-aware to spot an undermining spirit at work. So she catches hold of these doubts, names them as subversive forces burrowing away at her hope as foxes burrow at the roots of vines destroying the chances of fruit. And recognition is enough to deal with the intruders.

We too doubt even the good news of salvation. Sometimes we find ourselves responding to the acclamation 'Christ is risen' with 'Ah but ... is it too good to be true?' instead of 'He is risen indeed!' Awareness of these little foxes is often enough to see them off, averting the havoc such doubts cause in the vineyard of faith.

**For prayer and
reflection**

**Memorise this
verse and use
it whenever the
good news of
God's love for you
seems just too
good to be true
or more than you
dare hope for.**

Choosing **to commit**

What does it mean to commit our lives to Jesus? At the beginning of our relationship with Him it may mean declaring that He is mine and I am His. Later in the Song the woman's declaration is inverted, as she realises: 'I am my beloved's, and my beloved is mine' (6:3, NKJV). As the relationship deepens she moves from feeling proudly possessive of the man to surrendering her entire being to him. To save means to make whole and she recognises that union with him is her salvation. She resolves to remain one with him come what may.

How does this deepening happen for us? Haltingly it seems. As we get to know this Lord we have asked into our hearts we want more of the loving humanity we see in Him for our own lives. But we want other things too and while these distract us from total surrender we are like the Israelites whose attempts to serve many gods steered their lives this way and that, and all the time away from the one true God. That is until Joshua told the Israelites it was time to choose: 'Now fear the LORD, and serve him with all faithfulness. Throw away the gods your forefathers worshipped beyond the River and in Egypt, and serve the LORD. But if serving the LORD seems undesirable to you, then choose for yourselves this day whom you will serve' then he declared his own decision: 'But as for me and my household, we will serve the LORD' (Josh. 24:14–15).

Jesus is the Saviour of our souls. We belong in Him, and He in us, if we so choose. For His part Jesus has already committed Himself entirely to our service. He declares that He is ours and we are His with the words: 'I will be with you always' (Matt. 28:20).

**Song of Songs
2:16–17**

'My lover is mine and I am his.' (v.16)

For prayer and reflection

Jesus invites you to be part of Him, made whole in Him. Respond by making the Song of Songs 6:3 your daily prayer.

When God **seems absent**

**Song of Songs
3:1–5**

'Have you seen
the one my heart
loves?' (v.3)

**For prayer and
reflection**

**If hesitating in
prayer, imagine
you are the
woman at the well
(John 4:1–26).
As you give Jesus
water tell Him
what troubles
you. Listen for
His response.**

e all know the anguish of loss. It is part of what it means to be alive. But sometimes we feel we have lost God. It could be that we have been careless with this relationship, letting pressures squeeze out our prayer from daily or weekly routine. Perhaps there is something troubling us that we have not brought to God in prayer. God sits quietly like a good friend until we are ready to say what is on our mind.

But there are times when He steps back; when the insights in prayer and the warm feelings we enjoyed in worship seem like a distant memory. God is like a mother. After enjoying lots of quality time with her infant she busies herself with something else. She stays within reach of the infant but does not give her full attention to the child. The mother knows that this is a good way of encouraging the development of a secure and confident individual.

God wants secure adult children; men and women who can leave the dependency of childhood to enjoy a loving relationship with God and other people. Consequently, as the Christian life progresses, for some there are fewer glimpses of God close up and personal, fewer times when the presence of Christ is almost tangible, like sweet honey on our lips. When this stage comes, it is common to find Christians hurrying after this or that new thing as though to ask 'Have you seen the One my heart loves? – can you deliver to me those sweet days of intimacy I long for?' God hopes instead that we will embrace our identity as grown-up children. Then we will hear the Father tell us: 'You are always with me, and everything I have is yours' (Luke 15:31).

A **discerning heart**

**Song of Songs
3:5–11**

'Come out, you
daughters of Zion,
and look at King
Solomon wearing
the crown …' (v.11)

Soon after Solomon became king, God appeared in a dream and bade him ask for whatever he wanted. Aware of the awesome responsibility of kingship, Solomon asked for 'a discerning heart to govern your people and to distinguish between right and wrong' (1 Kings 3:9). God was pleased to grant this wise request and also gave Solomon riches and honour, 'so that in your lifetime you will have no equal among kings' (1 Kings 3:13). Some of this splendid wealth and prestige is described in today's passage.

The appearance of Solomon in the Song led one interpreter to suggest that it is the story, not simply of a woman and her lover, but of a more complex *ménage à trois*. Perhaps Solomon abducted a beautiful maiden, attempting to win her love by seduction. She resists his wealth and power, staying true to her love for a shepherd boy. This unlikely interpretation does usefully accent the fidelity of our maiden. Such fidelity is exactly the grace King Solomon bids the Lord give him when he asks for the grace of discernment. The truth is that the ability to discern right from wrong must be accompanied by the will to choose the right and cleave to it no matter the consequences. For the maiden, the right choice was to remain true to her shepherd. For King Solomon the right course of action would always be the one in accord with God's will for His people.

For each of us the gift of faith comes with the same responsibility of fidelity to God's will. The grace of a discerning heart is a petition we all need to make. We cannot discern the right course of action unless we first commit ourselves to taking it.

For prayer and reflection

Ask God for the grace to discern in each situation of choice what is for His greater glory and the resolve to do it.

Eros!

**Song of Songs
4:1–8**

'Your two breasts
are like two fawns
… that browse
among the lilies.'
(v.5)

Imagine these verses read aloud in church. How would you feel? Uncomfortable? Not surprising, since for centuries the Church taught a hierarchical division of the person into two parts – body and soul. Love of God and love of mankind were sanctified, but the passionate, physical love shared by two people was deemed dangerous and defiling. Which is why to this day many couples leave Christ outside their bedroom. Yet in marital sex we transcend 'self' to join physically and spiritually with the person God has given us. This communion has the power to draw us from fragmentation to unity.

However it is by no means the only expression of the at-one-ment God desires for us. Worship is another. Chapter 4 of the Song is a sensual hymn of worship offered to the woman. Because we have regarded the intellect as superior to and more godly than the physical and emotional we have many fine hymns and psalms that allow us to proclaim the faith to one another in song. Psalm 100 – 'All People That On Earth Do Dwell' is a stirring example of good theology while 'Jesus Calls Us O'er The Tumult' captures Christ's life and ministry and reminds us all of His daily call on our lives. In recent years new songs with words directed *to* God rather than describing Him *to ourselves* have enhanced worship. These allow us to engage our minds without neglecting our senses through which we experience intimacy.

Singing songs like 'Have Thine Own Way, Lord' and 'Within The Veil' encourage the lover in us to feel our honest passion for the Beloved. Suddenly we know with body, mind and soul the desire God gives us for at-one-ment with Him.

For prayer and reflection

Read aloud chapter 4 of the Song. Borrowing its passion, choose a favourite praise song and sing it to God all day.

WEEKEND

Contemplating Jesus

For reflection: John 20:19–23
'The disciples were overjoyed when they saw the Lord.' (v.20)

Lovers gaze at each other often. Gospel contemplation is gazing leisurely using our senses to flesh out a scene. Take the scene in John 20:19–23: Christ appears to His friends hiding in the upper room.

Sit comfortably, read the verses slowly a few times (aloud is good) then close your eyes. Imagine the scene.

Ask yourself: what do I see? Perhaps a low roofed room sparsely furnished and with people standing around in small knots. What do I hear? Perhaps wailing or quiet sobs, speculative whispers or the sound of your own heart thudding. What do I smell and taste? Fear has a smell and it has a taste too. Or perhaps you smell the faint perfume of spices used to anoint the body of a loved one. Jesus has a fragrance, perhaps this enters the room before He does. What is touching me? Perhaps you are shoulder to shoulder with others becoming aware of Jesus and crowding round to hear His words. Perhaps you are touched when He says: 'Peace be with you.'

Love of Jesus deepens when we take time to gaze at Him. Try it and see.

God's passion, our response

Song of Songs
4:9–16

'You have stolen
my heart, my
sister, my bride;
you have stolen
my heart with
one glance of
your eyes ...' (v.9)

The Song conveys a passionate story of love even though it has no coherent plot and lacks both the structure and movement of a conventional romance. The couple's intense love for each other is neither unrequited nor frustrated, yet still there are twists and turns to be met. They suffer trials and sorrows as well as great joy and fulfilment on a journey that is not straightforward.

The whole Bible tells the thrilling story of God's passionate love for us. It chronicles all the usual ups and downs of any intimate relationship, as the history of Israel unfolds. God's chosen people were often distracted by other gods. More seriously, they frustrated the spontaneity of God's love with twists of arrogance and turns of complacency. Often they just misunderstood or underestimated the intense desire God felt for them. Through it all God was faithful. Humanity had captured God's heart and nothing would make Him renounce it. When sin stood between God and humanity this love story reached its climax. The beloved Son hung on a cross for the sake of the love that stole His heart before time began.

Gazing down at us with compassion, He prays: 'Father, forgive them, for they do not know what they are doing' (Luke 23:34). Our frailty meets with forgiveness and our hearts, often confused and faithless, finally comprehend our own longing: 'Lord you have made us for yourself and our hearts are restless until they rest in thee.' This confession of Augustine's is ours too and is as irresistible as the glance of the woman in the Song. It captures God's heart anew each time we make it.

For prayer and
reflection

**Lord, I can hardly
believe that I have
stolen Your heart
so completely.
Help me live in
grateful joy for
Your patience
with all my
ambivalence.**

Opening doors

Song of Songs 5:1–6

'I looked for him but did not find him. I called him but he did not answer.' (v.6)

The girl, for all her passionate love, cannot be bothered to open the door to her lover when he knocks. She has retired for the evening and getting up to open the door to him would mean dressing again and dirtying her newly washed feet. Then, too late, a change of heart comes. Opening the door she finds her lover gone. Regret hits her like a fist in the stomach and she feels faint.

Jesus tells us that He is standing at the door of our hearts and that 'If anyone hears my voice and opens the door, I will come in and eat with him, and he with me' (Rev. 3:20). It is tempting to assume that having opened the door once to invite Jesus into our lives this passage cannot have much to teach us. But aren't we all sometimes like the girl in this poem – not in the mood when Christ seeks our company? It is easy to become complacent, to act as though the grace of God in our lives is something we have a right to control. Just as we control the central heating in our homes with a thermostat, turning the heat up and down for our own comfort and convenience, switching the whole system off when we are away from home.

Christ comes to us at will and sometimes He knocks at the door of a room within our heart to which He has not yet had access. And sometimes we pretend not to hear Him. Though it is never too late to respond to Jesus, it is certainly presumptuous to keep the Lord of all creation waiting until the mood takes us. God calls us to surrender the whole of our lives to the cause of love and begs us not to keep any part of our heart closed to His healing presence.

For prayer and reflection

When trouble has taken you unawares, what were the signs and how did you ignore them? Resolve, with God's help, to open every door to Christ.

Enemies within and without

**Song of Songs
5:7**

'They beat me,
they bruised me;
they took away
my cloak, those
watchmen of
the walls!' (v.7)

The girl runs through the streets searching frantically for her lover. She collides with the officers of the watch who, objecting to the noise she is making as she calls out, accuse her of disturbing the peace. They treat her roughly and laugh as, battered, bruised and naked, she finally escapes to make her way home. But remember that this is a dream and every character is some aspect of the dreamer, every symbol addresses personal concerns. Perhaps the young woman's dream was prompted by some gnawing anxiety that the passion she felt for her lover was not quite respectable. The law dealing with prostitutes demanded the ritual exposure of a prostitute's nakedness and this may be how the watchmen dealt with her.

Jesus had no such doubts about the veracity of His feelings for God and the Father's love for Him and for us. He disturbed the peace of many with His passionate teaching and soon came to the attention of 'those watchmen of the walls'; men who knew the law and were happy to stretch it to breaking point in order to punish Him for a ministry they found dangerously radical. The world deals harshly with those whose passion for God will not be quieted.

We, too, if we follow Jesus, can expect this world's hirelings to mock our commitment and pour scorn on our values. But we should not be surprised if the most zealous law enforcer turns out to be an internal watcher. This part of ourselves cautions us against complete faith in God's love for us, treats us harshly and is content to watch us treat others harshly too.

For prayer and reflection

Pray that you might remember your dreams, and note down any when you waken. In prayer, work with the feelings in the dream to discover God speaking through it.

Our faith **questioned**

'How is your
beloved better
than others … that
you charge us so?'
(v.9)

Peter gives this advice: 'Always be prepared to give an answer to everyone who asks you to give the reason for the hope that you have' (1 Pet. 3:15). Sometimes this questioning is done aggressively, yet we are charged to answer 'with gentleness and respect' (1 Pet. 3:15). More often, as in the Song, it is done scornfully. We are considered unreasonable when we cannot agree that the revelation of God in the life, death and resurrection of Jesus is no more significant for the world than the wisdom of other faiths. This makes it all the more important that we each have an answer to the question, 'How is your beloved better than others?'

Without being harsh or disrespectful of other religions, our testimony can nevertheless be confident in the completeness of God's revelation to humanity in Christ. Our hope does not lie with a God who is far off or circumscribed by laws. We do not rely on a deity summoned by aesthetic practices. Nor is our beloved a guru of self-actualisation. Our hope is 'God with us'. Our Beloved is better than others because He is the One who has come close to us. He wanted to understand the human condition and out of that compassionate understanding offer us unconditional forgiveness of all our wrongdoing and healing of all our dis-ease. Ours is a hopeful God who looked at creation 'And saw that it was good' (Gen. 1:10).

He looks to us to work alongside Him. Inviting us to *be* what we *are*: made in His image and co-creators with Him in an enterprise of hope still to be completed. It's good news very different from anything offered by the religions and philosophies that may question us.

For prayer and
reflection

**What is God's
hope for your
family, friends
and neighbours,
for your
community,
country and
world?**

Jesus **the Man**

**Song of Songs
5:10–6:3**

'His mouth is
sweetness … he is
altogether lovely.
This is my lover,
this my friend …'
(v.16)

**For prayer and
reflection**

**God, grant me
the grace to know
Jesus better so
that I might feel a
deeper attraction
to His Person and
cause and a desire
to follow Him
more closely.**

We can only really bear witness to God's goodness when we know Jesus well. But knowing Jesus is difficult, especially if we are so focused on His divinity that we overlook His humanity; for it is His humanity that makes Him 'God with us'. Ignatius of Loyola is just one of many saints who discovered that by spending time in imaginative contemplation of the gospel we can get to know better the carpenter from Nazareth and the message He left His home and work to tell. Ignatius discovered that when we get to know Jesus more we find ourselves attracted to Him, and being attracted to Him we want to follow Him more closely.

This getting to know Jesus has the power to transform us from believers into companions. The crowd who followed Him from one village to another were believers, but the disciples who left everything to be with Him were His companions.

Each Gospel is good news told with a particular theological perspective and evangelical mission. Mark's Gospel is good news for those who want to meet Jesus the Man. It was the first Gospel to be written and perhaps because of this it is the least varnished collection of memories about Jesus.

It is also the shortest Gospel so it is easy to read straight through at one sitting. Do this and you will encounter the emotional dimension of Jesus: His anger (Mark 11:15–17), His compassion (Mark 1:40–42), His sense of fun (Mark 12:13–17), His frustration (Mark 6:1–6), and His willingness to learn from other people (Mark 7:24–30). This is our lover, this is our friend and we can get to know Him by spending time praying with the Gospel of Mark.

WEEKEND

Spirit of light or darkness?

For reflection: 1 John 4:1–6
*'Every spirit that acknowledges that Jesus Christ
has come in the flesh is from God ...' (v.2)*

Writing to a persecuted church, John advocates caution, 'because many false prophets have gone out into the world'(1 John 4:1). False prophets also inhabit the inner world of our experience and emotions; laughter and tears, love and indifference, deep feeling and transitory mood. Not all insights or impulses are of equal value. Some beckon the unwary on to disaster. Careful examination will help us to follow only those inspirations that increase faith, hope and love.

So look over a day, giving thanks for all of it (even the uncomfortable bits) and ask the Holy Spirit to help you notice those actions and intentions inspired by Christ's Spirit, and those dictated by other interests. Give thanks for the first and learn what you can about yourself and your own false prophets from a careful examination of the second. Then pray for the day ahead:

Thank You for this day given to me to praise, reverence and serve You. Grant me the grace to live each moment as one who knows that Jesus Christ has come in the flesh.

Celebrate your virtues

'… my perfect one, is unique, the only daughter … the favourite of the one who bore her.' (v.9)

Self-worth is a gift parents give when they notice a child's virtues and talents. If she is celebrated as the lover celebrates his beloved in the Song, then the gift of self-worth will take root and its fruit will last a lifetime.

But what of those whose parents did not notice when their child was patient, loyal, kind or generous, who forgot to celebrate a talent for music or for making friends or telling a joke? Such people need to hear how precious they are in God's eyes. Pray for any you know, and in the spirit of the Song celebrate their unique virtues and the giftedness they bring to the lives of those around them.

Perhaps self-worth is something you find yourself lacking. Perhaps you even thought that God expects you to cope with life while being unsure of your own value. If so, now is the time to let God nurture the child within you who still longs to be celebrated. Look out a photo of yourself aged around three – a child full of goodness. Champion her virtues and talents by noticing them. The talents and virtues we esteem in others are actually our own. It is not envy that causes us to notice them in other people but resonance. Prove this by sticking a list of them with the photo above your bathroom mirror, for example. Whenever you look into the mirror read the list and, with the help of anyone else who uses the bathroom, begin to notice each quality in your own life.

For each grace you discover give thanks by saluting the three-year-old you. Over time the un-esteemed child can learn to trust that what you notice about her is true and begin to celebrate her own uniqueness.

For prayer and reflection

Hear God tell you that you are a favourite daughter, unique in all creation.

Toe-tapping prayer

Today's reading and yesterday's (6:4–13) are two of four passages in the Song that elaborately celebrate the beauty of the beloved. The others are: 4:1–15 and 5:10–16. This form of poetry is called *wasif* a word meaning 'description'. The *wasif* formed an important part of ancient wedding celebrations. The bride danced before her guests while they sang to her of her incomparable beauty and grace. Dance has always played a part in the worship of the Hebrew people. Remember how Miriam danced on the banks of the Red Sea, and when David danced before the ark as it processed towards Jerusalem. Both were joyfully and exuberantly applying their bodies to the task of adoration.

Try this form of prayer for yourself when you want to tell God how great is your love for Him. You will probably want to take the advice of Jesus to go apart to some lonely place when you try it out for the first time! Then select a favourite hymn or chorus. Choose one that lends itself to movement, addressing God rather than describing God to the assembly, and expresses your feelings for Him. Play it over a few times while you close your eyes and imagine yourself interpreting the words and music with simple movements.

If you are physically able, try out the moves and have fun improving them until the whole thing flows and you can enjoy this form of praise. Then take some time to catch your breath and notice what new insights this physical adoration has given you into the greatness of God and the love you feel for Him.

Song of Songs 7:1–9

'I said, "I will climb the palm tree; I will take hold of its fruit." ' (v.8)

For prayer and reflection

If you enjoy dancing in prayer consider introducing some friends to it.

Live now!

**Song of Songs
7:10–8:4**

'If only you were to
me like a brother,
who was nursed
at my mother's
breasts!' (v.1)

The woman wishes for the one circumstance that would allow her to display affection for the man in public. If he were her brother it would not offend propriety to hug him in greeting or hold his hand in the street. 'If only' is a game without any winners because it dreams of things that cannot be. 'If only we had not quarrelled', 'If only I had studied harder for that exam or practised more for my driving test'. God is not in our desires for what might have been possible 'if only'. God is too busy creating and recreating to look back. Or perhaps you thought creation was an act in the distant past; done and dusted.

Though God began the work of creation by creating out of nothing He continues by using each and every circumstance of our lives. Our joys and sorrows, our victories and defeats, our good choices and bad, can all become part of God's plan for the world and for us. God does not say, 'If only she had not done that or gone there or chosen that partner I could have blessed her life.' Instead He blesses us by redeeming all our losses, creating something unexpected and new out of them.

Co-operating means in every circumstance keeping ourselves like moist clay in God's hands so that He can mould us and make us into the shape that will perfectly express who we are and thereby glorify God in us. 'Today, if you hear his voice, do not harden your hearts as you did at Meribah ...' (Psa. 95:8), pleads the psalmist.

'If only' is not merely a game with no winners, it is a way of hardening our hearts to the true call of God in the midst of our real experience and present circumstances.

**For prayer and
reflection**

**Lord, help me to
find You in each
situation however
trying, and in
this way keep
my heart moist
and ready to be
shaped into the
Christ form.**

Love is …

H ere is a passionate speech any woman might make to her lover. Read the whole passage aloud to appreciate the strength of its conviction and the depth of its emotion. Elizabeth Barrett Browning declared similar feelings of passionate love and deep commitment to Robert Browning in one of her *Sonnets from the Portuguese*:

> … I love thee with the breath,
> Smiles, tears, of all my life! –
> and, if God choose,
> I shall but love thee better after death.

Yet the promise made in today's focus verse claims more for love than even this beautiful poetry does, although clearly Elizabeth experiences love as a constant presence, transcending the joys, sorrows and transience of life.

For our lovers it is also, and more enduringly, a strong, unyielding force. It seems they are past the point of sending messages to one another eulogising the beauty and sweetness of their love. In these closing verses the woman challenges her lover and the reader to embrace a love that does battle with disaster, death, wealth and compromise. Love for this couple has been a hard won victory over everything that sought to hinder or pervert it, as is Christ's love for us and as ours for Him should be.

The love we are challenged to place as a seal over our hearts is the love Christ demonstrates for us in determined victory over death. Paul describes it both poetically and forcefully: '… neither death nor life, neither angels nor demons, neither the present nor the future, nor any powers, neither height nor depth, nor anything else in all creation, will be able to separate us from the love of God that is in Christ Jesus our Lord' (Rom. 8:38–39).

Song of Songs 8:5–7

'Place me like a seal over your heart, like a seal on your arm; for love is as strong as death.' (v.6)

For prayer and reflection

Pray to recognise every temptation to sentimentalise love, and resolve to place Christ as a seal over your heart.

Learning from **strong women**

Song of Songs
8:8–14

'But my own
vineyard is mine
to give …' (v.12)

One of the most exciting aspects of our study of the Song is our encounter with a strong woman: 'I am a wall,' she declares to the world, 'and my breasts are like towers' (v.10). What confidence she enjoys in herself!

When it comes to serving Christ in the world through His Church we may lack her confidence to bring our own style of leadership or ministry. So we try to conform to the traditional, male models of how leadership has always led and ministry always ministered. Ironically, while many women need to explore ways of bringing their own unique gifts to Christ's Church, many men could usefully explore Christ's call to humility. Sometimes the men can have too big a vision for themselves in God's plan and too much confidence in their natural abilities.

Meanwhile women can have too small a vision and not enough confidence that Christ can work through them. To correct any imbalance it's helpful for us all to spend some time with the strong women we meet in the Bible; those who know they have a vineyard to give, a contribution to make. Those who appear long enough to tell their stories include Ruth, Naomi, Esther – and the woman who wept at Jesus' feet; the vineyard this woman gave to Jesus was her heart (Luke 7:36–50). Broken with sin it was still hers to give or hold back. She chose to give it with such honesty and vulnerability onlookers were aghast. But Jesus told them, '… her many sins have been forgiven – for she loved much' (v.47). He instantly recognised that here was a devotion so strikingly different that her story would be told in memory of her wherever the gospel was declared.

For prayer and reflection

Ask God to help you discover your own ways of serving Christ, and give you the courage to make your contribution with integrity.

Ruth – a place in God's purposes

Beverley Shepherd

Beverley is a long-standing member of the Women's Ministry team of CWR. As an experienced trainer, mentor and facilitator, she has a wealth of experience in the field of personal and team development, working with a wide range of secular organisations. One of her passions is the encouraging and equipping of Christians in the workplace and she is an associate speaker for The London Institute for Contemporary Christianity. A regular speaker at conferences, Beverley has written several books including *Insight into Stress* and *Created as a Woman*.

WEEKEND

Ruth – a place in God's purposes

For reflection: Ephesians 3:14–15

Over the next few weeks we will be looking together at the book of Ruth. It is a love story and, as women, the thought of studying such a book naturally warms us. Yet if we look at it only as a love story between Ruth and Boaz we will miss much of its richness. It is part of the ongoing love story of God for His people; it challenges us to examine how we live in a society that has turned away from God. The very heartbeat of this book is covenantal love and faithfulness – between God and His people and between individuals.

Ruth is a love story that embraces your life and mine as we seek to be part of God's salvation purposes for this world. It is a love story that reveals something of the heart of God for us – His people.

So let your heart be warmed by the thought of this look at Ruth – but be prepared also to respond to God's love for you and be challenged to live this out in your own personal context.

If you have time today you might like to read through the whole book of Ruth.

In the **days when** ...

'Once upon a time' is the age-old formula for our children's stories – placing them beyond time and free of context. Yet the story of Ruth starts, 'In the days when the judges ruled'. This sets it somewhere between 1380 and 1050 BC, ie after the Exodus out of Egypt and entry into the promised land, but before the era of the kings – Saul, David, Solomon and so on. It's a time when judges were appointed to lead Israel and save them from their enemies.

Throughout the book of Judges there are two refrains: the first is 'the Israelites once again did evil in the eyes of the LORD' (eg 3:12; 4:1). Because of this evil God repeatedly brings judgment on His people by giving their enemies victory over them and, as at the start of the book of Ruth, through famine.

The second refrain is 'In those days Israel had no king; everyone did as he saw fit' (17:6; 21:25). The people developed a 'pick & mix' attitude to spirituality as is evidenced by Micah in Judges 17, who designs his own religion to suit himself. Worship of Yahweh, the one true God, was mixed with idolatry and pagan religions to produce an ungodly cocktail. The lack of true godliness in people's homes was reflected in unfaithfulness in relationships, violence on the streets, women being raped and an ailing economy.

What is God's way forward in such a context (not unlike our own)? Is it grand political strategies, radical economic policies or more police on the streets? No, though these have their place. The story of Ruth dares to suggest that the hope for Israel and for us lies in sacrificial committed love in our relationships and ultimately in God's covenant love for us. Each one of us has a part to play in God's salvation purposes!

Ruth 1:1–7

'In the days when the judges ruled, there was a famine in the land ...' (v.1)

For prayer and reflection

Dear Lord, please help me to hear You speak through the pages of this book of Ruth, and open my heart to receive and apply its truths. Amen.

Godly **decisions**

Proverbs 3:1–8

'Trust in the LORD with all your heart and lean not on your own understanding.' (v.5)

What is in a name, we might ask. When we come to the book of Ruth the answer would be 'a lot!' We are told that a man went from Bethlehem ('The House of Bread') to live in Moab. A rational decision when there is no bread in The House of Bread due to famine and presumably there is plenty in Moab – especially if you have a family to feed. Yet famine is a sign of God's judgment and Moab was dubious territory for the people of God (Deut. 23:3–6); so has Elimelech, whose name means 'My God is King', really submitted this decision to God? Or has he 'leant on his own understanding'?

The continuing story supports the latter conclusion as he and his sons die – presumably the fate they were hoping to escape back in Bethlehem. To further emphasise this, the whole town is stirred and recognises Naomi when she eventually returns to Bethlehem with Ruth (1:19), so few, if any, had died. There may not have been plenty in the place of God's provision – but there was enough!

For prayer and reflection

Dear Father, help me to daily trust in Your goodness and provision. I ask for Your wisdom when making decisions for myself and my family. Amen.

Despite his name, Elimelech does not trust in God's provision for his family. Instead he takes matters into his own hands and moves his family to Moab. It is a temptation we all face when making decisions. Yet we are required to 'not be wise in our own eyes' and to ask God for His wisdom, wisdom that we are promised we will receive (James 1:5). When, through our busyness or oversight, we fail to do this, God is merciful – yet if we are deliberately disobedient to His written Word or proud of our own self-sufficiency, then we bypass His wise direction and reap the consequences. Today let us choose to submit to His leading and 'in all our ways acknowledge Him'.

Sovereignty and **suffering**

Psalm 77:1–20

'Has God forgotten to be merciful? Has he in anger withheld his compassion?' (v.9)

Life is unfair – why should Naomi be called upon to suffer so much? First she is uprooted from her home and friends to go and live in Moab, an alien culture where Chemosh, not Yahweh, is worshipped. Then her husband dies, and within the next few years she loses both her sons. For a woman in that society, the loss of your men folk meant not only the deep pain of bereavement, but also the loss of your status, your means of provision and your role – you were thrown onto the charity of strangers.

Naomi had gone to Moab full, but is now empty (1:21). No wonder she declares in 1:13, 'the LORD's hand has gone out against me!' and 'the Almighty has made my life very bitter' (1:20). Yet here are the very seeds of hope – ultimately these are statements of God's sovereignty. God is both Lord and Almighty.

Although you may be battered by circumstances and suffer great loss, God is still in control – there is someone to whom you can address your anguished questions: 'Why?' 'How long?' 'Do you care?' 'Have you forgotten to be merciful?' God answers our questions, not with words, but with a cross. Through the cross of Christ, God declares: 'I love you deeply, My mercy is unfailing – I know and share your pain and anguish.'

The Christian life is not trouble-free – we experience the same hardships as non-believers, and it is right that we should grieve. Yet we do so in the knowledge of His sovereignty and in the security of His mercy. More than this, we know that God shares in our suffering and comforts us in our loss.

No, God has not forgotten to be merciful, as Naomi is to discover.

For prayer and reflection

O Merciful Lord, in my loss and pain, please draw close. May I know Your comfort and Your healing. Thank You that You are in control. Amen.

Repentance and returning

Isaiah 30:15–21

'In repentance
[returning]
and rest is your
salvation, in
quietness and trust
is your strength …'
(v.15)

When Naomi makes the decision to go back to Bethlehem (Ruth 1:7), she is doing more than just 'going home', she is returning to full dependence on God rather than on the seeming plenty of Moab. To repent means to turn back or return to God in total dependence and trust in Him. This results, Isaiah tells us, in a quietness and stillness in our spirits, rather than anxious thoughts, and renewed strength as we lean on the Almighty.

When I am lost while driving I hate turning back – 'Surely,' I reason, 'if I just go on a little further, it will all work out.' Often this is just stubborn pride, a refusal to admit that I have gone wrong, or failure to study the map before setting out. If returning to God leads to quietness and rest, why do we delay? For the same reasons I find when driving – being too proud to admit that we have got it wrong. It takes humility to acknowledge that we should have looked at God's map before we started.

It took Naomi ten years to return, and yet the good news is that it wasn't too late! God is always ready to welcome us home when we turn back to Him. Notice that although the decision to return may have taken only a moment, the process of getting back to Bethlehem took much longer. There would have been the goodbyes and letting go of all the friends in Moab, packing up what she could carry and leaving the rest of her possessions; and then the journey itself – fearful for a woman travelling alone. Yet, from the point Naomi's heart has turned back to God, she can commit her way to Him and trust in His provision – provision that included a beloved travelling companion.

For prayer and reflection

O Lord, today please help me to admit where I have got it wrong and gone off track, and give me the humility to return to You. Amen.

Covenant love

Ruth expresses her devotion to Naomi in covenantal form. This is no mere 'I'll travel with you for as long as it suits, and then move on', it is a commitment 'for better or for worse'. Ruth is expressing the very heart of God, for without total commitment, no true intimacy is possible.

God offers us a loving and intimate relationship, but He specifies the basis for that relationship: covenantal commitment. It is truly 'for better, for worse, for richer, for poorer, in sickness and in health, to love and to worship, till death do us join'.

I recall the day that God challenged me to commit myself fully to Him. I had been a Christian for nearly ten years, but viewed my relationship with God as a contract: I kept the rules and He delivered wellbeing (according to my definition) and answered prayer. It was the lack of 'wellbeing' in my life that had led me to accuse God of not fulfilling His side of the bargain! His answer was to pull the rug out from under my feet: 'Bev, there never was a bargain or contract, only a covenant. Will you commit to me in covenantal faithfulness, for better, for worse ... till death do us join?'

I knelt in the Prayer Room at Waverley Abbey House and prayed that prayer. I wish I could tell you that it was a moment of pure delight – it wasn't! It was a moment of desperation; I had nowhere else to go. Yet, as I was to later realise, God made those same vows to me, and knowing that we are bound together in covenantal commitment has been foundational to my growing intimacy with God.

Ruth 1:8–18

'Don't urge me to leave you … Your people will be my people and your God my God.' (v.16)

For prayer and reflection

Beloved Lord, I choose to rip up any contract I thought we had, and commit myself to You in covenantal love from this day forward. Amen.

WEEKEND

The will to love

For reflection: 1 John 5:1–5

What is love? If we were to listen to the way the word 'love' is used on TV, in magazines and in newspapers, we would conclude that love is an 'intensity of feeling'. Sometimes love is portrayed as clinging desperately to another person declaring, 'I cannot live without you.'

This is not love, it is merely the desire to have our needs met through another. The Bible sees love differently – God, who is the originator of love, describes it as an act of the will: 'This is love for God: to obey his commands' (John 5:3). Obedience is not a feeling – it is a decision. Obedience has at its root the verb 'to listen'. We cannot be obedient to God without giving time to listening to Him through His Word and through prayer.

Just as with God, our love for others will show itself in giving them attention – in listening. Why is this costly? Because it involves setting aside our own agenda and focusing on the other person.

This weekend let me encourage you to show your love for God and for others by listening.

Naomi or Mara?

A woman once asked me to help her complete a 'Lonely Hearts' advert. She was having difficulty describing herself – 'Should I call myself a widow or a divorcee?' she asked. 'Which are you?' was my reply. In fact, the circumstances of her life gave her claim to both titles, but the real issue was what she felt the labels said about her – how they defined her identity.

The circumstances of our life can change our sense of identity, as those who have gone through divorce, bereavement, illness or redundancy can testify – we no longer seem to be the person we once were. Naomi struggles with this too. Her name, meaning pleasant, no longer seems an apt description of her life; 'Mara', meaning bitterness, seems more appropriate. Loss can leave us feeling very empty as Naomi expresses: 'I went away full, but the LORD has brought me back empty' (v.20), yet our very emptiness can be God's opportunity to fill us with something new. We need to grieve our loss, but emptiness is not the last word – for God, whose creative activity took place when the earth was formless, empty and dark (Gen. 1:2), is at work.

If we allow the joys and sorrows of this life to define us we will forever be registering a name change. Yet these are not the basis of our identity. 'Fear not, for I have redeemed you; I have summoned you by name; you are mine' (Isa. 43:1). The unchanging basis of our true identity is that we are redeemed and called and we belong to the living God.

As Selwyn Hughes said: 'You don't know who you are until you know whose you are.' You and I are the beloved daughters of the living God!

Ruth 1:19–22

'Don't call me Naomi … Call me Mara, because the Almighty has made my life very bitter.' (v.20)

For prayer and reflection

Creator, You who formed me, redeemed me and indwell me by Your Holy Spirit – I am Yours. Thank You that this is my unchanging identity. Amen.

God's **timing**

....

Ruth 1:22–2:4

....

'Just then Boaz
arrived from
Bethlehem …' (2:4)

I am not naturally a patient person. In fact, having completed a psychometric profile as a part of a course I was taking, I was a little unnerved to find the report describe my attitude to time as 'Ready, Fire, Aim!' I have to constantly remind myself that God's clocks keep perfect time.

We see examples of His perfect timing in this passage: the barley harvest was beginning at the very time that Ruth and Naomi arrive in Bethlehem (1:22) and then Boaz arrives in the fields just as Ruth is gleaning. These are not coincidences – God is working His purposes out. He takes careful aim before He fires and my role is to await His timing. To await God's timing involves submission. Waiting is an acknowledgement of my dependency on God and it confronts me with the illusion of my own control. God is not to be hurried. Our life has to keep time with His clock.

I love to dance, especially the waltz. When waltzing, the woman submits willingly to her partner's lead. He determines which sequence of steps they dance, which route around the room they will take and also gently halts their progress when there is a danger of colliding with another couple. The woman's role is to keep in time and to follow – she cannot see where they are going, only where they have been. Trusting your partner is key.

When we doubt God's perfect timing we are tempted to take the lead and then expect Jesus to keep in time with us! God will not co-operate with this and we will find ourselves dancing alone. Jesus says, 'Follow Me and keep time with Me – dance by faith, not by sight. Enjoy the unforced rhythms of My grace' (see Matt. 11:28–30, *The Message*).

....

**For prayer and
reflection**

....

**Lord, thank You
that as I look
back over my life
I see Your perfect
timing. Help me to
trust Your timing
for the future.
Amen.**

God's **concern for the poor**

When the Lord spoke to Moses and gave him various laws for the people of God, He built in provision for the poor, the widowed and the alien. This is so important that God does not leave it to a whim of generosity on the part of His people, but ensures that it is written into the very structure of society. It is on the basis of this law that Ruth (poor, widowed and an alien) knows she has the right to go and pick up the leftover grain to provide for Naomi and herself.

Notice that Ruth takes the initiative to claim this provision – she asks permission of both Naomi and the foreman, then goes out and works hard, only having a short rest. This would have been tiring work in the hot sun, yet God has also provided Ruth with the energy and strength to do this physical work. However, His provision for her extends beyond the general (law and health) to the specific provision of 'coincidentally' choosing Boaz's field in which to work.

Work is a gift from God – it was given to us before the Fall (Gen. 2:15). We know from Genesis 3:17 that our toil will often be painful, for the context of our work is cursed; yet God provides us with the skills, ability and energy to do our jobs. Work is still God's primary means of enabling us to provide for our families and to be generous to the poor, both through our taxes and giving.

It is not always easy to see our work as God's gift, especially when we have a difficult boss, unrealistic deadlines or inadequate resources. In my experience, thankfulness for my work can change my attitude and re-energise me to face the difficulties of the day.

**Ruth 2:1–7,
Leviticus 19:9**

'… do not … gather the gleanings of your harvest … Leave them for the poor …'
(Lev. 19:9–10)

For prayer and reflection

Lord, thank You for the work You have given me to do today, the strength to do it, and the ability to bless others through it. Amen.

Water **for the thirsty**

. . . .
Ruth 2:8–16
. . . .

'You have given me comfort and have spoken kindly to your servant …' (v.13)

✓

Yesterday we noted that Ruth had worked hard at a task that would have left her tired and thirsty. Boaz encourages her to go and drink from the water jars whenever she is thirsty, yet he does more than this, he also speaks to her thirst for kindness. Ruth is most commonly described in this book as 'the Moabitess' – she is the foreigner, with no friends or family except Naomi. She has voluntarily chosen to leave behind all that is familiar and commit herself to Naomi and Naomi's God. Yet this is not without cost. In a society where most relationships are formed through family connections she only has Naomi, who is herself bereft of close family, as her companion.

Ruth's response to Boaz's concern and kindness shows that this was water on dry ground. His words also indicate that her sacrifice has not gone unnoticed – either by Boaz or by God.

Words have incredible power to both hurt us and to heal and encourage us. Paul emphasises this in his letter to the Ephesians when he writes: 'Do not let any unwholesome talk come out of your mouths, but only what is helpful for building others up according to their needs, that it may benefit those who listen' (Eph. 4:29).

Daily we have a choice how we use our words. We can use our words to criticise, slander, wound, discourage and isolate others. Many of you know what it is like to be on the receiving end of this. Or we can use them as Boaz did, to befriend the lonely, to protect the vulnerable, to recognise godly sacrifice and to pray blessing on each other (vv.11–12).

Just think what power we have been given to bless and to comfort through our words today!

. . . .
For prayer and reflection
. . . .

Lord, please guide me in the use of my tongue and protect me from the unkind words of others. Amen.

Godly **men**

'The name of the
man I worked with
today is Boaz.'
(v.19)

A
t the beginning of chapter 2 we are
introduced to Boaz as a 'man of standing' – a
man who is straightforward and honourable.
His name means 'in him is strength'. As we read on we
discover that this is a man who has good relationships
with his employees (v.4), who notices the stranger
(v.5), who provides protection and provision for the
disadvantaged (v.9), who honours godliness in others
(v.12), who includes the foreigner (v.14) and who is
generous to the poor even beyond the requirements of
the law (v.16). No wonder Naomi declares, 'Blessed be
the man who took notice of you!' before she even knows
his name.

We learn that he is an older man, a landowner,
and perhaps a widower. He is a distant relative of
Naomi's husband and a kinsman-redeemer. A kinsman-
redeemer was responsible for protecting the interests
of needy members of the family, for buying back land
sold outside the family, and for purchasing the freedom
of any family member sold into slavery. There is no
indication in chapter 2 that Boaz has any romantic
aspirations concerning Ruth – his behaviour flows from
a godly character. His notice of Ruth is due to what he
has heard of her sacrificial love for Naomi (2:10–11).

More and more I am aware of the need of both
spiritual and practical protection by godly men. Whilst
God is our ultimate protector, He works through others
to shield our vulnerability. The feminist agenda of
the last few decades has given us many benefits and
freedoms but has, perhaps, made men unsure of how
to offer us this vital protection. May we learn to affirm
the godly men in our lives, and to receive protection
from them.

**For prayer and
reflection**

**Dear Lord, thank
You for the godly
men You have
placed in my life –
please bless them
today. Amen.**

WEEKEND

The power of love

For reflection: Acts 1:1–11; 2:1–4

The Church's birthday – Pentecost – is when we celebrate the gift of the Holy Spirit to all believers, a gift of power. It is power with a purpose: 'You will receive power when the Holy Spirit comes on you; and you will be my witnesses in Jerusalem … and to the ends of the earth' (1:8).

The most loving thing I can do for my non-Christian friends and neighbours is to tell them about Christ. Other things I might do for them have value only in this life, whereas their relationship with Jesus has eternal significance. Yet why do I need power for this? Because 'the god of this age has blinded the minds of unbelievers, so that they cannot see the light of the gospel of the glory of Christ …' (2 Cor. 4:4). Even though my friends may not agree with what I am saying, they are often open and interested when they realise that my motivation is love.

Yes, we need God's wisdom as to how and when to speak, but the power to love and to witness is God's birthday present to His Church. Thank You, Lord!

God's **hand**

Naomi constantly alerts us to God's hand at work in this story of Ruth: '... the LORD had come to the aid of his people by providing food for them' (1:6); 'May the LORD show kindness ... May the LORD grant ... another husband' (1:8–9); 'the LORD's hand has gone out against me!' (1:13); 'The LORD has afflicted me; the Almighty has brought misfortune upon me' (1:21). And now, at the end of chapter 2, she again sees the Lord's hand at work in the 'coincidence' of Ruth working in Boaz's field and Boaz taking notice of her. '[The LORD] has not stopped showing his kindness to the living and the dead,' she declares in 2:20. No, Naomi, the Lord never stopped showing His kindness to you, for even when you settled in Moab – even there God's hand guided you and His right hand held you fast (Psa. 139:9–10).

Are you ever tempted to doubt God's kindness to you? The Hebrew word is '*hesed*' – His loving kindness and faithfulness. Or do you doubt that He is in control? As Naomi affirms – God is Almighty – He is the all-powerful God who is able to change the circumstances of your life in an instant, should He so choose. And this Almighty God loves us – He uses the circumstances of our lives to draw us into deeper relationship with Him and to develop His character within us.

Job, whose life contained one long series of bereavement, financial loss, illness and criticism by friends, affirms that God is in charge and that no plan of His can be thwarted. He is, in your life and mine, working for the good of those who love Him and who have been called according to His purpose (Rom. 8:28).

Job 42:1–6

'I know that you can do all things; no plan of yours can be thwarted.' (v.2)

For prayer and reflection

Almighty God, I affirm that You are the Sovereign Lord. No plan of Yours can be thwarted and You are working Your purposes out in my life. Amen.

Our hand

Ruth 3:1–6

'My daughter, should I not try to find a home for you …?' (v.1)

The book of Ruth shows us a wonderful interplay of divine sovereignty and human responsibility. Yesterday we looked at God's sovereignty in our lives – that no plan of His can be thwarted. What should be our response to this; passive acceptance and fatalism? No! God calls us to work hand in hand with Him to bring about His purposes. At the end of chapter 2 we see Naomi's eyes being opened to what the Lord is doing in Ruth and Boaz's lives and she decides it is now time to do her part! There is always a danger when we talk of human responsibility that we will go ahead of God; Naomi waits to see what He is doing before she makes her move.

Naomi would have been aware of God's provision of levirate marriage (coming from the Latin word meaning 'brother-in-law'). This required the brother-in-law to marry the widow of his deceased brother if no heir had been born; the widow was not to remarry outside the family. The brother was to raise an heir for his dead brother so that his brother's name might be perpetuated and the family inheritance secured (Deut. 25:5–10). Although Boaz is not Ruth's brother-in-law, he is one of her nearest male kin, and she does therefore have some claim on him to fulfil this duty to her dead husband. Naomi is also aware of her own responsibility, as Ruth's nearest relative, to arrange a good marriage for her.

Notice these helpful principles for action:

1. Observe what God is doing through the circumstances of your life.
2. Is the action required of you in line with God's law?
3. What are your responsibilities?

God has called us to be partners in working out His plans!

For prayer and reflection

Dear Lord, I ask for the wisdom to observe what You are doing in my family's life, and my own, and to work with You. Amen.

Audacious **obedience**

Ruth 3:7–15

'Spread the corner of your garment over me …' (v.9)

Ruth takes my breath away. Not only did we see the abandonment of all she had known and loved to follow Naomi and Naomi's God, now we see her trusting implicitly in Naomi's decision to set up a very unusual meeting between Boaz and Ruth. She was to dress as a bride (washed and perfumed) and not as a servant girl and then go to the threshing floor where men, having had a good meal and plenty of wine, would be sleeping. She is gambling her reputation and her chastity on the godly character of Boaz.

I imagine that she didn't sleep a wink, wondering if Boaz would wake, and needing to be ready if he did. Naomi had said that Boaz would know what to do, but Ruth, with godly boldness, asks him to marry her and be her levir. The term 'spread the corner of your garment over me' is a request for marriage, but there is also a wonderful play on words here – the same words mean 'cover me with your protective wings'. In Ruth 2:12, Boaz prays for Ruth saying: 'May you be richly rewarded by the LORD, the God of Israel, under whose wings you have come to take refuge.'

Boaz is to be the answer to his own prayer! God's protection of Ruth is going to happen through Boaz spreading his garment over her and marrying her. Her rich reward is going to be the family life that they will enjoy together.

Is God calling you to audacious obedience in some area of your life? When God is in control, no obedience is truly reckless. In fact the only really safe place to be is in the centre of His will – as Ruth discovered on the threshing floor.

For prayer and reflection

Dear Lord, give me the boldness I need to follow step by step as You lead the way – wherever that path may take me. Amen.

Prior **commitments**

1 Corinthians 6:12–20

'You are not your own; you were bought at a price.' (vv.19–20)

While they were still in Moab, Naomi gave her daughters-in-law the choice to go back to their mothers' homes. They were released from all obligations to Naomi and to their dead husbands. Orpah took this freedom, but Ruth made a covenantal vow and committed herself to stay with Naomi until death.

This commitment meant that Ruth was no longer free to 'run after the younger men'. She was obligated instead to either remain single or to marry a man who would accept that Ruth and Naomi were a package deal, someone who would take Naomi into his house and care for her as well as for Ruth.

When Boaz says, 'This kindness is greater than that which you showed earlier' (3:10) he is not depreciating himself as a husband, he is recognising her kindness to Naomi. He knows that he is perhaps the only man who will accept this package deal and who shares Ruth's sense of family responsibility.

You and I have a prior commitment – we were bought with a price, the price of Christ's death on the cross. We have renounced the choice of returning to our mother's house and have covenanted ourselves to be His through life and into death. This choice means we are not free to bind ourselves to anyone who will not accept that we are a 'package deal' with God. If this seems a hard sacrifice then look again at Ruth – her example shows that God is no woman's debtor. Jesus said,

'I tell you the truth ... everyone who has left houses or brothers or sisters or father or mother or children or fields for my sake will receive a hundred times as much and will inherit eternal life' (Matt. 19:28–29).

For prayer and reflection

Dear Jesus, thank You that I am Your beloved and You are mine – we are a package deal! Amen.

A woman of **noble character**

....

**Proverbs
31:10–31**

....

'A woman who
fears the LORD
is to be praised.'
(v.30)

When Ruth makes her request on the threshing floor, Boaz says: 'All my fellow townsmen know that you are a woman of noble character.' The word '*hayil*', translated as 'noble', is a word denoting worth. It is also used of the woman in Proverbs 31 – a capable woman (*hayil* implies ability and efficiency) and a woman of moral worth. The word is most often used in the Old Testament of God – the helper of His people. This is not a weak woman, but one who ably stands alongside her husband.

It would seem that most women's reaction to Proverbs 31 is one of discouragement. Here is 'Superwoman' – an impossible role model to whom I can't live up. Yet if we understand her secret we will find that she is a good example for us and not one to be daunted by.

What is her secret? Her relationship with the Lord. 'Charm is deceptive, and beauty is fleeting; but a woman who fears the LORD is to be praised' (v.30). The fear of the LORD is the source of true wisdom (Prov. 1:7) and so it is no wonder that this woman is clothed with strength and dignity and can laugh at the days to come.

Today 'wisdom' is offered to us from a variety of sources – friends, TV chat shows, the problem pages of magazines, self-help books – yet the wise woman looks to God and His Word. God longs to speak wisdom into our lives – will we listen?

Although Ruth was probably physically attractive, the main reason that Boaz plans such a careful strategy (as we will see in chapter 4) to secure Ruth as his wife is that she is a woman of noble character – a wife worth having!

....

**For prayer and
reflection**

....

**Dear Lord, I
ask You for the
wisdom I need
for my family, my
work and my life.
Thank You. Amen.**

WEEKEND

The work of love

For reflection: 1 Corinthians 13:1–13

A definition of love which I have found helpful is: 'Love is the will to extend one's self for the purpose of nurturing one's own or another's spiritual growth' (Dr Scott Peck, *The Road Less Travelled*). 'Extending oneself' implies effort and action – love is costly. Paul spells out the very practical out-workings of love in his letter to the Corinthians – love is patient and kind, it is not self-seeking or rude …

Yet there are guidelines here as well; we are only to do what will nurture another's spiritual growth – this is not about creating an unhealthy dependency, nor is it about being a doormat. As those of you who are parents know, how you demonstrate your love for your children changes over the years. Initially you have to do everything for them but, in order for them to grow up into mature adulthood, you then have to stand back and let them do things for themselves. Sometimes the most loving thing we can do is to say 'No'.

Re-read 1 Corinthians 13 putting your name wherever it says 'I' in verses 1–3 and 'love' in verses 4–7. In which part did you find this most difficult?

Waiting

Y ou can imagine the scene – Naomi, probably having been up all night waiting, listening for the first sound of Ruth's return. And then here Ruth is, carrying six measures of barley, and Naomi's first words: 'How did it go?' – in the Hebrew literally, 'Who are you, my daughter?' Naomi wants to know if she is the prospective Mrs Boaz!

Ruth describes all that happened and then wise Naomi's advice is to wait. Again the Hebrew is instructive here as the word Naomi uses has at its root the verb 'to sit'. Sit and wait and trust that Boaz will settle the matter. They have both done their part, now the initiative passes to Boaz.

We don't know what was going through Ruth's mind, but I suspect that the degree of peace she experienced would have totally depended on how much she trusted both Boaz's commitment to her, and his character.

The same is true of us. When we place something in the Lord's hands, having done all that He requires of us, in prayer or action, then we can peacefully rest and prepare to receive His answer. Why? Because we know that He is committed to us in covenant love – a commitment that led Him to die on the cross for us; and that His Word is trustworthy.

Too often my prayers are of the 'delegation' variety, eg 'Lord, I'm placing this in Your hands, but if You haven't got it done by this time next week, then I'll do it myself!' God will not be delegated to – He is Lord and we are His servants. When we hand a person or a situation over to Him, we do so knowing that He is free to do what He chooses and when He chooses, and our role is to wait and to trust.

Ruth 3:16–18

'Wait, my daughter, until you find out what happens.' (v.18)

For prayer and reflection

Dear Lord, thank You that waiting is a time when I can deepen my trust in You and prepare to receive Your answer. Amen.

Kinsman-**redeemer**

Ruth 4:1–10

'Then I cannot redeem it because I might endanger my own estate.' (v.6)

To be a kinsman-redeemer to Naomi and Ruth involved personal sacrifice – the obligation to provide for both of them during their lifetimes. The more distant a relative you were – the more voluntary it was to take on the responsibilities of this redemption role. By a masterly strategy, Boaz links the role of kinsman-redeemer with that of levirate marriage – the responsibility to father an heir for Elimelech's property through Ruth. This could lead to future family disputes and endanger a man's estate. The cost was too high for the first kinsman-redeemer and he withdraws his claim. Boaz, however, is prepared to pay this cost – he understands sacrificial commitment and accepts its price.

We have a kinsman-redeemer – Jesus Christ. He willingly paid the price to buy us back from slavery to sin and make us a part of His family. The price was His death on the cross – 'In him we have redemption through his blood, the forgiveness of sins ...' (Eph. 1:7). Jesus' act of sacrificial love was voluntary and through it He secured a bride for Himself – the Church. This is why Paul writes: 'Husbands, love your wives, just as Christ loved the church and gave himself up for her ...' (Eph. 5:25). It is because we have been redeemed at such a cost that we have an obligation to live redeemed lives, and not live as if we were still enslaved to sin.

The love story between Ruth and Boaz, wonderful though it is, is merely a pale reflection of the greater Love Story – that of God and His Church. We are women who know what it means to have been loved sacrificially! Let us learn from Ruth, from Boaz and, supremely, from Jesus, the cost of love.

For prayer and reflection

Dear Jesus, my kinsman-redeemer, thank You for loving me sacrificially. Amen.

Blessed and **blessing**

Throughout the Bible we see the power of blessing: Isaac and his blessing of Jacob, Jacob's prophetic blessing of each of his sons. We should not be surprised at the power of blessing, for we are inheritors of the Abrahamic covenant (Gen. 12:1–3) where God declares that He will bless us and we will be a blessing to the whole world. The elders pray a wonderful blessing on Ruth and Boaz – a blessing that includes their reputation and their family life. This blessing is fulfilled through the birth of Obed. Ruth and Boaz are not just ancestors of King David but also of King Jesus! Through their union they are a channel of blessing to the whole world, fulfilling Genesis 12. The women recognise the great blessing Ruth is to Naomi. Naomi who was poor, bereft of family, embittered and empty, is now secure in the home of Boaz, her life renewed and her lap full with her precious grandson.

In Galatians Paul tells us, 'Understand, then, that those who believe are children of Abraham. The Scripture foresaw that God would justify the Gentiles by faith, and announced the gospel in advance to Abraham: "All nations will be blessed through you"' (Gal. 3:7–8). We are inheritors of that promise! We are called to both be blessed and to be channels of God's blessing wherever we go – including our homes, our places of work, our towns and our country. You and I are God's pipeline of blessing into this fallen world.

God longs to bless those around us, but He chooses to use us to do it. One of the primary ways we fulfil so high a calling is, like Ruth, in the sacrificial love and commitment we demonstrate in our relationships.

**Ruth 4:11–16;
Genesis 12:1–3**

'... I will bless you
... and you will
be a blessing.'
(Gen. 12:2)

**For prayer and
reflection**

**Thank You,
Lord, that I am
blessed – may I
be a blessing to
all the people I
have contact
with today. Amen.**

God's **great reversals**

Ephesians 2:11–22

'… you are no longer foreigners and aliens, but … members of God's household …' (v.19)

God is the Lord of great reversals – He is forever turning things around! In the story of Ruth we have some wonderful examples to ponder:

Bethlehem: The 'House of Bread' was experiencing famine in chapter 1 but now there is a plentiful harvest. This town, which had experienced God's judgment, is now a place of blessing.

Ruth: We meet her first as a widowed Moabitess, an outsider to the people and promises of God, and without provision. After the years of her marriage to Mahlon (whose name meant 'weak') she is childless. By the end of the book she is married to Boaz (whose name means 'in him is strength'), a mother, protected and provided for, and in the family line of Jesus. Not only is she one of God's people, but is greatly used in His salvation purposes!

Boaz, who perhaps considered himself past marriageable age, is now a husband and father.

Naomi: A widow, empty, bereft of sons and of hope, now has Ruth who is better to her than seven sons (the perfect family!) and renewed purpose (she is to care for her grandson). She had thought that the Lord's hand had gone out against her, but can now rejoice with the women who declare: 'Praise be to the LORD, who this day has not left you without a kinsman-redeemer' (Ruth 4:14).

We have experienced this in our own lives – we were once dead in our sins but are now alive in Christ; we were aliens to God's promises and now are part of His household; we were without hope and now have eternal hope. Praise be to God who has not left *us* without a kinsman-redeemer: the Lord Jesus Christ!

For prayer and reflection

Dear Jesus, thank You that there is no situation in my life that is beyond Your ability to turn it around. Amen.

Happy **endings**

I love happy endings! Yet the book of Ruth has more than just a happy ending – it ends with a wonderful new beginning: a family line that will extend via King David through to the birth of Jesus a millennium later. Little did Ruth realise that when she renounced home and country to follow Naomi and her God into a life of probable poverty and loneliness, that God, who is the Alpha and Omega, the A and the Z, had already written the end of her story. Through Ruth, the Israelites – who 'had no king; everyone did as he saw fit' (Judg. 21:25) – were to have both an earthly king and the King of kings.

God has already written the end of our stories. I was once speaking to a Romanian pastor whose life had been threatened by the secret police because of his clear preaching of the gospel – a very real threat as he knew, having just conducted the funeral of a fellow pastor for whom an 'accident' had been arranged. He told me his reply to the police was: 'You cannot threaten me with heaven!'

What is the end of your story and mine? We are going Home!

Now the dwelling of God is with men, and he will live with them. They will be his people, and God himself will be with them and be their God. He will wipe every tear from their eyes. There will be no more death or mourning or crying or pain, for the old order of things has passed away.

(Rev. 21:3–4)

If we, like Ruth, commit ourselves to God and to His purposes in our lives, then we can know that He has written for us the most amazing happy ending!

**Ruth 4:18;
Matthew 1:1–16**

'… Boaz the father of Obed, whose mother was Ruth …Jesse the father of King David.'
(Matt. 1:5–6)

For prayer and reflection

Lord Jesus, thank You that one day You will take me home to live with You. May I live today with this eternal perspective. Amen.

137

WEEKEND

The cost of love

For reflection: 1 Samuel 1:21–28

Love can be costly, not just in the effort required, but also in the pain of loss. Some people never love because of the fear of loss. I remember the day when God challenged me with regard to someone I dearly loved: 'Bev, do you love X enough to let him go?' With God's help I was able to let that person go, but not without many tears.

I wonder how Hannah felt when she took her young son to Eli. I believe that it was the knowledge that Samuel had been a gift from God that enabled her to give him back to God, as well as faithfulness to her vow. This is true of all our relationships – each one of them is a gift from God for however long He allows us. Genuine love does not seek to tie people to us, it respects and cultivates the individuality of the other person, even where this may be at the risk of loss (as when children leave home).

Just as Hannah let go of her son, so that eventually Israel might have a godly leader, so God sent His Son and willingly paid the cost of love, so that we could be saved.

Does my life have purpose? (1)

Jeremiah 29:10–14

'For I know the plans I have for you … plans to give you hope and a future.' (v.11)

Yes – *look at Naomi!* If we are ever tempted to doubt that our lives can be used by God for His purposes then let the story of Naomi encourage you. When we first meet her, her life reflects her name – pleasant: she is married with two sons. Then, due in all probability to the poor decision-making of her husband, she goes to live in Moab – 'exiled' from her home, her people and her religion. She loses her husband, her sons, her role in society, her financial security and her hope. Can God use this empty sorrowing woman? Yes!

It is from Naomi that Ruth learns about the one true God and she is so convinced by the example of Naomi's life that this God is worth following, that she is prepared to abandon her home to follow Naomi back to Bethlehem. It is Naomi who brings Ruth to Bethlehem and into the salvation purposes of God. It is Naomi who sees God's hand at work in the meeting of Ruth and Boaz and advises Ruth to go to the threshing floor. And ultimately it is Naomi who is given the care of Obed, King David's grandfather.

Naomi's story is echoed by that of the Israelite exiles in Babylon. Jeremiah prophesied that they would return to Jerusalem and that God would prosper them and give them back their hope. When the circumstances of their lives evidenced that God was punishing them and seemed to declare that He had forgotten them, God promises that He will bring them back from captivity and rebuild them. When was this to happen? 'You will seek me and find me when you seek me with all your heart' (v.13). Whatever the circumstances of our lives let us seek God and find both Him and His purposes.

For prayer and reflection

Lord Jesus, thank You that, if I seek You with all my heart, You have promised to be found by me and to give me renewed purpose. Amen.

Does my life **have purpose?**(2)

**Philippians
2:12–18**

'… for it is God
who works in you
to will and to act
according to his
good purpose.'
(v.13)

Yes – *look at Ruth!* If you are ever tempted to doubt that your life can be used by God for His purposes then let the story of Ruth encourage you. She is brought up in Moab, taught to worship Chemosh – a god who required child sacrifice – and, as a Moabitess, excluded by God's command from Israel (Deut. 23:3–6). A widow, without any close male relatives, she, like Naomi, is destitute.

Yet, at the point that she commits herself in covenant love to Naomi and to Naomi's God, and sacrificially leaves her home and family, she places herself under God's provision and protection and within His purposes. Ruth 'shines like a star' in a crooked and depraved generation. Her committed love for Naomi stands in sharp contrast to the faithlessness and depravity of the people of Bethlehem – so much so that Boaz and all his fellow townsmen knew her to be a woman of noble character. Through Ruth's son, and ultimately God's Son, the Word of life is held out to this world.

At the point that you and I commit ourselves in covenant love to Jesus and declare Him Lord of our lives, we not only put ourselves under His protective wings and know His provision, our lives have meaning and purpose. In the days when the judges ruled, how was God to carry out His salvation purposes for Israel and for the world? Was it to be through the daring exploits of Samson, the fleeces of Gideon or the wise counsel of Deborah? No, though all of these had their place. Supremely God's purposes are carried forward by a poor Moabite widow who pledged herself to the Lord and His people – yes, through Ruth!

**For prayer and
reflection**

**Lord Jesus, I am
no longer my own
but Yours. Please
take my life and
use it in Your
divine purposes.
Amen.**

God, my heavenly Father

Chris Ledger

Chris Ledger has worked as a counsellor, supervisor and trainer in the NHS, and now has a private practice. She enjoys speaking at Christian meetings and is a regular tutor on CWR's *Insight* days, and has co-authored several books in the *Insight* series. A Licensed Lay Minister at Greyfriars Church, Reading, Chris leads the Prayer Café and Prayer & Healing Teams.

God, my heavenly Father

1 John 3:1–3

'How great is the love the Father has lavished on us, that we should be called children of God!' (v.1)

At some time or another, perhaps we have asked ourselves the questions, 'What is God really like?' and 'Who is He?' All too easily our images of God can become distorted through life's experiences. The way we perceive God and what the Bible actually says about Him may be two different things. Many difficulties with life can be traced to misconceptions we may have of our heavenly Father.

What is your reaction when you hear the word, 'father'? Some may have an image of a father who was abusive, drunk or very critical. Others may automatically think of warmth, love and security. Our relationship with our earthly father will affect our relationship with our heavenly Father. Unconsciously we tend to attach feelings about, and impressions of, our earthly father to our concept of our heavenly Father. This results in a distorted understanding of our Father's love for us. So some may see God our Father as a distant, punitive judge, whereas others may think He is not remotely interested and doesn't love them at all.

For prayer and reflection

But let's remind ourselves from today's reading that the Father's heart is one of unstinting love. We are called children of God – hence we are His daughters. What a generous Father we have, for He has 'lavished' His love upon us – from His heart flows shower upon shower of blessings for each one of us ... His daughters. What a privilege!

What comes to mind when you think about God as your Father? Has your relationship with your earthly father affected your relationship with God? If so, how?

We will experience a closer presence of God as we deepen our understanding of Him as our Father. Hence my prayer throughout this month is that each one of us will grow in the 'Father–daughter' relationship, as we hear His tender words of love and learn of His total acceptance in deeper ways than we have ever known.

Abandoned, but **not orphaned**

Sheila was struggling with life. Sitting on the edge of her chair, she whispered, 'My mother died in childbirth and my father abandoned me. I don't know what it is to be loved by a father – I spent years in and out of children's homes.' Over the next few months, Sheila slowly began to learn that although her parents had forsaken her, her heavenly Father had not forgotten her. Jesus' words, 'I will not leave you as orphans; I will come to you' (John 14:18) really ministered to her.

These words were spoken at the Last Supper on the night before Jesus died. Jesus had informed the disciples that He was about to leave them (John 13:33). Anticipating how bereft, lonely and heartbroken they might feel after His death, He recognised that their emotional reaction to the loss of His presence would be like a child's pain at the loss of its parents. Hence He uses the image of 'orphans'. A future without Him would be a shattering prospect for the disciples. Therefore Jesus promised them a gift – 'another Counsellor to be with [them] for ever – the Spirit of truth' (John 14:16–17).

Although many of us won't actually have been orphaned, I wonder how many of us have *felt* orphaned? The pain of loneliness and abandonment, whenever it arises, can penetrate deep into our hearts. Maybe we have been separated from our father by a long-term posting abroad; through divorce; a long spell in hospital; or perhaps he was just never around. However there is good news! As Christians we are not orphaned – for the Spirit of truth reveals to us that our heavenly Father has adopted us as His daughters.

Psalm 27

'Though my father and mother forsake me, the LORD will receive me.' (v.10)

For prayer and reflection

Ask the Holy Spirit to reveal to you the times you have felt orphaned. Bring the pain to your heavenly Father, asking Him to pour His healing love into that place.

Adopted as a daughter

Romans 8:12–17

'… you received the Spirit of sonship. And by him we cry, "*Abba*, Father."' (v.15)

For prayer and reflection

Do you believe that Christ's blood was the price paid for you to be rescued? Can you hear the Judge of All declaring, 'You are my adopted daughter'?

A couple wanted to adopt a child. After a long process of interviews, their baby girl finally arrived. At the end of the probationary period the parents had to go to court to sign the adoption papers. They faced a stern judge who, before he would sign the papers, asked them if they would be as committed to their adopted daughter as they would if she were their natural one. 'Yes,' was their measured reply. Stepping down from his seat of honour, the judge handed them the certificate of adoption, saying, 'I too have an adopted child; what you are doing is a wonderful thing.'

Although the judge might at first have been perceived as stern and distant, we see him stepping down from his high position to reveal himself as a loving, adopting parent. Sadly, many of us may see God as a stern, cold judge for whom we are never good enough. But this is a distortion of who God is, for God stepped down onto this earth in the human form of Jesus and lovingly adopted us.

In New Testament times, an adopted child was one deliberately chosen by his adoptive father to inherit his goods and continue his family name. If the young person being adopted came from a family of slaves, his new father bought his freedom from slavery.

What a powerful image this is! It reminds us that Jesus paid the price on the cross to rescue us from slavery and thus we are now adopted into God's family. We are no longer orphans or slaves; but are daughters – *His* daughters. Spiritually we have been adopted by our heavenly Father and therefore can use the Jewish child's term of affection, 'Abba' meaning 'Daddy'.

WEEKEND

Wonderfully made by my Father

For reflection: Psalm 139:1–17

sn't life a miracle? To think that God created us and knew us from the moment of conception. We are part of His overall plan – we are no accident. The same Creator who formed the beauty of this earth, from the delicate snowflakes to the pounding seas, created us. Isn't it amazing to think how God could possibly have put so many cells together to create a human being? '... you formed me in my mother's womb ... I was sculpted from nothing into something' (Psa. 139:13,15, *The Message*).

Apparently there are 5,000 different aspects of our personalities alone that He has combined together to make each one of us a unique person. No wonder we are very different. God sees each one of us as a master-work of His creative ability. 'God saw all that he had made, and it was very good' (Gen. 1:31).

Reflect on the miracle of your birth and thank God that He has created you to be someone completely unique. Your heavenly Father rejoices in the fact that no one else smiles, talks or thinks the way you do – He is proud to be your Father.

✓

Ephesians 1:3–14

'For he chose us in him before the creation of the world …' (v.4)

Tell your heavenly Father how you think and feel about being chosen by Him to be His adopted daughter, and then pray: 'O God, thank You that You are my Father, may our relationship grow deeper every day.'

My Father **chose me**

If we are to grow in our relationship with our heavenly Father, we desperately need to take hold of the wonderful picture of God that these verses give us. He has blessed us with every spiritual blessing (v.3); chosen us (v.4); predestined us for adoption (v.5); and lavished His riches of grace upon us (v.8). No wonder He's called, 'the glorious Father' (v.17)!

Our Father doesn't just bless us with a measly blessing or two! He is so generous that He has blessed us with *every* spiritual blessing. Because this blessing is spiritual in nature it will also include *every* blessing of the Holy Spirit. Therefore we are blessed when we allow the Holy Spirit to testify to our spirits that we are daughters of our heavenly Father.

We are daughters because God chose us; not because He had to, but because He loves us so much He wanted to. Sometimes it is difficult for us to receive His love as we are tempted to think that we have to be good enough, or have to have particular qualities, or achieve specific goals to have been chosen. But having a Father–daughter relationship doesn't depend upon us, for Jesus said, 'You did not choose me, but I chose you …' (John 15:16).

Deep within us there is a need to know that we are wanted, chosen and loved, because this satisfies a profound emotional need. If our earthly fathers haven't communicated this to us, then we often end up feeling insecure and suffer with anxiety. But once we know in our hearts that our heavenly Father has taken great pleasure in choosing us, then our anxiety lessens and we become free from the pressure to prove that we are worth choosing.

My Father **loves and accepts me**

I can't accept myself'; 'I don't like myself'; 'I'm inadequate'; 'I'm a failure'; 'I'm fat'. I frequently hear these words in my counselling room, as women struggle with low self-esteem. Many of us have a real problem in accepting different aspects of ourselves – emotions, intellect, behaviour, personality traits or our bodies. What part of yourself do you find the most difficult to accept? It's important to acknowledge these areas otherwise we may ignore or reject the parts of ourselves which we can't accept – and this will cause difficulties in relating to ourselves, others and God.

Jenny became very angry with herself when she didn't do things perfectly, and would end up berating herself for not being good enough – she certainly didn't feel good enough for God. Consequently she became very low. As she began to see herself in the light of God's love, recognising that He still accepted her even though she wasn't perfect, she was able to embrace that part of herself she found so difficult.

In today's passage, we learn that Paul regarded himself as undeserving to be called an apostle (v.9). But he recognised that only the grace of God could help him accept such imperfection, for he was nothing except what God had made him to be. 'By the grace of God I am what I am ...' God has created each one of us; He knows our strengths and weaknesses. By His grace He loves and accepts every aspect of our being, warts and all!

Let's learn to be gracious to ourselves, accepting the areas of our lives and personalities we don't like, and allowing our Father's unconditional love to stem the flow of negative self-criticism.

1 Corinthians 15:9–11

'... by the grace of God I am what I am ...' (v.10)

For prayer and reflection

'Grace means there is nothing God can do to make us love Him more ... there is nothing we can do to make Him love us less.' (P. Yancey)

My Father **values me**

1 John 4:7–16a

'This is love …
that he [God] …
sent his Son as an
atoning sacrifice
for our sins.' (v.10)

Years ago a young mother was carrying her baby in her arms across the Welsh hills, when she was caught in a blizzard. She took off her outer clothes, wrapping them around her baby to save him from the chilling cold. Unfortunately, before help arrived she died, but the baby was found to be alive and well. She valued her son so much that she was willing to die so that he might live. What a demonstration of a parent's love! Years later that child became the Prime Minister of Great Britain, David Lloyd George.

God showed how much He values each one of us when He allowed Jesus to die so that we might live. We know how much that cost Jesus, but think how much it cost God, too. Such is His love that He bought us freedom from punishment through the shedding of His Son's blood on the cross. The fact that God allowed His Son to suffer so much on the cross reveals just how much He values you and me.

But many of us struggle to accept this spiritual truth for we often base our sense of value and self-worth on the things we do, rather than on who we are. Many fathers put more value on what we achieve … careers, status, abilities … rather than loving and valuing us simply for who we are.

As a result we sometimes find ourselves behaving in manipulative ways to make other people value us. This is one reason why many of us become people pleasers, as we feel valued when we are pleasing others. Let's remind ourselves that God's love expressed in Jesus' death is where we will find our true value, so that our relationships with others can flow from that.

For prayer and reflection

Heavenly Father, please give me a deeper revelation of the suffering and agony Christ endured for me, so that I may grasp how much I'm valued by You.

My Father **nurtures me**

What image does the word 'love' conjure up for you? In 1989, after Ceausescu's dictatorship ended in Romania, thousands of Romanian children were found to have been abandoned at birth and left in orphanages where they were often neglected. On TV news we saw pictures of these unwanted children imprisoned in cots, like caged animals, rocking to and fro to comfort themselves. They had no one to pick them up in loving arms and tell them how much they were loved. Many of them didn't live to see their teenage years because they were so psychologically traumatised by abuse and neglect when young, that they simply died from a lack of love.

We have been created by God in love, to love and to be loved. It is difficult to grasp the depth and breadth of God's love as He is beyond our comprehension, but today's verse tells us that God is love. Are you comfortable with love? Perhaps you struggle with this word as you were brought up in a home where you never experienced cuddles or heard the words, 'I love you'.

When our earthly father fails to give us a sense of nurture with intimate hugs and words of endearment, something in us will also die. In the absence of a nurturing love we may try to defend ourselves against the pain we feel, by developing addictive tendencies, eating disorders, or uncontrollable anger, to name but a few. But our nurturing heavenly Father wants to embrace us in His arms with the same cherishing love as a hen shows when gathering her chicks under her wing (Luke 13:34). He longs to hold you in His arms and enfold you with His love, so don't push Him away.

1 John 4:16b–21

'God is love. Whoever lives in love lives in God, and God in him.' (v.16b)

For prayer and reflection

Oh God, thank You that You are someone with a Father's heart, a Father's love and a Father's strength for each one of us. Enable me to come to You with the confidence of a trusting child.

My Father **forgives me**

1 John 1:5–10

'If we confess our sins, he is faithful and just and will forgive us our sins ...' (v.9)

Your earthly father and your perfect heavenly Father are two different people. Perhaps your earthly father kept score of everything that displeased him and every failure, and knew exactly the right time to throw it back in your face. The truth is that we may have made a mess of things but our heavenly Father will never crush us or stamp on us. On the contrary, He wants us to know that whatever we have done He will always be our forgiving Father. We don't have to live under the condemnation of past sins.

When Adam and Eve sinned in the Garden of Eden they hid. Feeling guilty and ashamed they sewed fig leaves together to hide their nakedness. Their relationship with God was broken. We too can hide away from God and although we will not use literal fig leaves we may wear spiritual fig leaves to cover our nakedness and shame. The basis of all mankind's problems is self and when we rebel against God we deny Him the right to be God in our lives and to that end we also deny Him the right to be a loving Father to us, His daughters.

Therefore, in order to establish a closer relationship with our Father it is important to confess our sins to Him. When we are honest, saying sorry for our actions, and repenting of our shortcomings, He lovingly and graciously cleanses us 'from all unrighteousness' (v.9) and frees us from our guilt and shame.

Our Father will never throw things back in our face by condemning us or rejecting us for, 'as far as the east is from the west, so far has he removed our transgressions from us' (Psa. 103:12). He forgives and forgets.

For prayer and reflection

'All have sinned and fall short of the glory of God' (Rom. 3:23). Therefore let's confess our sins to our Father and receive His cleansing love.

WEEKEND

Loved by my Father

For reflection: 1 Corinthians 13:4–7

Everybody is doing it – or so it seems! From the heads of big businesses, to many 'celebreties'. Even a popular magazine marketed this latest DIY fashion, 'How to meditate: you can teach yourself in a matter of minutes'. It has been scientifically and psychologically proven that given the right technique, meditation produces the 'feel-good factor'.

However, meditation, as understood in the Christian tradition (eg Psa. 48:9) produces far more than just the 'feel-good factor'. Meditating on the Word of God enables us to develop an ever-closer relationship with God. Perhaps it is possible to teach ourselves to meditate in a matter of minutes, but meditation needs to be sustained for a much longer period for it to be effective.

Over this weekend let's experiment with meditating ('chewing the cud') in different ways, using this phrase: *My heavenly Father loves and accepts me.* Try repeating these words as a 'mantra'.

Meditate on the word 'love' and remind yourself of love's characteristics found in today's passage.

Think about all the areas of your life in which your Father accepts you. Enjoy chewing over these words!

Where is **the real me?**

Psalm 77:7–9

'Has God forgotten to be merciful?' (v.9)

H ow are you?' are the words that greet you as you go into church. The honest reply would be, 'Lousy!' but putting on a smile you reply, 'Fine, thanks.' The mask is on! Behind the mask is pain and emptiness but we let no one see the real us. One lady confessed to acting as a clown in order to cover up how sad and vulnerable she felt inside – this mask protected her. She felt that if people discovered her real self, she would be rejected.

In Margery Williams' well-known story, *The Velveteen Rabbit*, the rabbit asks the old worn-out skin horse, 'What is REAL?' The horse replies that when a child 'REALLY loves you, then you become real'. Like the rabbit and the horse, we become real as we are loved. As we cultivate an intimate relationship with our loving Father we will begin to have the courage to take off our masks in His presence, daring to be transparent and vulnerable. Then we shall come to see ourselves as He sees us. It is only when we feel safe and accepted by our Father that we can take off the masks we wear in our everyday life.

For prayer and reflection

What masks do you put on? Are you able to be real with your Father? Consider writing to Him, describing those secret places where you feel vulnerable.

Have you ever wanted to be honest with your heavenly Father, and tell Him exactly what you are thinking or feeling? But you hesitate ... perhaps you are frightened of what He will think of you. However, you don't have to pretend and wear a mask, for He already knows the secrets of our hearts (Psa. 44:21). In our reading it is refreshing to find David so transparently real with God. We sense his pain as he cries out, 'Has [God] in his anger withheld his compassion?' (v.9).

Love tanks

Some years ago I came across the book, *How to Really Love Your Child* by Dr Ross Campbell.* Discovering his concept of 'love tanks' was very illuminating and has helped me not only in parenting my daughters, but also in counselling broken people. A 'love tank' is the author's way of describing emotional tanks that every child is born with. God created a child not only with physical needs: to be fed and watered, but also with emotional needs: to be loved and cherished. Because a child is unable to fill up his own emotional tank he will automatically look to his parents to fill it up with love. The degree to which you will feel good about yourself will depend upon the degree to which your 'love tank' was filled up when you were a child.

All children need to be loved, affirmed and given attention in order for their 'love tank' to be filled. This is vital for healthy life and good relationships. When we have enjoyed good formative years and our 'love tank' is filled we grow to be well-balanced people, enjoying intimate relationships. But when we have experienced an absence of love and our 'love tank' is nearly empty we often end up struggling, particularly with relationships.

However, whatever our experience of being parented, our 'love tanks' will never be completely full as none of us have perfect parents. Therefore it is important to look to our heavenly Father to fill them as He is perfect in every way. God *is* love. Our Father delights in our existence and as we begin to see ourselves in the light of His perfect truth, we become free from the distorted view we have of ourselves.

* Scripture Press, 1987.

Isaiah 43:1–13

'… you are precious and honoured in my sight … I love you …' (v.4)

For prayer and reflection

Your Father wants to fill up your 'love tank' now. Reflect on these words, 'you are precious' (v.4); you are 'the apple of his eye' (Deut. 32:10).

My **prodigal Father**

'… his father saw him … filled with compassion … he ran to his son …' (v.20)

The word 'prodigal' means 'one who spends or gives lavishly; reckless extravagant'. This story is invariably called the 'Prodigal Son' because the son recklessly squanders his inheritance. But the parable is not only about a rebellious son, it is also about a father's love – the 'prodigal father' extravagantly pours out his compassion and forgives a son who least deserves it.

The son did not value his father for the intimacy that their relationship offered, but selfishly demanded his inheritance. Here we see first the prodigality of the father. Without anger or judgment he gives the money to his selfish and greedy son. We learn of the choices the son makes and the consequence of those choices – life in a pigsty – the ultimate degradation for a Jewish son.

When the son finally comes to his senses, his motives change from 'Gimme' to 'Change me'. His *heart* attitude changed from selfishness to humility and his *actions* changed as he chose to return to his father – a picture of true repentance. What was his father doing? Waiting for him with outstretched arms to welcome him back. The father's love was not based upon his son's behaviour, but flowed from a heart that was recklessly extravagant in pouring out undeserved blessings.

Whether we have chosen to turn our back on our Father, or have squandered the gifts and life He has blessed us with, when we return to Him, He runs to greet us with open arms. But sometimes our own attitude can hold us back and we can echo the words, 'I am no longer worthy to be called your son' (v.21). However, our Father not only welcomes us back but also gives us the royal treatment!

For prayer and reflection

In what areas of our lives are we selfish? What are the consequences? Repent and choose to change, knowing that our prodigal Father is extravagant in giving us a gift of grace.

So near, **yet so far!**

esterday we saw a father's heart full of compassion for a son who rebelliously left home for a distant land, and then returned in humility and repentance. Today, again, we see the father's love, as he pleads with his older son to change his attitude and join the party. Although the older son had stayed in his father's house, he had no intimate relationship with his father. Geographically he was near to his Dad, but emotionally he was far away from him. Outwardly, the older son looks so righteous and good, staying at home and serving faithfully in the fields for many years. But inwardly, we discern jealousy, pride and self-righteousness – inner attitudes that threatened to spoil his younger brother's joyful homecoming.

We may be very involved in church life, or serving our Father faithfully in the workplace, and to all intents and purposes we may give the appearance of a loyal, hard-working Christian. But what is going on inside our hearts? Are we like the older son? What attitudes create an emotional and spiritual distance that stop us from experiencing the Father's love at the very root of our soul?

I recognise that I can easily drift away from the Father's heart and find myself, like the older son, faithfully slaving in the fields, yet deceiving myself that I am living close to the Father. When my daughter first became very ill, I dutifully and faithfully became her carer, but inwardly I struggled with feeling jealous of other mothers who had healthy daughters. 'Woe is me,' developed into 'pity parties'! I was just like the older brother! In humility I repented and found that my relationship with my heavenly Father became more worshipful and intimate again.

Luke 15:25–32

'My son … everything I have is yours.' (v.31)

For prayer and reflection

Heavenly Father, help me to recognise where I'm like the older brother with attitudes of resentment, competition and jealousy. I repent of these attitudes and return to Your heart of love.

Take **responsibility**

Matthew 6:5–15

'But if you do not forgive men their sins, your Father will not forgive your sins' (v.15)

Our earthly fathers are only human and they are bound to have made mistakes with us, leaving us hurt and wounded. We may have had a strict authoritarian father; or an inadequate passive father; or an abusive father who emotionally put us down, or physically hit out in a deep-seated rage, or destroyed the very heart of our childhood – sexual innocence. As a result of being hurt, we may develop sinful attitudes or responses, and find it difficult to forgive.

Blaming your father for the problems you have in life may feel comfortable but it will increase a sense of separation from God. We learn that God holds us responsible for our response (even though it may be understandable) and if we refuse to forgive, we are cut off from our Father (v.15). Our relationship is fractured.

Forgiveness is not saying that what our father has done is OK, and it is not about forgetting a wrong, but it's about giving a gift of pardon to the dad who has hurt us. Therefore it is important to take responsibility and forgive our earthly father where appropriate.

Forgiveness keeps our emotional wounds clean of bitterness and is often a process rather than a once-only act. I have met women who have said they have forgiven their fathers, but in the process of counselling have discovered a deeper wound of pain and anger, and realise there is more forgiving yet to be done.

Forgiveness is giving to others what our heavenly Father has given to us – love and acceptance in spite of being hurt. Whenever you think of your Father and feel hurt, choose to forgive him, and love him with God's love.

For prayer and reflection

Ask God to reveal any memory of your father that needs forgiving. At the foot of the cross release your painful emotions, letting go of anger, and forgive your dad.

WEEKEND

My Father's song

For reflection: Zephaniah 3:17

These words, in their original context, refer to the restoration of the city of Jerusalem in the time of Ezra and Nehemiah. However, many people have taken the prophet's words and allowed them to speak into their hearts as they have sought an intimate relationship with their Father. We find three thoughts that reveal something of the Father's heart.

Firstly, the Father delights in us, taking pleasure in us because of who we are – not because of what we do.

Secondly, the Father quiets us with His love, by drawing us into a place of security – we don't have to struggle and strive.

Thirdly, the Father rejoices over us with singing. God is a Father who is so joyous in adopting us as His daughters, that He expresses His feelings in singing a special song over each one of us. Isn't that amazing!

Over the weekend reflect on how your Father delights in you. Invite Him to draw you closer so that you find that quiet place of peace where you can relax, then listen. Can you hear Him singing a song expressing how much He loves you?

Struggle **well!**

Ephesians 2:1–10

'For we are God's workmanship, created in Christ Jesus to do good works …' (v.10)

Have you ever asked yourself the question, 'What do I hope to achieve in life?' Are you motivated by personal ambition or do you behave in certain ways to protect yourself from fear of failure or rejection? It is important that we stop and remind ourselves of Jesus' pattern of motivation for His life. Speaking of His Father, He said, 'I always do what pleases him' (John 8:29). In wanting to follow Jesus' example, I am trying to approach every situation and every decision with a single, simple question, 'How can I please my Father?' But I find this a battle at times.

When we please our heavenly Father we will be fulfilling our own unique calling in life, for He has created us to do good works by using our individual gifts and talents. God doesn't do a 'Friday afternoon' job and create junk! Knowing that we are His workmanship, His priceless work of art, enables us to work without striving. Having a purpose in life is vitally important for us to function well, as this brings us a sense of significance. But it isn't always easy is it?

This is where many of us struggle: wanting to please our Father, but finding self gets in the way; wanting to use our gifts and talents for His pleasure, but not knowing how and when. However, let's give ourselves permission to struggle in trying to please our Father. 'The Christian's greatest struggle is the struggle not to struggle' (Arthur Burt). I read somewhere that to struggle well is a sign of maturity! So be encouraged when you feel pulled in all directions, trying to find God's purpose for your life – it could be a sign of maturity!

For prayer and reflection

Father, help me adopt an attitude of self-surrender as I try and please You in finding a purpose for my life. When it's difficult, help me to struggle well.

Trusting my Father

Let's ask ourselves some important questions. Do we trust God because He is God? Because of His character, His love and His grace? Because of His greatness and power? Because He says His promises are unchangeable, no matter what the outward circumstances? Or do we trust God for what we see Him do in answer to our prayers, or what we are believing for? If we don't see our prayers answered, then sometimes we can begin to question how much God really loves us. 'If my heavenly Father really loves me, then He would ... intervene and save my marriage; bless me with a child; provide me with a job ...'

Those with a deep faith will trust God no matter what the circumstances or what they are feeling, for they have got beyond the need for God to prove Himself. 'Feelings come and go and feelings are deceiving. My warrant is the word of God, naught else is worth believing' (Martin Luther).

We become secure in our relationship with our heavenly Father when we trust in what we know of God and His attributes, rather than solely in what we see and experience.

Feeling troubled and experiencing bouts of anxiety with my daughter very ill, I was asked by a friend, 'What are you trusting God for?' When I thought about this I realised that God might choose to heal her, but then again He might not. I recognised that the bottom line was that I could trust my heavenly Father to hold me in His hands in that situation, comforting and strengthening me every day. Trusting that He fully knew the future brought me a deep sense of peace that He was in control.

John 14:1–4

'Do not let your hearts be troubled. Trust in God ...' (v.1)

For prayer and reflection

Loving heavenly Father, when I feel life is beyond my control, help me to trust in Your unfailing love and know Your everlasting arms are underneath me.

My Father **affirms me**

'You are my Son, whom I love ...' (v.11)

Flicking through a children's catalogue recently (looking for books for my grandchildren, not for me!), I came across *My Very First Book of Princesses*. This jogged my memory to recall how, as a child, I used to dream of becoming a princess. Like many little girls I dreamt of becoming a beautiful person, wearing wonderful clothes and having special privileges. I can't say that the first two have come true! But I do feel immensely privileged that my heavenly Father is a King and thus I am His princess. My friend used to positively glow when her dad called her, 'My little princess'. Words of endearment are powerful and I can still remember the pride on my father's face as he used to say, 'You are a wonderful daughter' and the subsequent warm feelings that arose within me, making me feel great.

No doubt Jesus also felt good as He heard His Father say, 'You are my Son, whom I love, with you I am well pleased.' Jesus had lived obscurely in Nazareth for 30 years and on this, His first public appearance, we see His Father encouraging Him by affirming His identity. His Father knew that after His baptism, Jesus would face a wilderness experience where He would be tempted by the devil. What better way to be prepared than to have the affirming words of His Father ringing in His ears, 'You are my Son, chosen and marked by my love, pride of my life' (*The Message*).

We may not have had affirming words spoken over us by our earthly father, but we can learn to tune in to hear the voice of our heavenly Father. 'You are My daughter; My princess. I am proud of you and I love you.'

For prayer and reflection

Heavenly Father, thank You so much for speaking words of affirmation into my life. Help me never to block them out – I am listening to You.

My Father **corrects me**

I wonder how many of us have heard that infamous sentence, 'Just wait until your father gets home'? The thought of our father walking through the door to discipline us may have provoked different images and feelings. The word *discipline* may conjure up negative connotations for those who were once disciplined in a hurtful fashion. Whereas the use of the word *correction* found in some other Bible translations may suggest a more positive note. None of us are born perfect and therefore we all need a certain amount of correction to become mature and whole. So, is it possible to be disciplined in ways that build up rather than tear down?

Yes! Our heavenly Father has our best interests at heart and will correct us in order to mould us to become all that we are meant to be. Just as precious metals are purified as they go through fire, so our characters are purified as we go through the fire of correction. This isn't exactly fun, but *because* God loves us so much He corrects us. When we harbour attitudes or exhibit behaviour patterns that do not honour our Father He may correct us through His Word, His Spirit, through His people or through circumstances.

How do you respond to God's correction? Some may despise correction and run away from it saying, 'Well, I'll do it my way anyway.' Others may become totally discouraged, 'Oh, I can't do anything right.' But God loves you so much He doesn't want to see you destroyed; nor does He want to see you press the self-destruct button; He wants to help you to become everything you were designed to be. Therefore let's rejoice in His correction.

Hebrews 12:4–13

'... the Lord disciplines those he loves ... what son is not disciplined by his father?' (vv.6–7)

For prayer and reflection

'Whom the Lord loves, he corrects.' How have you experienced the truth of these words in your own life?

My Father **protects me**

Psalm 91

'Surely he will save you from the fowler's snare … I will protect him …' (vv.3,14)

All children want to feel safe … that is why they snuggle under their daddy's arm. They want to feel that their big, strong father will protect them from harm. Living in our unsettled society today with dangers potentially lurking round every corner, it is important that we learn to take 'refuge under his wings' for 'He will cover you with his feathers' (v.4). In spite of the threats to our physical safety, our Father offers us a totally safe living environment that is spiritual in nature. When we enter into a personal relationship with God through Jesus, He will allow nothing to snatch us out of a relationship with Him (John 10:28–29). As we dwell 'in the secret place of the Most High', we are completely safe. Whatever is going on in life around us we are protected forever.

This psalm also describes other ways in which our Father shelters us from harm, for He protects us 'from the fowler's snare' (v.3). That is, from anything that may tempt us to wander away from the life our Father has for us. Let's be honest; there are probably many ways that the enemy tries to lure us away from God's ways. But our Father loves us so much that even when we are tempted, He protects us by providing a way of escape (1 Cor. 10:13).

Marion was burdened by debt owing to her love of consumerism and heavy use of credit cards. Feeling guilty and ashamed of her behaviour, her relationship with God suffered. When she realised that her Father was offering a way of escape, she hesitantly cut up her cards and returned to shelter under the protection of her Father's arms.

For prayer and reflection

In what areas of your life are you being tempted? Your Father will protect you, but you have to do your part. What is the escape route He provides?

WEEKEND

A time to embrace my Father

For reflection: Romans 12:1–2

'Take your everyday, ordinary life – your sleeping, eating, going to work, and walking around-life – and place it before God as an offering. Embracing what God does for you is the best thing you can do for him.' (Rom. 12:1, *The Message*)

Have you ever considered embracing our Father's world by reflecting on the created life around you, and being attentive to hearing Him speak to you through His creation? This weekend try to fit in a slow 'walk-about' and ask God to speak to you either about a specific concern you may have, or about something He wants to show you.

Walk slowly, taking a few deep breaths, and use your senses to become aware of what is around you.

- Use your eyes to look at shapes, textures and colours.
- Listen to sounds and silences.
- Use touch to become aware of different textures: a flower, a stone, a wall.

If something attracts your attention, stop and reflect on this, asking, 'Is God saying something through this?' Then listen to Him. Enjoy embracing your Father through His creation.

A **compassionate** heart

'Praise be to … the Father of compassion and the God of all comfort.' (v.3)

Sue found the concept of God as a compassionate heavenly Father difficult to accept. 'I had an awful dad who was so cold. I'd love to think that God was different – but how can I? I just can't believe.' Gently she was encouraged to look at Jesus, for He is the expression of the Father in human form. 'The Son is the radiance of God's glory and the exact representation of his being …' (Heb. 1:3). By observing the way Jesus related to people and by understanding how He functioned, we see an emerging picture of a warm, accepting, compassionate Father. Jesus once said, 'Anyone who has seen me has seen the Father' (John 14:9), and we find in the Gospels many examples of how Jesus revealed the Father to us.

Jesus saw the leper, not only physically disfigured but rejected and isolated by society. 'Filled with compassion …' (Mark 1:41), Jesus reached out and healed him. Seeing the predicament of two blind men, 'Jesus had compassion on them and touched their eyes. Immediately they received their sight …' (Matt. 20:34). Jesus saw a large hungry crowd, 'I have compassion for these people … they have nothing to eat' (Matt. 15:32). We also see Jesus taking little children on His lap and talking to them; the disciples thought He was too busy to bless them, but He wasn't. He cared about them. And He cares about us.

Whenever you feel lonely or rejected, trapped or lost in life, or hungry for a greater revelation of the Father's love, gaze at Jesus. For He will show you a loving and tender Father whose heart throbs with a compassion that will touch your life.

For prayer and reflection

'Turn your eyes upon Jesus, look full in His wonderful face; and the things of earth will grow strangely dim in the light of His glory and grace.' (Helen H. Lemmell)

Love **crosses barriers**

John 4:1–26

'You are a Jew and I am a Samaritan woman. How can you ask me for a drink?' (v.9)

We ended yesterday with the thought that we can see more of what the Father heart of God is like as we look at Jesus' love and concern for people. Jesus came to reveal God to us and in today's reading we catch a glimpse of God's Father heart for the outcast and the immoral.

Jesus, a Jew, meeting with a Samaritan, a woman, was extraordinary. Why? Racial hatred was rampant between these two cultures – the Jews despised the Samaritans – and here was a Jew, meeting not just with a Samaritan, that would have been difficult enough, but with a Samaritan woman. The Jews declared Samaritan women unclean from birth, and thus religious Jews would feel contaminated by any contact with such a woman. But Jesus broke the rules of Jewish piety and elevated this Samaritan woman to a place of value.

In doing so He showed her that God cares for men and women equally. Jesus was not ashamed to be seen talking to her. In fact He went out of His way to demonstrate a real love to her, knowing that she had been rejected by others because of her promiscuous lifestyle. He saw beyond her brusqueness and sarcasm. He saw an empty heart. She longed to be loved and cared for, and to be someone special. Jesus pours love and grace into a broken and wasted life and she begins to see God in a new light. Jesus has revealed His Father, a loving and accepting God.

What sort of thoughts and feelings does this story stir up in us? Some of us may consider ourselves second-class citizens, or perhaps we have a past we would rather forget. Whatever arises, allow God's Father heart to meet with you in Jesus.

For prayer and reflection

'If anyone is thirsty, let him come to me and drink' (John 7:37). Thank You, Jesus, that Your love is being poured into my thirsty spirit.

My Father **weeps with me**

John 11:17–37

'When Jesus saw her weeping … he was deeply moved … Jesus wept.' (vv.33,35)

I am sure we have all found ourselves in situations of such pain that tears flow. Tears naturally arise from sadness; perhaps from the loss of a loved one, a broken relationship, difficulties with children, or other experiences of loss. In my twenties, I remember my father giving me a hug once when I was upset. He obviously felt my pain as there was a tear in his eye. To experience someone supporting me in such a way was comforting. Knowing that God our Father also feels our pain is very reassuring.

In our passage today, we see the Father's compassion reflected in Jesus' response to His grieving friends. Martha and Mary were upset as their dear brother, Lazarus, had died four days previously. When Mary saw Jesus, she fell at His feet in floods of tears. Jesus was so deeply moved at the sight of His friend's suffering that He too burst into tears. These tears were not the professional tears of the hired mourner or of the inwardly detached spectator … they were spontaneous. He felt the sisters' pain, and His tears at that moment authentically expressed His inner emotions. What an insight into the heart of God. And what a comfort for us when we suffer. Jesus' whole life demonstrated the Father heart of God. Our Father is not sitting back, indifferent on the throne of heaven … He is deeply troubled for us when we are hurting. He weeps with our pain.

Are you going through a tough time at the moment? What have you lost? A relationship? Purpose? Confidence? Are your wounds causing you to weep? Just as Jesus asked to see Mary (v.28), so your Father is inviting you to come to Him with your tears and pain.

For prayer and reflection

Come to the Father as a child in need of a father's love and comfort, and tell Him what you are hurting about and how you feel.

Whose child are you?

Our heavenly Father delights in being our Dad. He stands with outstretched arms inviting us to come to Him through faith in His Son, Jesus Christ. He wants us to be His child and to know the love and security that entails. We may have been hurt, abused or rejected. We may have been abandoned or overlooked by our earthly father. But, as we have seen over the last month, our heavenly Father is an entirely different character. He is an awesome, majestic God, the Creator of this world, yet He craves a relationship of love and intimacy with each one of us. This is the supreme relationship for which we were created. Are you growing closer to your heavenly Father? Relationships are like flowers; they need to be watered, fed and nurtured. So how can we continue to nourish an intimate relationship with our Father?

'… to all who received him … who believed … he gave the right to become children of God.' (v.12)

Firstly, agree with what the Word of God says about you. Every fibre of your being has been created for intimacy with God. It is important to remind yourself that regardless of your behaviour, God's character of love and grace never changes.

Secondly, don't listen to lies! When you can't sense your Father's presence, don't listen to the lie that says, 'God doesn't love me because I don't *feel* He is close.' Instead, listen to His truth.

Thirdly, dwell daily in your Father's embrace. When you feel overwhelmed by your thoughts or emotions, admit to Him that you need His help. 'Father, I feel discouraged by insecurities and fears. I need Your fathering arms to embrace me with comfort and strength.'

Then, as you realign your heart with the Father's heart things will change. Love will touch your spirit.

For prayer and reflection

Your heavenly Father wants to be what you have always desired – a Dad who will always love you. Will you allow God to father you?

Galatians – free at last

Liz Hansford

Liz Hansford lives in Javea, Spain, where her husband John is the Pastor of the International Baptist Church. Before moving to Spain she was frequently on radio. She is the founder of Empowering Women, an organisation dedicated to reaching the thousands of expat women in her area with God's love. Liz is also involved in local church ministry, prayer ministry and writing for both secular and Christian markets. She has four grown-up children and four grandchildren.

Galatians – free at last

Galatians 1:1–5

'… sent … by Jesus Christ …' (v.1)

Good, where do you want me to be? What do you want me to do? How do you want me to do it? When do you want me to go?

Since I'm personally a creature of indecision and uncertainty, it's an area that I struggle with – but not the apostle Paul. He's sure of what God has called him to do and to whom he is to go. He is called to the Gentiles (of whom the Christians in Galatia are a part) and he is to preach Jesus to them. That's it in a nutshell.

Meantime, Peter, James and John are to focus on the Jews (2:8–9). It's called targeting territory – and those in sales know all about it. But God is a strategist, too, and He plans who we are to reach and how we are to do it.

So how did Paul know exactly what his part was? The answer's simple: Jesus spoke to him personally. He made the commission clear and direct without the involvement of anyone else – 'not from men nor by man' (v.1). And he returns to this again in verses 11 and 12.

Why does this matter so much? Well, Paul's apostolic authority was on the line. 'We know better than you,' was the cry of the Judaisers. 'You've got it wrong.' And their premise was if you discredit the man then you discredit his message. But Paul is saying, 'I am a reliable source because God spoke to me directly.' The message hasn't been reshaped by committee, nothing's got in the way of God and His voice, I haven't been persuaded by men to modify it a little or make it more immediately appealing. This is it and it stays the same – Jesus 'gave himself for our sins to rescue us' (v.4).

For prayer and reflection

Lord, You sent and Paul went. You're sending me somewhere, too, with exactly the same message. Help me to hear and go in just the same obedient and responsive way.

WEEKEND

Any post for me?

For reflection: John 8:32–36

I wonder who picked the letter of Galatians off the mat one morning in Turkey and settled down for a quiet read with a cup of coffee. A strong cup I hope – for this is one strong letter. 'Don't mess with the truth', is Paul's cry. Don't add to it, don't get waylaid with rules and regulations; don't be taken in by people who tell you there's more you have to do to please God. If you get sucked into that kind of look-alike gospel you're just fools and it's bad news not good news you're believing in. Instead, it's grace all the way – from Galatians 1:3 to 6:18. God giving and us receiving.

If you have time, look through the whole epistle this weekend.

This was probably Paul's first letter and he realises that all will be lost if, at the very beginning, the gospel gets modified into another kind of self-help religion. We have amazing freedom in Jesus and in that freedom we have the power of the Spirit to live as God intended.

Have you chosen freedom in Him or are you sometimes drawn back into legalism? Focus on all that you've received in Christ.

Not the real thing

Galatians 1:6–10

'… a different gospel – which is really no gospel at all.' (vv.6–7)

'm afraid the picture's a fake. I know it looks good but it isn't genuine.' Just about the last thing you'd want to hear if you had made your way to Sotheby's with the family heirloom which had been passed down to you from your great-granny. So how come you were fooled? The essence of a fake is that it looks so remarkably like the genuine article that the ordinary woman in the street is easily taken in.

And that's why Paul is so emphatic in these verses. What the Galatian believers had been conned into believing wasn't so very different from the original gospel as preached to them by Paul – or at least so it seemed. It was subtle, it was plausible, it was reasonable. And it was downright dangerous. It's 'semi-amazing grace plus works, how reasonable the sound,' as Chuck Swindoll says.

It's what is mistaken for the gospel still in many places today. Having been brought up in a fairly liberal church, I first encountered the idea of a living faith in Christ with all its repercussions in my late teens. Before that I knew I had to be good, obey the Ten Commandments and go to church, but there was nothing of the dynamism of a life-changing, empowering relationship involved.

For prayer and reflection

Lord, help me to hold on to what is priceless: the truth of Your undeserved love for me.

Without hesitation I leapt into a new-found faith and I can recall my closest, equally church-going, friend saying, 'You just believe a different version of Christianity now.' But there *is* no different version. We can certainly express it differently – whether culturally or denominationally, but the core is the same. And, according to Paul, anyone who threatens its purity is to be 'eternally condemned'. That's how important it is. Paul doesn't want us to pass on a fake from generation to generation.

Testing for truth

Where do you get your truth from? It's an interesting question. As I sat down to think seriously about this myself, I had to confess that I so implicitly trust my preacher husband that I take much of my truth from him. If he says it then I believe it to be true – despite the fact that he encourages all of our congregation to check out Scripture to see whether these things are true (Acts 17:11). The longer you're in a particular church group the more likely it is that you'll become slack in your thinking and too dependent on a mere human being to dispense truth to you. And that's a risky thing.

We long to belong – and sometimes belonging can be the determiner of what we choose to believe. Our friends follow a particular teaching and we go along with it – unsure whether what's being taught is truth and hesitant to say anything in case we're cold-shouldered. A close friend of mine was at one time part of a somewhat exclusive small Christian group. She is a strong-minded woman but the group's views of women silenced her completely and, though I would scarcely have believed it possible, she and her husband towed the party line until the group closed down.

In an age where absolute truth is scorned and we have a weak grasp of God's Word, we are particularly prey to anyone who chooses to announce he has a revelation from God. There is only one safe place to get our truth and that is 'from Jesus Christ' (v.12) and today that means from Scripture. Christ reveals Himself and the truth that we need to believe in His Word.

Test what you believe and what you hear by setting it alongside Scripture.

Galatians 1:11–12

'… the gospel … is not something that man made up.'
(v.11)

For prayer and reflection

Lord, help me to truly examine what I believe and weed out from my thinking anything that isn't of You, and especially anything that's merely man-made.

Slowly does it

**Galatians
1:13–24**

'Then after three years, I went up to Jerusalem to get acquainted with Peter …' (v.18)

How much time do you spend alone? How much time do you spend waiting – and I don't mean in supermarket queues or at traffic lights? How much time do you spend being slow?

The Slow Food organisation is the antithesis of the 'fast food' culture of the West, and the idea behind Slow Travel is to 'enjoy a deeper level of experience by staying in one place longer'. The simple correlation for the Christian is to stay in one place long enough to hear God and thus to enjoy a deeper level of experience with Him.

So what has this to do with today's passage? Sometimes we imagine Paul busy, always on the move, active and evangelising with an energy that we can only dream about. We picture him setting off to preach the gospel directly after his conversion, having had a quick visit from Ananias (Acts 9:11–19). But that's not the way it was.

The first thing he does is go to Arabia and Damascus (Gal. 1:17) for three years! On his own (v.16)! He hasn't yet met the other apostles and worked out a plan of action. Instead his focus is on time alone with God. What an amazing choice!

He may have been parallelling the three years the disciples had had with Jesus, but we can only speculate: three years listening to God, three years thinking and praying, three years reading the Old Testament Scriptures, three years realigning your whole life and your former values. Three years out of the picture is not three years wasted.

Three years of quietness adds depth to the soul. A person who takes time to think as well as speak, to meditate before acting, is a wise person, a person who has given God time to speak.

For prayer and reflection

How much time have I spent slowly this week? How much time have I wasted moving faster than God wanted me to?

Danger on the inside

I magine the situation: you have no Bible, or at least not as we know it (only the Old Testament is currently available), and you live in a town called Antioch, tucked in the southernmost tip of today's Turkey, approximately 350 miles from Jerusalem. You're an emerging Christian leader but you're out on your own. It's around AD 40, and travelling at a speed of 30 miles a day, the roundtrip to talk to your fellow leaders will take you about 23 days, and a lot of blisters. You can't have a quick chat about key issues that might need clarification, and remember, what you believe hasn't been documented yet and is therefore open to being tampered with – which is what happened.

'False brothers' infiltrated the Church and tried to peddle their 'better' version of what we should all believe. They took advantage of the distance that Paul was from the other apostles to muddle new Gentile believers and confuse them. They wanted all believers, whatever their background, to follow the Old Testament, Jewish practices of circumcision, Sabbath observance and food laws. These were to be a bolt-on essential, without which one couldn't claim to be a Christian at all. Paul says, 'We did not give in to them for a moment' (v.5).

If he had, what kind of Christianity would we all be following today? It wouldn't be Christianity at all. It would be a wearying religion – something that depends on us: our performance, our rule-keeping, our effort. Does this pattern of adding on to the gospel happen today? Yes, of course it does! If any group or church makes a bolt-on extra, a requirement in order for you to be part of it, then your freedom in Christ has gone.

Galatians 2:1–5

'… false brothers had infiltrated our ranks to spy on the freedom we have in Christ Jesus …' (v.4)

For prayer and reflection

Lord, I don't want to be burdened with obligations that rob me of freedom and make me tired. Help me to abandon them for joy and release in You.

In **perfect unity**

Galatians 2:6–10

'… they recognised the grace given to me.' (v.9)

A member of our church recently told me of yet another minister, just six months in his present charge, whose members 'don't like him now'. 'Satan's at work,' she says – and I agree – but I wonder how much is merely 'fleshly', how much is due to the notion that we hire and fire and 'they' must meet our personal criteria. This is a far cry from the attitude of the apostles as seen in today's passage.

The leaders at Jerusalem ministering to Jews, and Paul from Antioch ministering to Gentiles, worked things out without playing for status or power. Nobody tried to topple anybody else. Nobody felt his nose put out of joint because God had gifted someone else. Nobody seems to have felt jealous or threatened. There's no record of anyone saying, 'You must defer to me – after all I am the Lord's brother', or 'I was one of the three closest to Jesus so I know best'. Compare all of that to contemporary church practice!

Paul was the outsider, yet the Jerusalem leaders worked completely for co-operation. There are four key phrases here: '*they saw* that I had been entrusted with the task …' (v.7); '*they recognised* the grace given to me' (v.9); *[they] gave* me and Barnabas the right hand of fellowship'; and '*They agreed* that we should go …' (v.9).

Unity requires us to let someone else lead and have freedom to operate. Unity is hard work for we have to be alert to personal agendas creeping in and self-importance taking over. Unity is hard because personalities preen and strut. Unity is hard because we want our own way. Unity is hard because foolish talking takes over. Unity is hard because Satan is at work. Woe betide us if we play into his hands!

For prayer and reflection

Lord, keep me from being a part of disunity in anything I say or do.

WEEKEND
Fear

For reflection: Psalm 34

Fear is a dreadful enemy. It paralyses, for it imagines the worst possible consequences. It breaks relationships, for it spends time looking at itself rather than others. It makes you lie, for it believes that the truth will cause unpopularity. It procrastinates, for it convinces that later will be easier. It cringes in subservience and silence because of possible consequences. And ultimately it can destroy a person and all her potential.

Peter was prey to it. Remember when he denied knowing Jesus – that was out of fear. And in Galatians 2:12 when he separates himself from the Gentiles, he acts in a way totally contrary to what he believes, because he is afraid. He goes along with what others want to hear. But thankfully he had a friend to challenge him.

Fear needs challenging. It needs confronting, otherwise it will hide forever. Let us strengthen and challenge each other not to do anything out of fear, but to live in the openness, courage and strength that is there even for the most timid, in the name and the power of Jesus Christ.

Penalty points **cancelled**

**Galatians
2:11–21**

'… I live by faith in the Son of God, who loved me and gave himself for me.' (v.20)

✓

One thing I need to do as a teacher is repeat anything that's really important, to make sure everyone's really heard. So, check out verses 16, 17 and 21 in this passage and see what Paul mentions four times, just to make extra sure the Galatians have heard. The word in question is 'justified' or 'made righteous'. And if this is all beginning to sound too theological, please stay with me, it's absolutely crucial to your wellbeing!

Remember those ads about penalty points, with a despairing husband contemplating the loss of his driving licence and therefore job and income? Remember the drink-driving ad where the car appears from nowhere into a garden and a little lad's life is ended?

Dreadful consequences. Consequences that horrify – but it's too late. In life you can't wind back time and make it different. But in God's amazing long-term plan, it's possible for selfish, sinful actions not to produce their normal deserved results. What justification does is stop the consequences we deserve in terms of God's assessment of us. It doesn't stop the sin, but it stops the results.

Normally, the only way to get out of paying the price is to claim innocence: 'I didn't do it'; 'It wasn't my fault'. But God's plan requires us to tell the truth, 'I did it,' and then to walk away scot-free. Absurd, upside down, amazing.

Justification is a legal declaration of innocence. It's as if the penalty points are cancelled, the anticipated and catastrophic result doesn't happen – even though we are responsible.

Justified is the exact opposite of condemned. With justification condemnation goes, as do blame, disapproval and guilt – all in one go. It says that you are legally free from blame.

For prayer and reflection

Thank You that You have done for me something I could never have done for myself. All I need do is believe and receive.

Faith works

'After beginning with the Spirit, are you now trying to attain your goal by human effort?' (v.3)

'Me do it,' says two-year-old Jessica, with a determined look, when I hold out a hand to help her down some particularly steep steps. So I remove the proffered hand and applaud her progress. After all, I don't want her to be dependent on anyone's hand when she's 12. And when I'm 90, I will probably want her to help me down the odd flight of steps. But there are some things neither she nor I, whatever our age or experience, will ever be able to do for ourselves.

And that's what's gone wrong for the poor benighted Galatians. They began in dependence on the Holy Spirit and then they thought they'd grow up a bit and do it for themselves. 'No way,' says Paul. The strange dynamic of the relationship we have with God is that we will still be totally dependent on Him till the day we die. How you begin is how you carry on, right to the end. In fact, true maturity in the Christian life is through becoming even more dependent than you were yesterday, not less.

The Galatians had moved to lives of religious obedience. And tearing themselves away from the satisfying feeling that they were contributing to their own salvation was hard. Every bit as hard as it is for us.

'Look,' Paul says, 'you've already experienced how it works. All you had to do was believe and you received the Holy Spirit, just like that! Keep on doing it that way and it will be fine. Try on your own and you'll never make it. And in case you're imagining that Abraham pleased God by law-keeping (the argument the Judaisers were propagating), you're wrong. God blessed him simply because he believed. Faith works, self-help doesn't.'

Am I experiencing as much of God's power as I once did, or have I slipped into partial self-dependence, slipping and struggling in my own strength?

Bound to fail

Galatians 3:10–14

'… so that by faith we might receive …' (v.14)

I reckon I can scarcely get from home to the school where I teach 10 miles away without breaking the law. It's not that I'm a deliberate criminal, just that I slip quite inadvertently over the speed limit. And as far as my mouth goes, I wonder if I could manage more than a few hours without saying something the Lord would rather I hadn't. Add my thoughts, the stuff I've left undone and my selfishness, and it makes a pretty messy picture. Imagine a video of your entire life (including your secret thoughts) replayed, not just to God, but in full view of all your friends too. Anybody feeling smug? Anybody feeling comfortable?

The fact is that if we choose to live by the law, judge others by law, focus on law, we are bound to fail. Why? Because we have to keep '*everything* written in the Book of the Law' in order to succeed. Alert to every last possibility of sin, we'd be stressed out with observance, compliance and worry.

I recently watched a TV programme showing parents pushing their little children towards success. Allowed no real childhood, they were trained, driven towards perfection and achievement, and the cost for those who did not make it to the very top was despair and depression.

God does not want Christians to feel like that, for He is a much kinder parent. He already knows we cannot be perfect, so He himself has 'redeemed us from the curse of the law'. Christ has done it all for us and we now live 'by faith' that that is enough. No worries that it's inadequate. Neither our future nor our present depend on keeping rules. Instead, He lifts us up in His own hands to receive blessing, not condemnation.

For prayer and reflection

Lord, I long to be a happy, blessed, receiving believer, no longer struggling with myself. Grow my total trust in You, so that I can fully live in relaxed blessing.

I will, you shall

WEEK 28 THURS

The distinction between 'I will' and 'you shall' is at the heart of this passage. First, God made a series of promises to Abraham – '*I will* make you very fruitful ... *I will* establish my covenant with you ... *I will* give you ...' (Gen. 17:3–8); whereas to Moses He gave the law, the Ten Commandments, '*You shall, you shall, you shall not*' (Exod. 20:1–17). The promise is all about what God will do, the law is all about what man has to do. The question this passage raises is, how do they fit together?

For a start, 'The law ... does not ... do away with the promise' (v.17). But since God started with a promise (to bless mankind through Abraham) and ended with a promise (to give salvation freely, through faith alone) why did He give the law at all? What was the point?

'There's no such thing as absolute truth, you live your way and I'll live mine', is a fairly generally held viewpoint today, and it's because of that kind of thinking that the law was given. In God's moral universe there are absolute truths and there is a right way to live. The law makes this clear and through it we become aware that we're constantly failing. Living without law would be like trying to do maths without rules. It would be like trying to drive in a world without roads. No markings, no guidelines, nothing clear.

The law is also there to keep some kind of moral constraint on us, it 'kept [us] in protective custody' (v.23, NLT), to stop us messing up as much as we would otherwise have done.

Finally, it led us towards Christ, as a teacher leads a pupil towards truth. It is a kind of pointer in the right direction (v.24).

Galatians 3:15–25

'So the law was put in charge to lead us to Christ ...' (v.24)

For prayer and reflection

Lord, thank You for guidelines to help me live, but thank You even more that to be accepted by You doesn't depend on keeping them all.

181

Beautifully dressed

'… all of you
… have clothed
yourselves with
Christ.' (v.27)

Why I should want to wear designer labels is beyond me. With brand names clearly visible on so many clothes, I remember once, in my naivety, saying to a class of 14-year-olds, 'Why do you want to give free advertising to whoever manufactured your clothes?'

'So that everybody will see where you got them, Miss,' was the reply. 'If you can afford them, people like you more and you get more respect.' So apparently it's not the colour or the style of your clothes that matters but who made or designed them.

So it is in the spiritual realm. We are wearing Christ. We are covered by His designer label; in fact, we *are* His designer label. Even if I am in poverty, I am clothed in Christ; if I am affluent beyond words, I'll be no better dressed, for I am already wearing the very best – I am clothed in Christ. If I am a teenage girl my latest fashion will be what Christ clothes me in – Himself. If I am an old man, shabbily dressed and in a nursing home, I will be as beautifully dressed as that teenage fashion-conscious girl, for I am wearing Christ. It is as if I have put on an all-enveloping coat so that nobody notices what my sex or background or social status is. These things no longer matter, they have absolutely no significance.

We tend to see church growth happen only within social groupings – like attracting like – 'white middle class', 'inner city', and so on. But this ought not to be so. One of the truest signs that the Christian Church is living like it ought is that a totally diverse mixture of people live and work harmoniously together without even noticing the differences between them.

**For prayer and
reflection**

**What do I notice
immediately –
someone's social
status or whether
they are 'wearing'
Christ?**

WEEKEND

A Cinderella story

For reflection: Ephesians 1:3–6 and John 1:12–13

Imagine a young offenders' institution, and inside a group of hardened teenage girls – sullen, disinterested, lethargic and hopeless. Pinched faces, blank eyes, arms stabbed with needle marks, fingers browned with nicotine.

One day the big double doors are opened and the girls are suddenly and unbelievably told, 'You're free to go.' They gather their few pitiful belongings and stumble out into the street. A stretch limo draws up, the window rolls down and a kindly voice says, 'The prison's closed. I closed it personally, you're free. Hop in the car.' They hesitate. People like him don't offer girls like them a ride.

Then the voice says, 'I'd actually like to adopt you all. Make you part of my family, daughters in fact, and give you all the things you've never had.'

All too much? A con, a scam? No! Jesus takes us from slavery (Gal. 4:3) and the prison of the law (3:23) into freedom – and then one step further into daughterhood (4:7). Not content with setting us free, He has made us part of His own loved family.

Celebrate this weekend that you are God's daughter, His rightful heir.

How to be a **popular preacher**

'Have I now become your enemy by telling you the truth?' (v.16)

Recently I noticed an advertisement in the evangelical press which bore the words 'Wanted, minister, boring preachers need not apply'. It made me gasp – with concern for the poor soul who might unwittingly be lured into employment in such a church and with despair for the church in question that had that as its top priority and was unashamed to go public with it. OK, nobody wants to be sent to sleep every Sunday – but is entertainment value what we're really looking for? Is it the preacher's job to keep us all happy?

I imagine the new pastor of that particular church nervously stepping into the pulpit on a Sunday morning, trembling as he opens his mouth lest he not be reckoned to have delivered the desired goods that day. I imagine the congregation, score cards in hand, like ice-skating judges: 5.4 for illustrations, 5.9 for content, 4.0 for length – over 25 minutes again! Would he ever dare challenge them, rebuke them, make them feel uncomfortable? Not if he values his pay cheque rolling in at the end of the month!

That was Paul's concern here. He saw the Judaisers ('those people', v.17) trying to flatter the congregation with smooth words which weren't true. Paul, on the other hand, had told them the truth and it was unpalatable. Once they had welcomed him as if he 'were an angel', now they had been swayed by the words of others and their opinion of him had changed. In fact telling them the truth had made him their enemy.

It's very easy to please a congregation by never challenging them, but a true pastor who really cares for the sheep will challenge and occasionally rebuke. Remember, God's Word is meant to be like a two-edged sword!

For prayer and reflection

How do you react when your minister preaches unpalatable words? Do you take offence or do you let Scripture do its sometimes painful work?

Children **of promise**

Galatians 4:21–31

How safe and secure do you feel in your Christian faith? Perhaps you fear that you may slip out of God's loving arms, or maybe you wonder whether you meet all the standards. Today's passage shows us how safe a foundation we are on – the promises of God and the work of the Spirit.

In the Old Testament, God promised a son to Abraham and Sarah and in due course that son, Isaac, was born. However, while she was waiting for this event, Sarah's faith in God got a little shaky, so she did things her own way and produced a son, Ishmael, by means of Hagar, her servant. Hagar's son was the child produced by human effort (trying hard, law, representing the old covenant). Isaac was the result of God's promise (freedom from law, all done by God, new covenant).

In Jesus' day, many felt no need of Him because they already believed that, being descended from Abraham, they were sure of God's acceptance and didn't need to be made free. In John 8:31–44, Jesus firmly corrected this idea. The new inheritors of the promise are those who are born not into a physical family but a spiritual one – by the Spirit of God. As Galatians 3:29 tells us, *we* are Abraham's seed – his rightful heirs, the 'children of promise' (4:28), born spiritually into God's family.

Just as Isaac was 'the son born by the power of the Spirit' (v.29), so we too received the Spirit and began with the Spirit (3:2–3). In other words it was something we could never do by human effort – that is why we can feel secure. We are His children through the work of the Holy Spirit and He will keep his promise to us just as He kept it to Sarah.

'Now you, brothers, like Isaac, are children of promise.' (v.28)

For prayer and reflection

Lord, confirm my faith in You today and show me how secure I am. Give me a fresh awareness of Your Spirit in me, my mark of acceptance in You.

Leaving the past behind

. . . .

Galatians 5:1–6

. . . .

'It is for freedom that Christ has set us free.' (v.1)

The first verse of this passage used to puzzle me. Wasn't it stating the obvious? If you've been set free then obviously you are free – end of story. But the truth is there's a difference between being set free and staying free.

Imagine a high mountain, steep-sloped all the way up to the top. At the top is the cross of Christ. As you climb, there is no way you can see what lies on the other side of the mountain, all you can see is the way you have come; in Christian terms, the way of law-keeping. Once you reach the cross, the great vista ahead opens out – a life of freedom and release. If you choose to lay down the burden of law-keeping at Christ's feet and let Him do it all from now on, then you can move on into the new landscape ahead.

What's offered is a 'Sound of Music', mountain meadow leaping and singing kind of freedom on the far side of the mountain. It's a thing to celebrate; a joyous, abandoned, ecstatic freedom. The heaviness of obligation is left behind with Jesus. He has taken the heaviest burden of all – living with rules.

For prayer and reflection

'So you want to go back to Egypt,' says the song title. Ask yourself today whether you have totally abandoned any idea of a safety-net of your own making.

But, sadly, some choose to hover at the top, afraid to leave the law behind, worried that more might be required of them, tied to the old way of living – just in case. They imagine that it's safer to keep a little control of things themselves. Trusting Christ for everything seems like burning their bridges, and keeping the law as well becomes a kind of safety-net. So they end up looking backwards, 'trying to be justified by law', and find themselves falling back down that mountain, 'fallen away from grace' (v.4).

True or false

'You were running a good race. Who cut in on you …?'
(v.7)

Strong stuff in today's reading, with the idea that whoever is leading the Galatians away from the truth should castrate themselves! That's how seriously Paul takes the danger of error. For when error is allowed a little leeway, it has a tendency to grow and multiply and do real damage.

You can sense both Paul's anger and his distress for these people who had been making such good progress and growing well. They had been 'cut in' on (v.7), persuaded (v.8), infected by a falsehood which was spreading (v.9) and 'thrown into confusion' (v.10). Total disorientation was the outcome. Voices of persuasion had worked powerfully so that the people didn't know where they were or what they should believe any more.

'Look at it this way,' says Paul, 'if circumcision is still OK, then why would anybody want to persecute me?' No, his persecution was happening because he was a very real threat to the old faith of Judaism – because believing in Christ couldn't possibly run alongside the law. Christianity is offensive to human pride, for it shows up how ineffective we are at doing anything for ourselves spiritually.

But one thing is sure, there is a price to be paid for leading believers into such a mess. Paul says that those who do so will 'pay the penalty'.

He uses this same idea of yeast leavening the dough in 1 Corinthians 5:6, where it is applied to sin. Both sin and error spread in a matter of hours and affect every part – just like yeast. That is why both must be challenged and stopped. Usually they work by word of mouth. And so each of us must watch both what we say and what we listen to so that we will not be led astray.

For prayer and reflection

Is my race as fast as it once was? If not, who or what has affected it?

Everybody's doing it

'But do not use
your freedom to
indulge the sinful
nature …' (v.13)

'Naughty – but nice' ran the slogan for cream cakes some years ago. And it worked a treat. It effectively said, 'We realise that you may feel guilty when you eat cream cakes, but set your guilt aside and spoil yourself.' There was a sense of conspiracy about it, a shared, almost mischievous, agreement to indulge together.

So, what about self-indulgence! How do we develop a Christian lifestyle in the context of freedom, especially if every other Christian is doing it? It's all too easy to end up indulging our sinful natures.

The sinful nature wants things – in particular stuff it doesn't need. It wants a good life with fun-filled leisure activities – membership of a gym, trips to the theatre, a good CD collection, time for TV. It wants money. It wants to speak freely – even if that means gossip. It wants to criticise and demand its rights. Some of these things are OK. But a life which could not be contemplated without most of them is a life given over to indulgence.

Not long ago, at a Christian conference centre, a member of staff in his early fifties shared his personal circumstances with me. He received pocket money and had a roof over his head, but no opportunity to save, no pension provision and no home for his family. A little later at the same conference, I overheard a woman tell another member of staff what a wonderful time she'd had test-driving a new Audi the day before. 'Much better than the BMW I'd planned to buy,' she trilled, with a delighted laugh. I cringed.

Freedom to indulge the sinful nature doesn't just mean moral lapses, it even includes speaking insensitively to someone who's struggling in an area where you've been blessed.

**'Where your
treasure is, there
your heart will be
also'. Lord, help
me to stand out
from the Christian
crowd in a way
that pleases You.**

WEEKEND

Biting and fighting

For reflection: Philippians 2:1–4,14

Contention in a group of believers is a miserable experience. Often it starts small: a misunderstanding gets out of hand, a personality takes over and people take sides, a minor doctrinal difference becomes a matter of life or death and a whole church erupts in dissension, with a split and an unpleasant coolness ensuing. Surely we can learn to separate, if we must, in love!

The irony is that in our fight for the right thing to *believe* we totally abandon the right way to *live*. It's easy to live in harmony when there isn't an issue or a personal problem, but the truest test of Christian love is when you find you disagree with another believer. It is then you have the best opportunity you'll ever have to show the world that faith makes a difference, 'By this all men will know that you are my disciples, if you love one another' (John 13:35).

This weekend, meditate on how you are showing love.

Is what you want to say really going to help the situation? Remember biting words and attacking speech lead to the destruction of more than a relationship. A whole church can be devoured if it gets out of hand.

Life in the Spirit

'But if you are led by the Spirit, you are not under law.' (v.18)

What empowers us to live the Christian life? Free-falling with no laws to stop us ending up in sin; how is it possible? Remember last Wednesday's reading about the mountain? On the before-Christ side of the mountain is the law and the 'pulling-yourself-up-the-hill' kind of relationship with God.

On the other side is a totally new kind of relationship with God, completely empowered by the Holy Spirit living within. His power has strength way beyond anything merely human and without Him it is utterly impossible to live the Christian life. He is no bolt-on extra – only for special Christians. 'Beginning with the Spirit' (Gal. 3:3), was how Paul described our starting point as Christians, whereas many of us might have said 'been converted' or 'saved'. But Paul focuses on a future life of empowerment rather than what we have been saved from. In fact, he doesn't envisage the possibility of a Christian life without the empowering Spirit at all.

For prayer and reflection

Thank God for the amazing power of the Spirit – beyond and above anything human or earthly. God's awesome presence dwelling within – alive, today in me!

Today's focus is on how we live now, with the Holy Spirit mentioned four times in today's three verses. He is 'the primary experienced reality' of the Christian life. We are to be involved in active co-operation with Him as we 'walk' (v.16, NKJV). Nor is it hit or miss whether we happen to fall prey to the flesh or live by the Spirit on any particular occasion.

While flesh and the Spirit are in opposition to each other, we are already on the other side of the mountain and are now 'led by the Spirit' and 'not under the law'.

Nor are flesh and Spirit equal forces, for as you go on walking by the Spirit, you will not carry out the desire of the flesh. We are on a 'long obedience in the same direction' (Nietzsche).

The **family likeness**

Galatians 5:19–21

once knew an elderly lady who sniped her way through life, regularly expressing critical opinions. Once, memorably, she railed against the minister who had been preaching through the book of James, 'How dare you preach to us about the tongue. We don't need that.' Condemned out of her own mouth – yet she didn't see it!

'… those who live like this will not inherit the kingdom of God.' (v.21)

How many of us fail to see what our own besetting sin is? We may not have fallen prey to drunkenness, witchcraft or debauchery, but perhaps the 'acts of the sinful nature' (v.19) are a little closer to home, in particular those that relate to the area of relationships. Paul mentions hatred, discord, jealousy, fits of rage, selfish ambition, dissensions, factions and envy. And the scary thing is that 'those who live like this will not inherit the kingdom of God' (v.21).

Why not? Remember back in chapter 4 where Paul talks of our inheritance? If we are God's children, His inheritors, we are meant to show the family likeness as a regular pattern of life. So, while we may lapse into such behaviour occasionally, it should be uncharacteristic behaviour.

A life marked by these sins shows difficulty in personal relationships. These include bitterness and jealousy when someone else is better than us at something, moments of blazing anger, a selfish focus on one's own interests and annoyance if we don't get the honour we feel we deserve, the destruction of unity or harmony, fragmenting into cliques and being the cause of divisions; attitudes of mind as well as the actions which spring from them. We need to guard carefully against such things and not assume that they are insignificant compared to, say, sexual sins. God puts them all together and so should we.

For prayer and reflection

Lord I need to examine my own life to make sure I am not complacent about how I think, speak or live. Please keep my relationships sweet and wholesome.

Learning **a new dance**

**Galatians
5:22–25**

'Since we live by
the Spirit, let us
keep in step with
the Spirit.' (v.25)

What does a Christian believer's life look like? Essentially it is a reflection of the character of God Himself. We are growing into His likeness. That is why it is only possible to be like Him if His Holy Spirit is resident within us. His Spirit produces His fruit. Some of us may be temperamentally quite patient, others find it easy to be gentle but the total package of spiritual fruit is grown when God works on us in our 'least like Him' areas.

It's remarkably easy to congratulate ourselves on the qualities in this list that we already have and gloss over the areas where we are weak. But God grows *all* this fruit on the same tree and the real sign of the Spirit's indwelling is a marked change in areas of personal weakness.

This fruit does not come so spontaneously as to be without co-operation and human effort. We are to crucify the sinful nature (v.24) and 'keep in step with the Spirit' (v.25). Both of these are active commands. Keeping in step suggests watching carefully and following – much like learning a dance routine. Where He walks, we go; how He moves, we move – close and co-operating. It's fluid harmony, not wrenching effort.

Eventually it becomes second nature – quite literally! For we have a *new nature* now since our sinful nature has been crucified. Following the Spirit's promptings becomes more and more unconscious – much like driving a car. Initially when we're learners we focus on the activities of clutch, gear and accelerator; later we do it without thinking. That is what gradually happens as God's Spirit takes over our human nature; we become more and more like Him.

For prayer and
reflection

**Lord, I know
which fruit of
the Spirit I'm not
manifesting. I
bring that area to
You and commit
myself to co-
operate until Your
Spirit produces
real change in me.**

Each **other**

What is your opinion of yourself? Honestly. In the secrecy of your own heart, how do you think you're doing spiritually? A decided failure – you've stumbled a few times and everybody knows it; limited and lacking in spiritual gifts; or do you feel you've made better progress than some others whom you could name? Each of these attitudes needs dealing with for none of them are compatible with being led by the Spirit.

We are to look out for each other and gently lift anyone who has fallen – 'mend' is the actual word used in verse 1, just as the fishermen disciples mended their nets. And if we are amongst those who do the lifting up and are more spiritually mature, we are to avoid pride and self-congratulation for they are provocative qualities (v.26) and conceit is ugly to both man and God.

We are to be so filled with love for the fallen one that we are like Christ Himself, offering loving arms to raise up. We are to share the especially heavy load (v.2) that someone else may be carrying – stresses, worries and cares. But the normal, daily 'backpack' (v.5) we are to take responsibility for ourselves, and not be so self-focused that we become an unwarranted drain on other believers. If we imagine ourselves to be insignificant we should not become envious (v.26), for that eats away at what God has actually given us.

How we think of ourselves and how we treat others is the truest test of whether we are walking in step with the Spirit. 'Self-centred Christian' is a contradiction in terms. If we are really living in the Spirit it will show clearly in gentle, self-effacing, godly love for each other, with not a trace of self-righteousness.

Galatians 5:26–6:5

'Carry each other's burdens, and in this way you will fulfil the law of Christ.' (6:2)

For prayer and reflection

Lord, help me to stop thinking about how everything will affect me. Take my eyes off my needs and give me the strength to be a Christian 'body builder'.

Sowing and growing

Galatians 6:6–18

'… the one who sows to please the Spirit, from the Spirit will reap eternal life.' (v.8)

One summer we went tubing on the Itchetucknee River in Florida. Mile after mile we lazed downstream, but for the last stretch there were warnings to pull into the left, ready for landing. Gradually, we edged towards the bank but watched as some women in an inflatable, ignoring the warnings, drifted on out into alligator-infested waters. They screamed as they disappeared from view round the bend – but it was too late. That is the kind of danger Paul has in mind in these final verses. A man reaps what he sows (v.7). And the truly dangerous thing is that most of us don't realise just how important daily sowing is. We are sowing for a final destination – the safety of the bank after a delightful journey, or the horrors of destruction (v.8) after a mindless, casual, unthinking journey.

Daily choices matter. What we become depends on how we behave. Imperceptibly we grow in holiness or remain stunted spiritually. And the choices relate to remarkably ordinary things. We are to choose to sow generously into the life of the one who teaches us from the Word (v.6). I remember being told about the dreadful manses provided by a particular denomination due to the congregations having got used to being collectively ungenerous.

Secondly, we are to do good to all – especially other believers. That may mean committing to a task in church life with gladness, or simply noticing another's need and doing something about it. These acts produce a harvest for you as well as for those you give to.

A truly spiritual life shows outwardly in selfless behaviour as you sow 'to please the Spirit'.

For prayer and reflection

Lord, I need to take action on this NOW and not drift along any longer. I want my life to be Spirit-led, pouring out to others and producing a harvest.

WEEKEND

Throwing the world away

For reflection: Philippians 3:7–11

How radical is your Christian life? Is it more of an outward show or a costly, deep-seated, far-reaching transformation? The outward show kind of Christian life is tolerably easy – except for the fact that it requires effort to look the part, whereas radical transformation goes way beyond the surface, is sometimes painful, but is powered by the Holy Spirit Himself. With this choice you throw the world away, in terms of storing up material things and the desire for power and fame; a loss that seems huge until you walk into the presence of God and see what you gain instead.

There are times when you lose direction and slip back into the ordinariness of earthly living – worrying about what others worry about, wanting what they have. But at the top of that hill the things of the world ceased to matter to us, and when you remember that you want to shout and leap and tell everyone. It is a matter for boasting.

What Jesus did outwardly has so affected you inwardly, by the power of His indwelling Spirit, that everything else fades into insignificance. Choose that new life, freedom and peace, today.

Finding God's perfect plan

Alie Stibbe

Alie Stibbe works as the Timetabling Officer at a college of further education. A mother of four, in her spare time she works as a freelance writer and translator, cultivates her potager garden, keeps chickens and quails, and is a trustee of The Father's House Trust: www.fathershousetrust.com

Finding God's perfect plan

' "For my thoughts are not your thoughts, neither are your ways my ways," declares the LORD.' (v.8)

For prayer and reflection

Lord, so often I have chosen to make the world's way my way. From now on I want to think and do things Your way – for Your renown.

We are going to spend the next month looking at the often perplexing subject of how we know God's guidance in our lives. In the West particularly, contemporary life presents us with a bewildering array of options, choices and opportunities; never before have women had such a great dilemma in trying to discern how God would have them spend the time and talents they've been given.

How do we know what is right in God's sight when we are faced with the barrage of different messages and aspirations that bombard us through the media? How do we know that we are making God's choices and not just following the spirit of the age?

Before we begin to try and answer these questions, it is essential for us to realise that our fallen nature affects the way we think. Our natural minds are at odds with our spiritual minds; our human nature does not automatically think the way God thinks and the things human nature values are not necessarily the things God values. If they were, then we wouldn't have the problem of knowing His will or discerning His guidance – it would be our natural instinct and I wouldn't be writing these notes!

The basic problem is our sinful human nature, a nature that seeks to satisfy 'self' rather than seek the kingdom of God. Today's reading encourages us to forsake our selfish ways and our selfish thoughts in favour of God's ways and thoughts. If we answer that call, then the Lord pardons us, has mercy on our human weakness, and we find ourselves in a position to begin to seek the way He wants us to live and the path He wants us to follow.

A future **and a hope**

This verse has been a life-line for me when I have had moments of struggling in my mind as to whether I am in the place God wants me to be, doing the things He wants me to do at any particular stage in my life. It reminds me that the Lord knows the plans He has for each of us and that they were laid out before we were even born (Psa. 139:16).

The wonderful thing about the Lord's plans for us are that they are tailor-made for each individual; they are plans that allow us to hope in the future, knowing that the Lord has been there ahead of us, preparing the way He wants us to follow. He knows where we should be going and what we should be doing and who we will become.

Our task as Christians is to ensure we live in such a way that we don't miss the 'hope and a future' the Lord has planned for us, due to being deceived by our human nature. One of the biggest deceptions in our day is the subtle understanding that God having 'hope and a future' for us means that we are going to be successful, rich, healthy, happy and free from any kind of trouble. Wrong. Remember what Jesus said: 'In this world you will have trouble' (John 16:33).

A future and a hope does not mean that we will not face difficulties – it means we will have the heavenly resources to turn these difficulties into opportunities for building the spiritual character that is required for tasks further down the road of life – tasks that the Lord knows only you can do, with the equipping He has provided along the way.

Jeremiah 29:1–14

'For I know the plans I have for you … plans to … give you hope and a future.' (v.11)

For prayer and reflection

Lord, thank You that I can trust You that Your plans for me are for good, even when I face difficult times. Thank You that You are in perfect control.

A **new direction**

Proverbs 3:1–12

'… in all your ways acknowledge him, and he will make your paths straight.' (v.6)

We have seen that human beings don't naturally think or act the way the Lord does, and yet that the Lord has a future and a hope for us. How do we reconcile the distance between these things? I have already mentioned that living a life yielded to God is the first step – confessing our sin and allowing the Lord to live in us by His Holy Spirit. It is very easy, however, to live the Christian life without seeking to put God first in everything – the Lord can be living in our lives, but we have not allowed Him to sit on the throne of our hearts.

So many of us miss the Lord's best for us precisely because we allow self to keep pushing Jesus into a quiet corner of our hearts and minds where we can't hear the radical demands that living in His love makes on our thinking and decision-making.

The way to combat this natural human tendency is to acknowledge the Lord in all your ways, rather than depending on your own limited and humanly-biased understanding and analysis of any situation. The wonderful promise for those who do this is that the Lord 'will make your paths straight'; in other words, you can't go far wrong if you bring Jesus into your decision-making.

Acknowledging the Lord in all your ways is a major step on the way to finding out if an idea is a 'God' idea or just a good idea; it prepares the broad canvas of the heart and mind so that it is ready and receptive for the Lord to fill in the detailed brushstrokes one at a time until the whole picture emerges.

For prayer and reflection

Lord, I want to acknowledge You in all that I am, think and do – and I trust in Your promise that You will then show me the way to live.

A **voice** behind you

When we belong to Jesus and we are seeking to put Him first in our lives – yielding to Him and acknowledging Him – His Holy Spirit comes and lives inside us. Our spiritual nature then begins to gain ground over our human nature so that we become increasingly attuned to God's ways and God's thoughts as each day goes by. This means that when we ask God for direction, we begin to recognise His voice echoing in our hearts *if we are listening out for it* (John 10:4).

The people in today's passage are promised that 'whether you turn to the right or to the left, your ears will hear a voice behind you, saying, "This is the way; walk in it"'. This is often our own experience as Christians; we can be surrounded by a range of alternative choices for action, all seemingly good to our own understanding, yet it is often only when we turn to face the left or right and have the courage to weigh up the full implications of each of those choices with hearts and minds yielded to God, that we hear the still small voice that says, 'No, not that way', and 'No, not that way either … but this way – straight ahead'.

So, learning to listen is another key to knowing God's guidance; those who are unwilling to listen aren't going to find the Lord's perfect plan for their lives because ultimately, in their heart of hearts, they know they don't want to do the thing God is asking, because it will mean putting their natural 'self' to one side. Listening and obedience are closely related; both depend on being yielded to God, the willingness to change and the submission of 'self'.

Isaiah 30:15–22

'… your ears will hear a voice behind you, saying, "This is the way; walk in it." '
(v.21)

For prayer and reflection

Lord, I want to learn to listen and commit myself to the obedience that listening implies. Teach me to recognise Your voice in the midst of the clamour around me.

A teachable spirit

Psalm 25

'He guides the humble in what is right and teaches them his way.' (v.9)

So far this week we have looked at four spiritual traits characteristic of those who truly seek God's will in their life; such people have hearts that are repentant, trusting, submissive, listening (attentive with a desire for action). The final spiritual characteristic that I think is crucial for those who want to know the Lord's guidance in their lives is humility.

Time and time again in the Bible we read that God opposes the proud (eg Luke 1:51). We become proud when we forget the Lord and begin to depend on our own wisdom and capabilities — such an easy thing to do when things are going well for us or we begin to believe our own publicity. And that's when things start to go wrong — when we turn our eyes away from Jesus and begin to prioritise other things over and above the kingdom of God.

Humility, on the other hand, is having a true understanding of who we are — sinners saved by grace, who owe everything to Jesus, and who have nothing to boast about except the cross of Christ (Gal. 6:14). It is the humble heart that is open to God's guidance, because the person with a humble heart has a teachable spirit that is listening for the Lord's voice and is ready to act on what it hears.

Perhaps you can feel the tension in your own life as we have discussed these spiritual characteristics this week. The human spirit compels us to look out for ourselves at all times — but the Holy Spirit woos us with the promise of a greater and different kind of prosperity and success if we do things the Lord's way.

For prayer and reflection

Lord, once and for all, crucify my pride. Give me a humble heart and a teachable spirit so that I might know Your ways.

WEEKEND

Putting off the old man

For reflection: Ephesians 4:22 (AV)

I heard a sad but true story a few years ago. A Christian woman found that her relationship with her unbelieving husband was becoming more and more difficult to bear. She was desperately seeking the Lord's will as to how to deal with the situation. She sought guidance in the Bible and was convinced that God was telling her to divorce her husband, which, without taking advice, she did. It turned out that the basis for understanding God's guidance for her life was Ephesians 4:22 in the Authorised Version, which reads 'Put off the old man' – which, in her social dialect, seemed obvious advice.

It is incredible that people can read the Bible so literally and uncritically, in an old translation, without seeing if their understanding of a verse and its context agrees with what is written elsewhere. Perhaps if the lady had read 1 Corinthians 7:13 and 15 and consulted with other believers, she would have weighed up Ephesians 4:22 quite differently. (If she had used the NIV, there would have been no problem at all.)

Do you read God's Word with your head as well as your heart?

The ultimate **guide book**

2 Timothy 3:10–17

'All Scripture is God-breathed and is useful for … training in righteousness.' (v.16)

Last week we examined which attitudes of the heart we need to cultivate in order to know God's guidance. These general attitudes are necessary if the specifics of God's guidance are to have any effect at all in our lives. These specifics are all found in the Bible, the book that Christians consider to be the inspired Word of God. Reading the Bible with the right spiritual attitudes in place enables us to know and do what we need to in order to walk in the ways of the Lord in our everyday lives.

The Bible is useful not just for teaching and training – showing us how to 'live the life', but also for rebuking and correcting – helping us put things right when we go wrong. Both these aspects train the individual believer in living the way the Lord wants so that we will be 'thoroughly equipped for every good work' – ie ready to do what the Lord has planned ahead of time for us to do.

I have come across many believers who treat the Bible in the same way we often treat the instruction manual for a new domestic appliance once it is unwrapped and plugged in – skim read the important-looking bits, throw it in the kitchen drawer and then wonder weeks down the line why the thing doesn't do what we thought it would do! If we would only carefully read the instructions – then we would know the applications and limitations of the appliance.

It is the same with the Bible – if we are to know God's daily guidance for living then we need to read and learn to understand the God-inspired text. It can be that simple!

For prayer and reflection

'I meditate on your precepts and consider your ways. I delight in your decrees; I will not neglect your word.' (Psa. 119:15–16)

God's **bottom line**

I've spent a lot of time recently trying to work out which of the 'rules' we live by are imposed on us just because of the structure of the society we live in, and which rules are God's indispensable bottom line. All this in an attempt to try and think through the boundaries of the role of Christian women in contemporary secular society – not an easy job, nor one I've solved yet! However, the rules we can't dispense with, whatever age or culture we live in, are the Ten Commandments – God's bottom-line guidance for living life His way.

When Moses presented the Ten Commandments to the people of Israel he told them to learn them and ensure they followed them. Now here's a challenge – can you reel them off? Have you really thought about what they mean as guidelines for your daily living? Have you thought about how Jesus interpreted some of the commandments, especially in relation to our thought life, not just our visible actions (Matt. 5:17–48)? Until we have mastered God's guiding principles at this very basic level and allowed the foundational ideology of the Ten Commandments to permeate our thinking, we are standing on very shaky ground in relation to answering the more subjective, stickier points of guidance such as, 'Shall I take that job offer?'

Held up to the light of the Ten Commandments, some difficult questions concerning guidance can be answered quite quickly. If a course of action comes into blatant conflict with our understanding of any of the commandments, we have an indication it isn't the right thing to do. Often though, things are not as clear-cut as we would like ... but it's a start.

Deuteronomy 5:1–21

'Hear ... the laws I declare in your hearing today. Learn them and be sure to follow them.' (v.1)

For prayer and reflection

Lord, I know my salvation doesn't depend on keeping the law, but I know there are principles there by which You still want us to live. Help me sharpen up my act.

A new **commandment**

John 13:31–38

'A new command I give you: Love one another. As I have loved you, so you must love one another.' (v.34)

Learning, understanding and applying the Ten Commandments is one way we can find guidance for living, but in addition to that, we need to familiarise ourselves and be clear about the way Jesus taught that children of God should live. Jesus summarised the Law of Moses in a few sentences: '"Love the Lord your God with all your heart and with all your soul and with all your mind." This is the first and greatest commandment. And the second is like it: "Love your neighbour as yourself"' (Matt. 22:37–40).

For Jesus, the key to knowing how to live according to God's guidelines was the law of love, which for Him was one of humility and self-sacrifice (John 15:13; Phil. 2:1–11).

The clearest expression of the law of love in action is Jesus' teaching in the Sermon on the Mount (Matt. 5–7); it means going the extra mile, giving your cloak as well as your tunic, and turning the other cheek. I have often thought there is more than enough scope for living out the Sermon on the Mount as a mother!

Allison Pearson, an English journalist, once commented that 'sacrifice is written in a mother's genes, and is found right next to the guilt chromosome'; and there is some truth in her observation. Although I am all for self-sacrificial love, I am aware that my self-sacrificial actions all too easily become motivated by guilt and not love. I've found that if I feel driven to something by guilt, rather than drawn to volunteer in love, then I seriously need to question if I should take the considered course of action. 'Hardening of the *ought*-eries' is a disease that severely hinders our ability to discern what the Lord would or would not have us do.

For prayer and reflection

Lord, create in me the sacrificial attitude that enables me to live Your law of love, and give me wisdom how to assess the guilty nature in my motives.

Standing firm

Outside the Gospels, the New Testament contains a treasure trove of resources for our guidance in the Christian life. The book of Acts, particularly, contains many descriptions of how Christians lived and died – wonderful models of behaviour and attitude that we can use as plumb-lines against which to measure our own experiences, attitudes, choices and actions.

The epistles are also full of more directive teaching. The recipients of Paul's letter to the Thessalonians were encouraged to hold onto his teaching, whether it was something he had said to them directly or something he had written to them. We will never know more than Paul's written words, but there is so much practical wisdom there that can help us if we hold onto it when the going gets tough.

Much of Paul's writings is quite straightforward and uncontroversial, but there are parts that can cause us much heartache as we try and understand what they mean in a contemporary context. This is especially relevant for women who want to be true to the Word, but also seek to live in God's fullness and freedom within the restrictions of their particular culture. This is why it is important that we not only cultivate spiritual attitudes that predispose us to receive God's guidance, but also welcome the Holy Spirit into our reading of the Word so that we might know the correct application of the truth in our own situation by the inner witness and peace of the Spirit in our hearts and minds. And don't forget your *minds* – it is crucial that we examine and think about the implications and applications of the difficult teachings we are encouraged to hold onto.

2 Thessalonians 2:13–17

'… hold to the teachings we passed on to you, whether by word of mouth or by letter.' (v.15)

For prayer and reflection

Lord, fill my critical faculties with the power of Your Spirit so that I can see clearly how to hold onto and apply Your Word in my situation.

Steeped in the Word

Colossians 3:12–17

'Let the word of Christ dwell in you richly as you teach … one another with all wisdom …' (v.16)

I make no apology for having spent all week looking at how the Word of God acts as our primary guide in life. Reading the Word familiarises us with God's character and enables us to hold our everyday decisions and major life choices up to the benchmark of His holiness. As we read the Word regularly it becomes part of us, and our inner attitudes and ways of thinking begin to change. This means that as time goes by we find we no longer need to make conscious decisions about matters that vexed us as young believers, because the change Jesus is making in the depths of our being makes the moral and ethical choice automatic.

I have often surprised checkout assistants by asking them to scan the wrappers of snacks that one of my children has consumed as we've gone round a supermarket. 'You shouldn't worry about that,' is the usual response, 'No one else does!' But Christians aren't 'no one else' – the Lord demands the highest standards, and being *honest* gives us an opportunity to share the gospel with the astounded recipient of that honesty.

The only way automatic moral guidance can become a part of our lives is by letting the Word of Christ dwell in us richly. We need to read it, understand and remember it. Then, when the crunch comes, we have a basic moral framework against which simple decisions can be made quickly and unconsciously, or against which bigger decisions can be held up for examination. Knowing God's Word also enables us to give informed guidance to others – especially important for those of us with children! If I say 'No', I like to be able to give a biblical reason why – 'training in righteousness' is not easy for parents or children!

For prayer and reflection

Lord, help me to hide Your Word in my heart that I might not sin against You. (Psa. 119:11)

WEEKEND

Know my anxious thoughts

For reflection: Psalm 139:23–24

Common sense is not such a common thing these days – but the Lord gave us common sense so we don't have to over-spiritualise every decision. For some decisions specific guidance is not required! It is very sad that some overzealous Christians – the kind who pray about which pair of identical jeans to put on in the morning – can lead non-believers into thinking that following Jesus means surrendering any form of initiative or independent thought.

Don't get me wrong, I *do* pray about what to wear, especially when I need to consider if the impression my outfit might make is in line with kingdom values – though it is impossible to legislate for the thought life of every male in the work place! *God is interested in the details of our lives* as well as the big issues, but spiritual maturity involves knowing which little issues are worth bothering Him with and which decisions He might consider we can make ourselves.

Take stock of your indecisiveness. Ask the Lord to help you master the place of common sense in decision-making.

Your **personal advisor**

'... the Holy Spirit ... will teach you ... and will remind you of everything I have said to you.' (v.26)

I hope the last two weeks' readings haven't been too cerebral! We need the right attitudes to take on board God's guidance, and we need to be reading His Word so we get the basics of how to think and live as a Christian firmly in place – but even that is not enough. When we are born again, the Holy Spirit comes and lives inside us, and it is the Holy Spirit who makes the Word of God living and active in the life of a believer in a way that the person who is not born again just cannot understand.

There is a whole world of difference between reading the Bible with the natural mind, and reading with the enlightenment of the Holy Spirit. The natural mind can understand the basics, but the Holy Spirit turns Bible reading from a two-dimensional exercise in black and white, to a multi-dimensional experience in full technicolour.

Jesus said to His disciples that when the Father sent the Holy Spirit, He would 'teach you all things and remind you of everything I have said to you'. This promise while primarily for the 12 disciples and the writing of the New Testament, was also for all Jesus' followers who would believe as a result of their witness (John 17:20).

This means that God's Spirit within us can bring to mind parts of the Bible that we have read when we most need that particular information – but remember, you can't be reminded of something you haven't already read! Having said that, I have heard of people being prompted by the Spirit to look up a particular Bible reference and, when they do, they have found that the perhaps unfamiliar passage spoke vividly into their situation.

For prayer and reflection

Lord, open my heart and mind to welcome and recognise the prompting of Your Spirit – all that You would remind me and teach me.

Listening to the Spirit

I t's all very well saying that the Holy Spirit will remind us of things and teach us things, but how do we know that the 'voice' we are hearing in our inner beings is the Holy Spirit rather than our own imaginations? In answering this I always return to John 10. Here Jesus likens Himself to the Good Shepherd, and His followers to sheep. In the same way that sheep know by experience the voice of the shepherd they can trust, Jesus' sheep – His followers – know His voice. And we get to know that voice by experience; at first the voice is new and unfamiliar but, like sheep, if we are listening out and hear it enough, then we get to recognise it over a period of time.

Think about people you know very well – perhaps friends, or parents, or your spouse – when the phone rings and you pick it up and they begin talking, you know who it is – they don't need to say who it is, even if it takes a minute for the recognition to sink in. You know it's them by the way they talk and the kinds of things they are talking about; and you know all this because you spend so much time with them and are familiar with their idiosyncrasies.

It's the same with the voice of God in our hearts – if we are walking closely with Him in intimate relationship, we don't need Him to say 'Hi! It's me – *God*, you know ... your heavenly Father! Listen up!' – *We know.*

This recognition doesn't happen overnight, it grows with time, like in any relationship – and it can die, like in any relationship where communication is not functioning. Our relationship with the Lord needs to be invested in if we want to recognise His voice.

John 10:1–15

'He calls his own sheep by name ... [they] follow him because they know his voice.' (vv.3–4)

For prayer and reflection

Lord, I want to know You more and more – help me recognise the unmistakable distinctiveness of Your voice. Help me to listen.

Altered consciousness

Romans 12:1–8

'… be transformed
by the renewing of
your mind … you
will be able to test
… God's will …'
(v.2)

Difficulty in decision-making and knowing God's guidance can come from allowing ourselves to be so steeped in the way the world thinks and by so valuing the things the world values that we find ourselves in a bitter inner struggle between those attitudes and the values and attitudes that matter to the Lord. It reminds me of the story of the hyena who came to a fork in the path through the bush. Both paths led to villages where he was bound to find food – but he couldn't decide which one to go down. In the end he chose to go down both. As the paths began to diverge, his legs got wider and wider apart until he collapsed in an aching heap unable to move a step in any direction.

Followers of Jesus face the same dilemma: two paths – the world's way and the Lord's way. We know we should choose the Lord's way, but we don't want to relinquish any of the so-called benefits we might find down the world's way. We end up in an exhausted heap unable to keep our feet on either path.

How do we solve this dilemma? The obvious answer is to choose the Lord's way, but that means rejecting the world's way and leaving it behind. And that is not easy – it is impossible to fight an enemy who has outposts in your head. We need to get the outposts of the world out of our heads and that can only be done by the transforming of our minds in the power of the Holy Spirit. Once your values are transformed at such a deep level, knowing and choosing the Lord's way becomes easier because the massive struggle to hold onto the things of the world has disappeared.

For prayer and
reflection

**'Let us throw off
everything that
hinders and the
sin that so easily
entangles, and
let us run with
perseverance the
race marked out
for us.' (Heb. 12:1)**

All things **work ... for good**

Recently we thought we had to make a very difficult decision. The run-up to the event was traumatic, the point of no return was traumatic and, even after knowing God's provision in very difficult circumstances, things remained traumatic on and off for the best part of a year. First of all it was very hard to understand why we had to face such a difficulty when we had tried to live faithfully – but bad things do happen to good people just because we live in a fallen world.

Giving the circumstances over to the Lord, we had to accept that there are times in life when there is actually no choice over how to proceed, the only decision is to 'let go and let God' – circumstances channel you where you don't want to go and guidance isn't even an option. In that situation you just hold onto the raft, go where the current takes you, keep your eyes open despite the temptation to shut them – and pray very hard, trusting that God knows where the rapids will take you and when they're going to end.

Hopefully, none of us has to face these crisis situations more than once or twice in a lifetime, but these trials are intense times of spiritual character building when you come to appreciate that God does work in all things – even bad things – for the good of those who love Him. Our experience has taught me to see the long-term perspective, the fact that it can take a lifetime to see the Lord work a thread of His purpose out, that all the knots along the way are there for a reason and that nothing – however devastating – can separate us from His love – that 'underneath are the everlasting arms' (Deut. 33:27), ready to catch us when life goes into freefall.

Romans 8:28–39

'... God works for the good of those who love him ... called according to his purpose.' (v.28)

For prayer and reflection

Lord – when trusting myself into Your loving arms is the only option for 'guidance' I have, may I know that You will never let me go.

The Word **and the Spirit**

Hebrews 4:12–16

'For the Word of God is living and active.' (v.12)

Christians believe the Word of God was written by people under the inspiration of the Holy Spirit. This does not necessarily mean it was dictated word for word, but that there is a living presence behind and in the text that makes it 'living and active' in a way that purely human-inspired texts are not.

When we are born again, the Holy Spirit comes and dwells within us and connects with the same living and active presence in the inspired text of the Bible. Suddenly we are able to see and understand things written there that the natural mind cannot perceive.

There has been much discussion among theologians about how the Holy Spirit opens the text to us in ways that academic methods cannot. But the answer remains that it is a mystery – but the witness of hundreds of generations of Spirit-filled Christians demonstrate that it is so. Listen to this testimony from 1817:

'I promised myself then never again to try and fathom spiritual things or eternity by reason ... when I was in doubt about anything, I went off by myself and talked it over with my Saviour like a child and prayed that His Spirit might reveal to me the truth ... I now searched diligently in the Holy Scriptures for guidance for my life. I did not trust my feelings, my inner light, unless they agreed with the teachings of Jesus and the apostles ... in this way things I had formerly wondered about became clear to me without further search ... the Lord guided and admonished me by His Holy Spirit.' [1]

Can you testify to the living active nature of God's Word in your life?

For prayer and reflection

Lord, by the infilling of Your Holy Spirit, 'open my eyes that I may see wonderful things in your law.' (Psa. 119:18)

[1] Hauge, H.N. *Religious Feelings and their Worth* (1817), trans. from Norwegian by Joel M. Njus 1954 (Ausburg, Minneapolis)

WEEKEND

When doubts set in

For reflection: 1 Kings 8:23

'O Lord, God of Israel, there is no God like you …
you who keep your covenant of love with your servants
who continue wholeheartedly in your way.'

Big decision over – you're miles down the road you believe the Lord has directed you on. You've done everything possible to ensure this was God's will, especially if it was something you wanted, too, because you didn't want to confuse selfish desires with God's desire. But now there's a sense of anticlimax; everything seems so mundane when held up to the light of the promised future and hope you had been expecting. Sound familiar?

Well, it does to me! Committing to a five-year part-time degree was no easy decision. All the lights had seemed green! Now, months down the line, I'm exhausted – was all this a mistake? But the Lord is our greatest cheerleader if we desire to *persevere* in our calling – today I had an e-mail that uplifted me, and renewed my vision.

Knowing God's guidance is one thing – but persisting when the going gets ordinary is another. Are you up to settling down for the long haul?

The audible voice of God

Acts 9:1–19

'… a light from heaven flashed around him. He fell to the ground and heard a voice …' (vv.3b–4).

I n the last two weeks, among other issues, we've thought about how the Lord guides us by His Word and by the Holy Spirit. These are the most usual ways we know God's guidance. Less usual is the Lord's direct intervention in the lives of His followers – the most direct way being His audible voice.

Saul's meeting with the risen Jesus on the road to Damascus is a primary reference point for this kind of experience. It is impossible to know exactly what happened, but it does appear that the people with Saul heard something (cf. John 12:29), although they themselves didn't see anything (cf. 1 Cor. 15:8). Thus it seems pointless debating the exact meaning of 'audible', but it is clear that the voice is audible enough to the person who is intended to hear it.

People who have experienced the audible voice of God say it can be actually audible or like an extremely loud thought that enters your head so suddenly and says something that cuts across what you were dwelling on in such a way that you know it couldn't have been self-generated.

This has happened to me a few times, but I remember one instance particularly. We had just moved into our first vicarage. I was standing in the part of the garden I had designated as a much longed-for vegetable patch – it even had my dream apple tree. As I hugged my arms round myself in satisfaction, a voice cut through my thoughts and said, 'Don't get too settled, you won't be here long.' I knew it was the Lord. I stored those words in my heart, and it was no surprise when four years later, a short stint for a vicar, we were on the move again.

For prayer and reflection

' "Today if you hear his voice, do not harden your hearts" … See to it … that none of you has a sinful, unbelieving heart that turns away from the living God.' (Heb. 3:7–8,12)

Angels, unawares and otherwise

I will have to be honest with you – I have never seen an angel, not a recognisable one wreathed in light, anyway. My experience with messengers from God is rather like when Abraham welcomed three unexpected, unspectacular visitors to his tent whose words changed the course of his life forever (Gen. 18). The 'angel' I met was a man in a supermarket who came and talked to me because I was wearing a Norwegian sweater; and I don't *ever* allow myself to be talked to by strange men in supermarkets!

As a result of something he told me, I ended up as a student at an academic institution I would never have even known about or certainly not approached of my own initiative, had I not met him. He was a kind of angel – a messenger from God sent to point me in the right direction at a time when I didn't know what I was to do next on an unknown journey I felt the Lord had gently nudged me to begin.

My husband, on the other hand, has seen an angel – in fact, it was probably Jesus. His experience was more like Peter's in Acts 12:7. Way before I met him, a tall shining figure walked into his room one night, beckoned towards him and said, 'Come, follow me.' From that moment on, my husband has been set on following Jesus whatever it costs and wherever it leads. An experience like that becomes a more than decisive part in knowing God's guidance, it is all-defining.

It seems to me that when a crunch decision is called for, perhaps a decision about a completely new direction in life, the Lord does send angels unawares – or otherwise – to make sure we get the message loud and clear.

Luke 1:26–38

'... God sent the angel Gabriel to Nazareth ... to a virgin pledged to be married ...' (vv.26–27)

For prayer and reflection

Lord, help me be aware of the way You speak to me through others, whether they are angels or otherwise.

Dreams and visions

Acts 22:2–21

'… praying at the temple, I fell into a trance and saw the Lord speaking.' (vv.17–18)

All our waking moments our minds are busy, busy, busy – we are preoccupied with many things – and if your house is like ours, it can be very hard to find any peace and quiet anywhere, even at the bottom of the garden. I think the Lord must find it very hard to get a word in edgeways in these situations, and that is probably why He sometimes speaks to us in dreams – when we are asleep and our minds are at rest; or in visions – when we are awake and are consciously focused on Him and nothing else.

The examples of dreams and visions we find in the Bible seem to fall into two main categories when it comes to the Lord using them as a means of guidance. In today's reading, Paul has a vision of the Lord speaking and is told to leave Jerusalem for his own safety. The Lord speaks to Joseph, the husband of Mary, in dreams in the night warning him to take Mary and the baby Jesus and flee to Egypt. There are other similar examples – and they are all of the Lord warning His followers, telling them how to avoid coming danger of one kind or another.

The other main kind of vision or dream in the Bible is of a commissioning nature. Isaiah's vision is probably the best known (Isa. 6); the whole experience ends with Isaiah committing himself to the Lord's purpose for his life with the words, 'Here I am. Send me' (v.8).

Visions and dreams are still the experience of believers. A lot of dreams are purely the result of too much cheese before bedtime – so thoughtful and prayerful discernment often needs to be applied unless the message is loud and clear!

For prayer and reflection

'For God does speak – now one way, now another – though man may not perceive it. In a dream, in a vision of the night, when deep sleep falls on men …' (Job 33:14ff)

Prophetic words

People are becoming more familiar with prophecy, although it is often viewed with suspicion as a means of knowing God's guidance due to the many occasions it has been mishandled and abused by inexperienced or manipulative individuals. Inspired speech, one of the gifts of the Holy Spirit, has been commonly confused with *foretelling* the future. Although there is a future-orientated element in prophecy – relating to the encouragement that comes with God having a future and a hope for us – it is *not a predictive gift.* Prophecy is also commonly confused with *forth-telling* the Word of God in the sense of preaching – but it is more than that, although preaching can have a prophetic edge to it.

Spirit-filled Christians understand prophecy as the direct and often spontaneous word of God to believers, which has a *creative* function; its revelations being consistent with the written Word of God and what we know of God's character. Prophetic words can be challenging, usually including a call to repentance, but this is balanced by words that *strengthen, encourage and comfort.*

I have always been very careful of any 'prophetic' word that is highly condemnatory or specifies a particular course of action – just because the giver declares, 'The Lord says ...', doesn't mean it is the Lord.

In my experience, prophetic words that have proven genuine tend to be words in which the Lord's Spirit woos my spirit; there is recognition of the Shepherd's voice, a resonance. We are right to treat prophetic words with caution, but we must be careful not to discard something that can confirm the sense of God's guidance we have received from other sources.

1 Corinthians 14:1–5

'But everyone who prophesies speaks to men for ... strengthening, encouragement and comfort.' (v.3)

For prayer and reflection

**'Do not put out the Spirit's fire; do not treat prophecies with contempt. Test everything ...'
(1 Thess. 5:19–22)**

How can I be sure?

1 John 4:1–6

'Every spirit that acknowledges that Jesus Christ has come in the flesh is from God.' (v.2)

The audible voice of God, angelic messengers, visions, dreams, prophetic words, signs or 'God-incidences' (as opposed to coincidences), verses that leap out of the pages of the Bible as if written in fire, promptings in our inner heart – when it comes to guidance and decision-making beyond the basic everyday directives for living that we read in God's Word, these are all the kinds of extraordinary markers we look for. The more of these we can point to in relation to a particular incidence for decision, the more assured we are that a particular turning at the crossroads of life is the one God intends for us.

But how can we be sure? The devil can masquerade as an angel of light (2 Cor. 11:14), quote Scripture (Luke 4:1–13), and prophesy such that we can be misled (1 John 4:1). In instances of 'extraordinary' guidance we are encouraged to 'test the spirits' – to discern between and recognise the Spirit of truth and the spirit of falsehood (v.6) – the latter being human fleshliness or demonic influence.

'Discerning the spirits' is a spiritual gift. Those who have this gift describe a sense of inner peace if something is from the Lord, or unease if it is not. If you are not sure yourself, share your concern over the guidance you have received with others you know who are of good character and have a proven track record in this area, especially those in leadership. To be trustworthy, a particular phenomenon must be consistent with the Spirit of Jesus, the Scriptures, what we know of how God has worked in the past and, most importantly, it must reveal, glorify and commend Jesus by drawing us closer to Him and produce fruit worthy of His name.

For prayer and reflection

Lord, keep me in step with Your Spirit, close to Jesus and immersed in Your Word so that I might be able to test and know the perfect will.

WEEKEND

The open door

For reflection: Hosea 2:15 and Revelation 3:8

The Lord can speak to us and guide us creatively, comfortingly and encouragingly through His Word. The experienced listener knows the checks and balances that need to be taken into consideration when reading, but also knows the Shepherd's voice and recognises the fire of the Spirit being fanned in the hearth of the heart.

A long time ago the Lord spoke to me about what lay ahead: 'I will make the Valley of Achor a door of hope' (Hos. 2:15), and 'I have placed before you an open door that no-one can shut' (Rev. 3:8). The Valley of Achor was a valley of tears, my years of post-natal depression, but here was hope of a future beyond the valley – a future that nothing could take away from me except my own fear to step through the already open door.

The critics would say that this was not the correct or original intention of these verses; but we need to hold *correct* in balance with *creative* because the Word of God is living and active, Spirit-inspired and used by the Spirit.

Has the Lord ever spoken to you prophetically through His Word? Look back and be encouraged.

Have you **ever been fleeced?**

'Do not be angry with me … Allow me one more test with the fleece.' (v.39)

No examination of guidance would be complete without looking at Gideon and his fleece. Gideon's story is so familiar in that 'putting out a fleece' has become an established part of believers' jargon; it is so familiar that it bears a critical re-examination to make sure we are not using Scripture as an excuse to slip into superstition.

God had promised Gideon a victory. The odds were so stacked against him that Gideon needed reassurance. He asked the Lord to send dew on a fleece but not on the ground. It happened. But one test was not enough. Just to be sure, Gideon asked the Lord for dew on the ground but not on the fleece. It happened. By the end of Judges 8, Gideon's enemies were defeated.

Often we use the example of Gideon's fleece to try and discern the right course of action: 'If you want me to do such and such, God, or if such and such is "right", then you do such and such, so I can be sure.' Is this right? Look at Gideon's story carefully: the fleece incident comes in a long series of other experiences of guidance including a meeting with an angel – *it is not an isolated event*, it happens in the wider context of other guidance. The fleece incident is Gideon's way of making sure *the promise he has already received from God* is true – it is not a means of divining God's will out of thin air; the fleece incident contains a double bluff, wet then dry – often our 'fleeces' have no check, as though we're doing a scientific experiment without a 'control'.

Now look at Luke 4:9–13. The devil tempts Jesus to use *a one-off test* to prove to Himself He is the Son of God. What does Jesus reply?

....
For prayer and reflection
....

Lord, help me not to put You to the 'foolish' test, but help me understand the true signs along the way – what needs weighing and what does not.

Stepping out in faith?

I really need more than a day to look at the role of faith in relation to guidance, but I will risk throwing the cat among the pigeons with one quick thought. I want to examine the commonly trotted out quotation *'The righteous shall live by faith'.*

I've met Christians who are desperately unhappy, trapped on a course of action because they believe they have had 'a word from the Lord', they have acted on this word 'in faith', and it has resulted in untold suffering for themselves and their families, throwing these individuals into a crisis. I will not deny that the Lord clearly calls some people to radical action and that He provides the practical and spiritual resources those people need. I am concerned about those people who have uncritically adopted 'the righteous shall live by faith' and thus have naively misunderstood a supposed calling.

The references about believers living, or 'being alive' by faith, except perhaps in Hebrews 11, pertain to the fact that through faith in Jesus' redeeming work on the cross and His resurrection from the dead, we have eternal life waiting for us on the other side of physical death.

Confusion arises when we apply faith to things temporal and desire to have 'a faith that moves mountains' here on earth. God is a faithful God who keeps His promises – He is trustworthy. But 'walking in faith' in this life is as much about assurance of our particular calling as believing that God is faithful to what He has called us to.

The key is to test your calling before you make the leap of faith. Then we can have the assurance, or faith, that God will provide all the various resources we need to do all He is asking of us.

Romans 1:16–17

'… as it is written: "The righteous will live by faith."'
(v.17)

For prayer and reflection

'The one who calls you is faithful and he will do it.'
(1 Thess. 5:24)

Good idea **or God's idea?**

1 Chronicles
17:1–15

'Nathan replied to
David, "Whatever
you have in mind,
do it, for God is
with you."' (v.2)

I would like to finish this series of thoughts by considering the possibility that God can put us in the situation we often put our own children in: presenting the choice between two or more *equally good things* and letting them decide. I have found it difficult if not impossible to find a biblical precedent for this; the reason being that events in any biblical character's life leading up to a particular point have usually involved the Lord leading them in such a way that the choice is normally between the Lord's best way for them and the 'wrong' way – even if the 'wrong' way is one that 'seems good to a man' (Prov. 14:12). Ultimately, it appears we can't merely depend on our own judgment; however redeemed we may consider our critical faculties to be.

The story of David and Nathan is an example of this. The Lord was with David – Nathan's statement to this effect is a general one. David had it in mind to build a temple for the Lord, and it seems there was no earthly reason why he shouldn't – the Lord was with him, so anything he did was 'guaranteed' success. But David's good idea wasn't a 'God idea'. So, despite the initial human encouragement to proceed, the Lord subsequently intervened through Nathan to make clear the 'God idea'.

This is encouraging for us, because if something appears to be a good idea but isn't a God idea, and if we are listening, we can trust the Lord to make the situation clear before we start on or travel too far down the road in the less than ideal direction.

So, guidance can be a spiritual minefield, but I am sure that the Lord will guide our steps if we are keeping our eyes on Him.

For prayer and reflection

'The Lord will guide you always ... You will be like a well-watered garden, like a spring whose waters never fail.' (Isa. 58:11)

Hebrews

Christine Platt

Christine's passion for writing started in Ivory Coast, West Africa where she worked with The Navigators. She now lives in New Zealand and enjoys all the freedom and opportunities that semi-retirement brings! Mission involvement is never far away. She travels regularly to East Timor, taking teams to support the church in its courageous witness to war-ravaged people. Her life goal is to make the Bible accessible, by both writing and speaking, so that people may understand more of God's outrageous grace.

Hebrews

'The Son is
the radiance of
God's glory ...
he ... provided
purification for
sins ...' (v.3)

**For prayer and
reflection**

**In your
imagination,
picture a throne –
and Jesus by your
side, ushering you
to go closer. Take
some moments
to savour the
privilege of being
utterly accepted in
God's presence.**

A friend wailed, 'Pray for me. God will listen to you. I'm such a failure as a Christian.' If you feel inadequate and unworthy in your relationship with God, welcome to the magnificent letter to the Hebrews! Only God (and the author) know who wrote it. Prime candidates are Barnabas or Apollos. We are indebted to this unknown scholar and lover of God, who paints a lavish portrait of Jesus as the all-sufficient way into God's holy presence.

The context is mysterious to us in the 21st century. Jewish people (Hebrews) had a system of making sacrifices which would cover their failures and allow them to approach God. Slaughtered animals, priests, blood and altars were familiar but, ultimately, inadequate intermediaries to surmount the barriers between God and the people ... But no longer!

The perfect priest and sacrifice arrived in the Person of Jesus. This fact required a huge mind shift for Jewish people. They'd relied on prophets and even angels, whom they believed brought God's word to them – such was the gulf between God and humanity. In their eyes a holy God could not be expected to communicate directly with flawed men and women. So the writer emphasises the supremacy of Jesus above all other attempts to bridge the chasm.

Jewish believers were probably over-conscious of the fear of the Lord, hardly daring to cross the holy threshold, whereas 21st-century followers of Jesus can be guilty of an over-casual approach to God, glibly sauntering up to His throne. We wouldn't do that with any human monarch. We need to balance these two truths: God is holy and, because of Jesus' sacrifice, He is approachable.

Pay **attention!**

I teach a Bible-based values lesson every week to a class of six-year-olds, who often need reminders to pay attention. I also need to warn them about the consequences of bad behaviour. This verse gives the first of five warnings in Hebrews: Pay attention ... so you don't drift away.

When I'm with the children I have to pounce on the first bit of disobedience otherwise it will escalate out of control. I've been too lenient in the past and the lesson became a mess – no one learnt anything.

No follower of Jesus suddenly decides to give up on God and go his/her own way. It's more of a gradual process, like a ship drifting onto rocks because the captain is dozing. It can start with a small compromise, laziness or a wrong choice and, before we realise, a life of faith has been wrecked. We're warned to pay careful attention to what we've heard. In this context, what we've heard is the gospel – God becoming man and paying the price of sin on the cross.

How can we ensure that we don't drift? Just like my six-year-olds, we too need to listen to our Teacher all the time. For believers, that means keeping in close communication with God – reading the Bible and praying on a daily basis, asking Him to search our hearts and then being quick to repent of whatever sin He shows us.

What if we've already drifted away from a close walk with God? The cross of Christ shows us that we can always come back. Repent and lay firm foundations to avoid drifting away again. One safeguard is to do all you can to develop friendships with encouraging Christians with whom you can pray over current challenges.

Hebrews 2:1–9

'We must pay more careful attention ... to what we have heard, so that we do not drift away.' (v.1)

For prayer and reflection

Pray these words from Psalm 119: '... don't let me wander off from your instructions. I have thought much about your words, and stored them in my heart so that they would hold me back from sin.' (vv.10–11, TLB)

WEEKEND

Jesus – the Rock

For reflection: 'Trust in the LORD for ever, for the Lord, the Lord, is the Rock eternal.' (Isa. 26:4)

As I write this, I'm in a retreat house on the storm-whipped north-east coast of New Zealand. Yesterday was a brilliant sunny winter day. During the night a gale blew up. How quickly things change. Yesterday I frolicked on the beach; today I'm huddled indoors. The whole house is quivering in the wind.

Life's circumstances can change rapidly for us. We can either allow the future to paralyse us with fear or use the uncertainties to draw us more closely into the arms of Jesus. He is our one constant stability – our Rock. His permanence can enable us to cope with whatever life throws at us. He is more than adequate to meet us at any point of need and guide us through any complex maze of decision-making.

Over the weekend, consider how these thoughts of Jesus, the Rock, can help you face the future with confidence, no matter what changes lie ahead.

My Brother Jesus

G rowing up with two older sisters I'd always wanted an older brother – especially one who'd bring his dishy mates home! When the Bible speaks of believers being Jesus' brothers, it means being heirs of the family inheritance. We, women, as Jesus' sisters, are also included in that inheritance.

'Both the one who makes men holy and those who are made holy are of the same family.' (v.11)

One of my sisters and I look so alike that people often mistake us for one another. How close is the family resemblance between us and Jesus? He is holy and makes His followers holy. I used to visit a prison in Africa and the inmates called me Holy Sister Christine. I certainly didn't feel holy (and probably not many of us feel holy all the time), but that is our status as members of God's family.

The amazing reality is that Jesus put aside His holiness and felt the full weight of sin, abandonment and misery. He'd never known moral failure, or that sick feeling when you've really blown it, or the crippling effects of guilt. In our place Jesus was bombarded with the world's grot and He took it all on His unblemished soul. No wonder He sweated drops of blood in dread anticipation.

As His siblings we all have equal status in His family. He is not ashamed of those who bear His stamp – the Holy Spirit. On a human level I try my best not to bring my family grief by my behaviour. How much more should we aim to live rightly to bring honour to our King, our older Brother. But how frail and flawed we are. This same passage contains hope for us when we fall. He is a 'merciful and faithful high priest' (v.17), who understands temptation and promises to help us withstand it (v.18).

For prayer and reflection

What temptation are you facing today? Remember – you are Jesus' sister. Reach out to Him for help to overcome it.

Think about 2 Corinthians 5:21: 'God made him who had no sin to be sin for us, so that in him we might become the righteousness of God.'

Jesus is the best!

Hebrews 3:1–6

'… Christ is
faithful as a son
over God's house
… we are his
house, if we
hold on to our
courage …' (v.6)

For the Jews, Moses was Number One. He brought them the treasured Law of God. He was unlike other prophets – God spoke to him face to face (Num. 12:6–8). Moses had the closest possible relationship with God.

In the book of Hebrews we learn that Jesus is greater than angels, greater than prophets and now greater than mighty Moses himself. Moses was God's servant in His house, whereas Jesus is God's Son over His house. I feel privileged to have been born this side of the cross. The revelation of God's plan and purpose is clearer now than it was in Old Testament times (1 Pet. 1:10–12). Jesus has been revealed as the fulfilment of promises and prophecies.

As members of God's household we need to 'hold on to our courage and the hope of which we boast'. Moses had some ups and downs in the wilderness, but he is remembered as being faithful. He persevered in his task of shepherding an estimated 5 million chaotic, frightened people. He held on to his courage and his hope. Jesus persevered in His ministry of teaching, healing, training and demonstrating the kingdom lifestyle, which culminated in His perseverance under trial and death. He too held on to His courage and His hope.

Perseverance isn't glamorous. You may need to persevere in some hidden ministry – caring for an elderly relative, holding on to faith despite catastrophic disappointments, coping with an unsatisfactory work situation or debilitating illness. Moses shows us perseverance in a flawed human being and Jesus shows us perseverance of the highest degree.

Let's follow their example, and hold on to courage and hope no matter what comes.

For prayer and reflection

Claim this promise for your particular need: 'And the God of all grace … after you have suffered a little while, will himself restore you and make you strong, firm and steadfast.' (1 Pet. 5:10)

Antidote to unbelief

I n the school where I teach, several children carry an Epipen with them. They suffer with severe allergic reactions, even anaphylactic shock. This can be lethal, but a quick shot of adrenaline sorts the problem out. The antidote to allergic reactions is adrenaline. The children keep their Epipen in their pocket and know how to use it in an emergency. They trust it to work for them.

This passage contains the second of the five warnings in Hebrews – this time concerning unbelief. Even though the Israelites had witnessed God's awesome power and provision in their flight from Egypt, they wouldn't believe that God would give them a victorious entry into the promised land. Everyone from that generation, except Joshua and Caleb, died in the desert (Num. 13:1–14:45).

The antidote for falling away through unbelief is daily encouragement. Joshua and Caleb pleaded in vain with the Israelites, but their voices were obliterated by a fog of unbelief and discouragement. Instead of encouraging one another, the Israelites discouraged one another. The result was lethal.

Just as it would be deadly for a child suffering from allergic reactions not to use the antidote provided, so it is deadly for our faith if we don't use the antidote God provides for us. We need to place ourselves in situations where we will be encouraged in our faith – in our own Bible-reading and prayer time, by listening to Christian radio, tapes, CDs when doing chores or driving, by participating in a small group, by having a prayer partner. And, in turn, we need to find ways of encouraging others. The stakes are high – our faith depends upon it.

Hebrews 3:7–19

'… encourage one another daily … so that none of you may be hardened by sin's deceitfulness.'
(v.13)

For prayer and reflection

Think of ways to ensure that you are encouraged DAILY in your faith, and also how you can encourage others. Don't allow busyness to crowd out the encouragement factor.

God's **searchlight**

Hebrews 4:1–13

'For the word of God … penetrates … it judges the thoughts and attitudes of the heart.' (v.12)

Churchill's gravelly voice intoning 'We shall fight them on the beaches … we shall never surrender …' galvanized war-torn Britons to cope courageously with fear, bombing raids, rationing and the dreaded telegrams informing relatives of their loved one's death.

Words have power – think of Hitler, Chairman Mao … How much more the Word of God! Hitler's words, though effective for a few deadly years, are now despised by every right-thinking person. But God's words are relevant and arresting for every generation; from the instructions given to Adam and Eve, at the dawn of creation, to the promises given to Abraham, to the Ten Commandments given to Moses, to the words of the prophets, and finally to Jesus' own words.

God's Word has the power to penetrate to the inner core of a person and reveal what's there. You can put on a fine outward performance for those around you, but you can never fool God. He sees the real you.

God knows all about those skeletons in your cupboard: the ones you know about and hide so carefully. He also knows about the ones you've buried so deeply in your subconscious that you have no recollection of them. Life events may cause those skeletons to rattle in the cupboard.

For prayer and reflection

Reflect on David's response in Psalm 51 when God revealed his secret sins (see 2 Sam. 11:1–12:25).

God wants to free you from the fear of the real you being discovered. It takes guts to open the cupboard and let out the rotting stench but, incredibly, we find that God is there, helping us to get rid of the corpse and clean out the cupboard. Rather than cowering in shame, we find that we are bathed in compassion, love and acceptance, which brings a new and deeper peace. How willing are you to allow God's Word to deeply impact your life?

Sympathetic High Priest

**Hebrews
4:14–5:10**

'... come bravely
before ... our
merciful God ...
we will be treated
with undeserved
kindness ...'
(v.16, CEV)

I f we've watched any films about Jesus' life, the last quality we would usually attribute to a high priest is sympathy! The images portrayed are stern, unyielding, ready to punish any slight misdemeanor. It seems that those high priests forgot that they too were frail human beings who made mistakes and 'blew it'!

In some inexplicable way, when Jesus, Son of God, left heaven, He took off His royal robes, symbolising His eternal kingship, and entered our broken world of dust and pain to experience it first-hand, as a man. Satan threw temptations at Him from every side, attacking Him when He was at His weakest, but Jesus never flinched from obedience to His Father. He not only experienced the same temptations we do, but infinitely more.

We give in to temptation long before Satan ever has to roll out the big guns. Jesus got the whole lot thrown at Him. If anyone has the authority and right to be stern with sinners, He has. But He remembers what it is like to be a frail human being and to be pestered by temptation, and He sympathises. Because He is at the Father's side, we can come bravely to God's throne where we will receive undeserved kindness. What grace!

In your dealings with your fellow inhabitants of this planet, are you sympathetic and kind? Do you treat people with undeserved kindness? It's easier to be kind to the 'nice' people, but the adjective here is 'undeserved'. Even in church communities, some people will try our patience to the utmost. If we focus on how much we've been forgiven, we'll find it easier to forgive others.

For prayer and reflection

Holy and compassionate God, forgive me when I judge others harshly. Help me to remember my own faults. Put within my heart the same kindness for others that You pour out towards me.

233

WEEKEND

Happy Birthday, Church!

For reflection: Galatians 5:25
'Since we live by the Spirit, let us keep in step with the Spirit.'

At Pentecost, we celebrate the birth of the New Testament Church. The Holy Spirit who had rested intermittently on Old Testament believers was now poured out to indwell every believer (Acts 2). The Holy Spirit was the powerhouse of the New Testament Church. He gave gifts for ministry and produced fruit in believers' lives.

As well as being a day for celebration, our own birthday marks an auspicious moment to reflect on the past and learn from our successes and mistakes so that we can embrace the future with greater wisdom and hope.

Take time this weekend, to praise God for the ministry of the Holy Spirit in your life. Try to identify the gifts He has given you and how you've used them. Could you develop them further? Consider the fruit of the Spirit – in which areas have you grown the most?

Give thanks and celebrate!

You will find teaching about spiritual gifts in Romans 12 and 1 Corinthians 12, and about the fruit of the Holy Spirit in Galatians 5:22–23.

Grow up! Stick with it!

**Hebrews
5:11–6:12**

'… by this time
you ought to be
teachers … You
need milk, not
solid food!' (5:12)

As a Child Health Nurse I encounter the acute distress in parents who fear that their baby is delayed in his/her development. Usually the child catches up and all is well, but occasionally there is an ongoing problem. The child needs extra care and may never become an independent adult. Much sadness.

There are many adults in our churches who remain spiritually stunted. William Barclay describes them as those with 'the lethargy of the lazy mind and the embattled prejudice of the shut mind'.[1] Again, much sadness. Scripture places great emphasis on believers continuing to grow (2 Pet. 3:18) – let's never be guilty of having a lazy or shut mind. A key phrase in education is: 'Be a lifelong learner.' As believers we are urged not only to learn but to apply that learning to life. This requires stickability.

Later in chapter 11 of Hebrews we'll see the Hall of Fame of faithful saints who 'stuck with it' to the end. Some are famous, others unknown, but all known and loved by Almighty God.

In between these two exhortations – 'Grow up' and 'Stick with it' – comes the third warning. This is described by William Barclay as 'one of the most terrible passages in Scripture'.[2] Believers are warned not to turn their back on Jesus and reject Him. There are several possible interpretations of this passage. Suffice to say that if we focus on growing and persevering in our faith and relationship with God, we can be sure that we will never fall away. God wants to meet with us in all stages of life. I get so inspired when I see 80-year-olds pressing on to know and serve God. Much joy!

For prayer and reflection

Lord, with Your help, I commit myself to being a lifelong learner with You.

[1]William Barclay, *The Letter to the Hebrews*, *The Daily Study Bible*, (Edinburgh: Saint Andrew Press, 1976) p.49.
[2]Ibid., p.56.

Waiting, **waiting, waiting**

Hebrews 6:13–20

'God cannot tell lies! And so his promises and vows are two things that can never be changed.' (v.18, CEV)

We're so fortunate to have the Bible. Think of Abraham waiting, year after year, for his promised son to be born. He had no record of God's dealings with humanity to encourage him, just God's covenant promise. So he had to wait … for 25 years! If he'd known at the beginning it would be that long it might have been easier to cope with. But he had to face ongoing disappointment which can crush the most optimistic among us.

Faith doesn't just seep into our souls by osmosis: it is forged in a furnace (1 Pet. 1:6–7). God didn't make it easy for Abraham. He was determined that Abraham's faith would gleam like gold; only then could he become the father of the faithful – and Abraham came out shining. He wasn't perfect – lying, lacking courage, giving in to pressure from his wife – but he is remembered as being faithful.

We have so much more to help us as *we* wait: not only God's promises, but also the biblical record of His faithfulness to His people through the peaks and troughs of life. Think of Gideon going to war against overwhelming odds with 300 men and God's promise. Think of Hannah and Elizabeth, both waiting for a child, hanging on to God's promise when, humanly speaking, it was impossible.

For prayer and reflection

Where do you need to exercise faith at the moment? Do you have a promise from God for that area of your life? Is there a biblical story that speaks into your situation? When you're tempted to give up, ask yourself this question: 'Would God lie to me?' Obviously not. So, what is He doing? He is building your faith. Instead of champing at the bit, ask a friend to pray over it with you. Try to see the situation from God's point of view.

Mighty God, help me to consider my difficulties as stepping-stones to greater faith. I choose to wait patiently and allow You to do Your work in my life. (James 1:2–4)

Building **bridges**

In a recent storm in New Zealand a bridge was totally washed away and a community became isolated. There was no way in and no way out. The residents stood forlornly on the river bank gazing over the torrent to the road on the other side which led to family, friends and food! The army was called in to erect a bridge and with immense relief and joy the residents were reconnected with life on the other side.

The Latin word for priest is *pontifex*, which means bridge-builder. Melchizedek is an Old Testament priest (Gen. 14:18–20) whose names, King of righteousness and King of peace, are considered here as prefiguring Christ (Jer. 23:5–6; Isa. 9:6–7). Righteousness must come before peace, just as a bridge must be in place before any reunion can occur. The dictionary definition of righteousness is 'free from guilt or sin'. Jesus' death and resurrection means that the bridge is in place, but we must cross it. There is no point pleading with God to give us peace, if we are not sheltering under the cross of Christ and earnestly desiring to walk in His ways.

The residents of the cut-off community needed no second invitation to race over the new bridge to enjoy all the goodies on the other side. Sadly, many ignore the bridge that Christ has constructed. They fail to recognise the benefits of crossing and seem content to remain cut off from the source of righteousness and peace. Yet anxiety, stress, guilt and wondering what life is all about are hallmarks of Western society. Christ is the answer. People need Him and they need to be pointed in the right direction in order to find Him.

Hebrew 7:1–10

'First, his name means "king of righteousness"; then also … "king of peace".' (v.2)

For prayer and reflection

Think of ways you can demonstrate the peace and joy that comes from being free from guilt or sin, so that your friends, family and neighbours might be drawn to cross the bridge.

The Complete **Saviour**

Hebrews 7:11–28

'… he is able to save completely … because he always lives to intercede for them.' (v.25)

For prayer and reflection

Sing John Newton's hymn 'Amazing Grace' softly to yourself, savouring your forgiveness and freedom. 'Amazing grace, how sweet the sound / that saved a wretch like me. I once was lost but now am found, / was blind, but now I see.'

After Jesus had created the bridge between God and humanity, He didn't then retreat to heaven and enjoy His majestic lifestyle. He remains, amazingly, at the service of ordinary men, women and children.

He 'lives to intercede for them'. It's not a part-time job or a hobby that He tries to fit in while simultaneously keeping the universe going. In His earthly life Jesus served humanity and gave His life to be the bridge. In heaven He still serves at His Father's side as our priestly representative and He is always interceding for His people. This makes Him the Complete Saviour – nothing else needs to be added to the salvation He offers and no one else can offer it (John 14:6).

Do you feel 'completely saved'? Do you ever wonder if God might decide that you're not worthy to enter heaven, after all? Karen had been a follower of Jesus for a couple of years when I met her. She had never felt worthy to take Communion, not because of any blatant sin, just a feeling of generalised guilt from the past. How tragic! Her incomplete understanding of the cross blighted her joy and freedom as a believer.

Have you embraced the cross to the extent that you know all your past, present and future sin is forgiven – completely done away with? God placed all that load of sin on Jesus at the cross and, because of the 'power of [His] indestructible life' (Heb. 7:16), He paid the price and was not defeated by death. He rose to resurrection life! And that's what He wants us to experience – forgiveness, acceptance, peace and victory – the calm assurance that all is well between God and us.

A whole new ball game

Moses, the Law, the Temple and the covenant (agreement) had, for centuries, been central to the lives of Jewish people. Their annual calendar revolved around various feasts. Their Temple set-up underscored the inaccessibility of God – the high priest entered the Holy of Holies just once a year! This letter sets out God's whole new ball game.

All that stuff, says the writer, is passé, just a copy of the heavenly reality, and has now been superseded. The original covenant between God and His people required their obedience to His laws – an externally imposed set of rules. Things rapidly went pear-shaped. The people failed to be consistently obedient, which nullified the agreement.

Jeremiah prophesied about this new covenant (Jer. 31:31–34), so the concept wasn't completely new to the Jewish people, but it required a complete turnaround in their thinking. God had always been the Holy One and they barely dared say His name.

Now God was saying: 'It's OK. Jesus, My Son, has made a better way. He has smashed the barriers between us so that we can be friends. I will forgive you and change your hearts so that from deep within you will want to obey Me. This is My new covenant with you. Will you accept it?'

Many Jewish religious leaders couldn't accept Jesus' teaching. Their minds were too rigid and their thinking too engrained. Is your mind becoming more conformed to Christ? Or are you holding on to negative thought patterns about Him, others or yourself? For years I couldn't really believe that God loved me just as I am. Eventually I had to decide whether I was going to believe what God said in His Word or call Him a liar.

Hebrews 8:1–13

'... the covenant of which he [Jesus] is mediator is superior to the old one ...' (v.6)

For prayer and reflection

Lord, I want my mind to be filled with Your truth. Help me to recognise wrong thought patterns and repent of them.

WEEKEND

Forgiveness is possible

For reflection: Hebrews 12:15
'See to it that no-one misses the grace of God and that no bitter root grows up to cause trouble and defile many.'

I grieve when I hear the statement 'I will never be able to forgive them'. I can understand people feeling like that when they or their loved ones have been deeply wounded, but unforgiveness is such a damaging emotion to harbour. It can cause physical, emotional and spiritual harm to the person and to those around them.

Just as God gave the Israelites certain rituals to perform when asking His forgiveness, it can be helpful to go through a ritual when we're seeking to forgive the humanly unforgivable. Even saying to God: 'I want to be willing to forgive' is a good first step. You could write the person's name and the offence on a piece of paper and present that to God, asking Him to deal with it. You could then burn the paper as a symbol of letting go of the past.

If you or someone close to you has a poisonous festering sore of unforgiveness, try to find a meaningful practice which will enable the healing process to begin.

Chapters 18 and 21 of John's Gospel tell the story of how Jesus forgave Peter for abandoning and denying Him.

It's all **about Him**

Hebrews 9:1–10

'… the Most Holy Place … had … the gold-covered ark of the covenant.' (vv. 3–4)

The writer casts a nostalgic eye back to the majestic beauty of the tabernacle (tent of meeting). He recalls God commissioning Moses to get the people to make a sanctuary for Him so He could dwell with His people (Exod. 25:8). God gave detailed instructions as to how the tabernacle was to be constructed and adorned. This was not a utilitarian structure – every aspect was rooted in symbolism.

The people worked with a will to complete it. They gave so generously (Exod. 36:3–7) that they had to be stopped from offering more! They wove countless metres of linen for curtains. The place glittered with silver, brass and gold. It was an amazing demonstration of beauty and creativity in the wilderness. Yet once it was finished the common people were excluded. The priests could enter the courtyard and the Holy Place, and the high priest entered the Holy of Holies once a year, arrayed in gorgeous robes.

How did the common people feel about that, I wonder? They gave, they used their creative gifts, they worked together as a team, yet they couldn't enter. Maybe they realised that all this was for God: He was the focus, not them. It reminds me of the words of the song: '*I'm coming back to the heart of worship … And it's all about you …*'[1]

The Israelites spent a year building the tabernacle. They were eager to get to the promised land, but were willing to postpone their journey in order to make a special place for God in the midst of their community. How often do we just get on with the job in ministry, before making sure that God is in the central place and that all we do revolves around Him and is inspired by Him?

[1] Matt Redman, 'The Heart of Worship' © Thankyou Music

For prayer and reflection

Lord, let Your will be done in and through my life. I choose to put aside my agenda.

How to **feel good**

'... the blood of Christ, who ... offered himself unblemished to God, [will] cleanse our consciences ...' (v.14)

For prayer and reflection

Think about how you can follow Paul's example: '... I strive always to keep my conscience clear before God and man' (Acts 24:16). A daily time of reflection and evaluation is a good start.

I've just been helping my nephew and his wife clean and repair their house after their 'tenants from hell' were evicted by the bailiffs. New plaster, white paint and much elbow grease are restoring it to its former welcoming state. My nephew's wife said, 'It now feels so much better in here.' A clean, repaired house feels good.

On a deeper level, the same can be said of our conscience. It feels good to have a clear conscience. It enables you to sleep at night, not wracked with guilt. The Christian faith is the only one that has an answer to the problem of guilt. Other religions urge us, in vain, to try harder to keep the rules. Some philosophies rationalise the wrong and say it's OK but, deep inside, the embattled conscience rises up to resist the numbing power exerted on it. It shrieks: 'It's not OK. You were created to live within certain parameters and to worship God. What you've done violates that. You can't pretend it's all OK!'

Our conscience is a precious gift of God and we need to treat it with tenderness. The apostle Paul writes of those 'whose consciences have been seared as with a hot iron' (1 Tim. 4:2). Continual refusal to respond to one's conscience creates ugly scars and renders the delicate mechanism inoperable.

What hope is there for sinful people? The sacrifice of Christ cleanses our conscience; deep, deep within He makes us clean and new. It feels good to be at peace with our Creator. Saying sorry to God and to people we've offended is hard and humbling, but a clear conscience is worth it all.

Obedience – here I come!

Jesus' aim in life was to do what His Father wanted Him to do. He even called obedience His 'food' (John 4:34). That's an intriguing claim. For me, food is a lip-smacking delight. It nourishes me. I consider it a three-times-a-day necessity and I anticipate it with unadulterated enthusiasm! In short, I couldn't do without it, and sometimes I even overindulge.

But, sadly, that's not always my attitude to obedience. At times it feels difficult, uncomfortable and even too hard. How come Jesus saw it so differently? He was not without His share of acutely difficult and uncomfortable obedience, yet He considered obedience a daily necessity. He recognised that it nourished His relationship with His Father and it gave Him deep satisfaction and joy.

I wonder whether it's because He didn't focus on the actual act of obedience and how hard that was, but looked to its results – a deepening loving friendship with His Father and, in the case of the cross, the astounding benefits it would bring to all of humanity.

Would that outlook help us when faced with costly obedience? Rather than bemoaning the difficulty or perhaps thinking that major self-denial is only for super-saints or missionaries, maybe we too should concentrate on the results. Obedience pleases our Father. Jesus promises to show Himself to those who obey – so we would enjoy a closer walk with Him (John 14:21). In most situations there would also be a benefit to other people.

If we simply obeyed the Great Commandment: Love God and love others (Matt. 22:37–39) – our world would be transformed. Are these benefits enough to spur you on to greater obedience?

Hebrews 10:1–18

'And so, my God, I have come to do what you want …'
(v.7, CEV)

For prayer and reflection

In what area of life is God asking you to obey at the moment? Try to break it down into small steps. Try also to focus on the outcomes. Start today.

Always **be your best**

**Hebrews
10:19–39**

'You need to persevere so that … you will receive what he has promised.' (v.36)

The fourth warning of this letter is stark: Don't drift away from your first enthusiastic response to Christ. That would bring you and God much grief. On the positive side we are urged to persevere to the end. As William Barclay puts it: 'Here is a summons never to be less than our best, and always to remember that the end comes'.*

The Hebrews had started so well and had coped valiantly with insults and persecution, as well as being robbed of their possessions. Humanity being what it is, we rise to the challenge when times are tough, but prosperity and luxury can sap our spiritual strength. On a moral and physical level, this was illustrated by the army of Hannibal of Carthage. This was the one army which had triumphed over the mighty Roman legions. Fresh from victory, they had to overwinter in Capua, a city of luxury. After some months of ease and enjoyment, they were so relaxed and laid back that they'd lost their edge – and this paved the way for their eventual defeat by the Romans.

I've also found that to be true. I work with a development programme in East Timor – one of the poorest countries in the world. On my visits there my spiritual life is in top-notch form. My prayers are urgent, passionate and full of faith, despite overwhelming obstacles. I joyfully cope with grotty living conditions. Back home, when life is more mundane, my prayers are a bit humdrum and I get irritated by minor discomforts.

How can we always be at our best? Let's remember whom we serve and that heaven awaits us. Life is short – the reward of heaven will be worth all the endurance.

For prayer and reflection

Mighty God, I want to be my best for You today. Thank You that I can look forward to enjoying heaven with You.

*William Barclay, *Hebrews (The Daily Study Bible)* p.128.

Faith **adventurers**

They made it! We applaud the victorious return of adventurers who circumnavigate the world by boat or trek across Antarctica. We admire those who launch out in feats of endurance and danger. This passage highlights three of God's mighty adventurers.

Noah, Abraham and Sarah didn't wake up one morning and think: 'What great exploit can I do today?' Their adventures were placed before them by God. Most adventures have an exciting beginning, a thrilling, successful ending (hopefully), but in the middle there is much hard slog.

Noah had months of painstaking hammering and sawing to build the ark, probably accompanied by sarcastic comments from his neighbours. Abram and Sarai (renamed by God, Abraham and Sarah) set off with enthusiasm to an unknown destination; much walking and unsettledness followed. Noah finished the boat and saw his family and a pair of all the animals on earth saved from destruction. The fulfilment of the promise of a new country for Abraham and Sarah came after their death. Some adventures of faith are realised on earth; some are not.

What kept these three adventurers going was their faith – grounded on God's promise to them – and a vision for the future which galvanised them in the present. Knowing that they were 'aliens and strangers on earth' and not here to cosily settle down, they launched out under God's guidance into an unknown future. Their ultimate longing was for their heavenly home.

What is God placing before you today? A new job, home, church, ministry, new addition to your family or even a new illness or disability? It has been said: 'Never be afraid to trust an unknown future to a known God.'

Hebrews 11:1–19

'… they were aliens and strangers … longing for a better country – a heavenly one.' (vv.13,16)

For prayer and reflection

Father God, thank You that I'm safe with You. I choose to walk with You in this adventure of faith.

WEEKEND

Images of heaven

For reflection: 1 Corinthians 2:9
'No eye has seen, no ear has heard, no mind has conceived what God has prepared for those who love him …'

A magical moment in C.S. Lewis's *Chronicles of Narnia* is when the children realise that the land of Narnia with which they are familiar is but a shadow of true reality (heaven). They leap up to embrace their new life with their beloved Aslan. God gives massive blessings in this life, but those blessings awaiting His people in heaven are in a whole different league.

Sometimes when I'm on the beach gazing at the dying rays of the sun or examining the intricacies of a shell, I wonder, 'What could be more beautiful than this?' My imagination struggles to conjure up visions of a city of pure gold bedecked with flashing jewels, and gates made of a single pearl – WOW!

One of my most precious images of heaven comes from Revelation 4. There is a throne with someone sitting on it: God is in the place of authority. The universe and our tiny planet are not left in chaos. God will accomplish His purposes, in His time, in His way.

During this weekend think about God on His throne. Be encouraged that He is in control.

Our awesome **ancestors**

Don't you love hearing stories of victory – of answered prayers, healing, deliverance? Yes, we exclaim – God reigns! Victory is ours! Hallelujah!

Less encouraging is reading about people being sawn in two, destitute, persecuted and homeless. Yet we'd be wise to remember that not all of God's people experience a wonderful deliverance. Many, even today, are martyred for their faith.

In the second century BC Antiochus IV launched a vicious persecution on the Jewish faith. Men and women were tortured in the most sadistic ways, but refused to recant.* Because of the heroic way they died, others were strengthened in their resistance and the Jewish faith survived. This meant that Jesus could be born into the Jewish culture at God's chosen time in history. The writer to the Hebrews reminds his readers of the ones who kept the faith alive. Remember, he says, your spiritual ancestors and use their example of faith as a stimulus in your own walk with God.

Each year we rightly remember those who fought and died in the World Wars. Because of what they did, many countries of the world now enjoy freedom. I sometimes wonder, would I have been brave and willing to lay my life on the line for my country? Similarly, how would I respond if I were risking imprisonment and torture by possessing a Bible or turning up at church? How much am I willing to suffer for Jesus' sake? Am I just wanting Him to meet my needs? To follow Jesus means to walk in His ways. He encountered much suffering and, in one way or another, so will all His followers.

*As narrated in the Fourth Book of Maccabees.

Hebrews 11:20–40

'… they were sawn in two … destitute, persecuted … They wandered in deserts and mountains …' (vv.37–38)

For prayer and reflection

Lord Jesus, I recognise that being a believer involves suffering. Help me to embrace difficulties and face them courageously with You.

Travelling **light**

Hebrews 12:1–13

'… let us throw off everything that hinders and the sin that so easily entangles, and let us run …' (v.1)

Cliff Richard croons, '... got no bags or baggage to slow me down'. He's 'travelling light'. He 'just can't wait to be with [his] baby tonight'. With that goal in view he's not allowing anything to hinder his progress. No one runs a marathon with a 40kg backpack (unless to raise a lot of money for charity!). To go far, we need to travel light, discarding anything that would slow us down or deflect us from our aim.

If the 'race marked out for us' in the Christian life is to become like Christ, we need to examine carefully any impediment in our pursuit of that goal. Unconfessed sin is the obvious first item. Sin, especially in our attitudes, 'so easily entangles' us. We can be deceived – unaware of its presence until it tightens its strangle-hold. We need to ask God to search our hearts and reveal our wrongdoings (Psa. 139:23–24).

But sin isn't the only problem. The apostle Paul tells us, '"Everything is permissible" – but not everything is beneficial' (1 Cor. 10:23). Some habits, some people we spend time with, some self-indulgences (while not coming under the heading of sin) might be hindering our progress.

I've just had lunch with a friend who spent the whole time bemoaning all the work she had to do in order to move house. The multiplicity of her possessions seemed to be weighing her down. Another friend recently remarked that she was increasingly drawn to simplicity in her lifestyle.

Jesus exemplified the pilgrim way of life: no bags or baggage slowed Him down. Pleasing His Father was His focus and He looked towards His real home – heaven. Are you living like a pilgrim?

For prayer and reflection

Ask God to show you what is hindering your progress at the moment. Make a plan to remove that impediment from your life so that you can 'run with perseverance' the race marked out for you.

Don't play with fire

As I write, another foot and mouth outbreak has been discovered in the UK. Farms have been cordoned off. Cattle are being slaughtered and burned in pits to eradicate the spread of the virus. Fire has a purifying as well as a destructive force.

When God revealed the first covenant, it was with terrifying fire on Mount Sinai (Exod. 19:18). The people shuddered with fear and begged Moses to be their intermediary. They dreaded to meet with this God. They sensed the insurmountable distance between them and feared what He might do to them.

As we've seen, the new covenant that Jesus ushered in eliminated that distance – God is now approachable. So why does the writer to the Hebrews still speak of God as a consuming fire? Surely God is now a forgiving deity and much nicer than the Old Testament picture of Him? In *The Message* Eugene Peterson translates the passage like this: 'For God is not an indifferent bystander. He's actively cleaning house, torching all that needs to burn, and he won't quit until it's all cleansed. God himself is Fire!'

This brings us to the final warning in this letter: Do not refuse to listen to God; otherwise His fire will act as a cleansing and purifying agent, destroying that which is impure. Those who stay close to God gain everything; those who refuse to lose everything.

Should we then fear this God as the Israelites did when they gazed in horror at the blazing mountain? No, not with abject fear, but we are to be thankful and worship Him with reverence and awe. We are to listen to Him and take seriously what He says.

Hebrews 12:14–29

'… let us … worship God acceptably with reverence and awe, for our "God is a consuming fire."' (vv.28–29)

For prayer and reflection

As you come to God in prayer, recognise that you are standing on holy ground. Find ways to help you express awe and reverence: kneel, take off your shoes, be silent in His presence, focus completely on Him.

Because **He's worth it**

'Keep on loving each other as brothers … entertain strangers … Remember those in prison …' (vv.1–3)

After 12 chapters of theology and explanation, the writer says: So what? Is all this teaching about how the New Testament is the fulfilment of the Old Testament just to improve our minds? God certainly does not want us to be ignorant of our heritage. Followers of Jesus should be able to give an explanation of the hope that is in them (1 Pet. 3:15). But the study of God and His Word is fruitless unless it results in action and in changed lives (Luke 6:46–49; James 1:22–24).

So, the writer says, because of all that Jesus has done for you in being the full and complete sacrifice for sins, this is how you should live:

- Love others as brothers and sisters
- Be hospitable
- Care for those in trouble – in abusive situations or in prison
- Be pure – honour marriage relationships
- Be content – not driven by materialism

These qualities are the result of being God's people, not an attempt to obtain that privilege. All the good works in the world cannot atone for sin (Eph. 2:8–9). But we, as followers of Jesus, should show by our lives that we live by different values to those of the unbelieving world around us.

However, this gives us no grounds to look down on others with a 'holier than thou' attitude. We are not better than anyone else. Rather, in humble dependence on God, we offer the fruit of His work in and through us to others.

It takes courage to stand out from the crowd and march to a different drum. The Western world is characterised by individualism – every woman for herself, because she's 'worth it'. We need to resist that siren call and turn our focus to live God's way … because He's worth it.

For prayer and reflection

Reflect on the list of qualities. Which area do you need to work on the most? Plan to take some action on it this week.

Ready and **equipped for action**

Hebrews 13:17–25

'May the God of peace, who … brought back from the dead our Lord Jesus … equip you …' (vv.20–21)

P hew! We've come to the end of the letter. Like any wise teacher, the writer finishes on a positive note. He leaves us with a threefold vision of God. Firstly He is the God of peace. How much we need that sense of inner tranquility today. In our generation we face exponential change and it's easy to get anxious or distracted. But believers have peace with God, no matter what chaos the wider world, or even our smaller personal world of family, friends and work, is in. There is a space inside each of us where we can know deep abiding peace.

The Hebrews who received this letter had suffered persecution (10:32–34) and, from the tone of the letter, more difficulties lay ahead. They definitely needed 'the peace of God, which transcends all understanding' (Phil. 4:7).

Secondly, God is also the God of life. He raised Jesus from death and took its sting once and for all time. Hallelujah! The old enemy, Death, need hold no fear for the follower of Jesus.

My favourite image is the third: He is the God who equips us for the challenge of living in this world today. This may have something to do with my task-oriented personality! I love the fact that God gives gifts for ministry and service, so if He sends us out to do a job, we can be sure that He will equip us for it. Have you identified the gifts God has given you, and are you developing them to the fullest?

What's even more special is that, while we are using our God-given gifts in His service, He is at work within us transforming us into the image of Jesus – building up the fruit of the Spirit in our lives. It's a win-win situation.

For prayer and reflection

Heavenly Father, I praise You that You are the God of Peace, the God of Life, and the God who equips. Thank You for the gifts You've given me. Help me to honour You in the way I use them.

Caring for your own vineyard

Marion Stroud

Marion Stroud has published 21 books and writes regularly for *Woman Alive* and other magazines. She has written and spoken widely on the needs of those who come to faith or regain their faith after marriage leaves them as lone worshippers in their families. She is a European trustee of Media Associates, working with them to train Christian writers in Eastern Europe and the developing world. She is married to Gordon, and has five adult children and 15 grandchildren. See more on her website www.marionstroud.com and read her blog *Living Life on Purpose* at marionstroud.blogspot.com

WEEKEND

Caring for your own vineyard

For reflection: Songs 1:5–6

'… my own vineyard I have neglected.' (v.6)

I was really struggling. 'Close your eyes,' the course leader had instructed. 'Imagine a seed in the ground. Watch it grow, breaking through the soil and becoming a tree or plant. Then ask it what it wants from you.' This was foreign territory for me. I tried again, but as my seed reluctantly pushed its way through the soil of my imagination, forming a very stunted bush, the exercise ended and the moment passed. My apparent failure really bothered me. 'Father,' I prayed the next day, 'why couldn't I make my "seed" grow?'

'My own sheep have I not kept,' seemed to be the reply.

Wondering if this was in the Bible, I turned to the Song of Solomon. The words in chapter 1 verse 6 leapt out at me.

'You couldn't make that seed grow,' God whispered in my heart, 'because you have been so busy caring for others, that you have neglected your own needs.'

I knew that this was true for me. How about you?

Try the seed-growing exercise. What happened? Is God calling you to do anything about it? We'll explore this together in the month ahead.

A wall **worth dying for?**

The news was bad. Jerusalem's walls, the city's vital first line of defence, had been razed to the ground and the gates destroyed. There was no security for the returning exiles. But what could he do? As cupbearer, Nehemiah had access to King Artaxerxes, but approaching him on his own account was a risky business. However, the broken walls troubled Nehemiah so much that after he had fasted and prayed, he risked his life by asking the king for permission to go and put matters right.

Cities rarely have walls today. But in many countries houses are like fortresses, with high fences, guards on the gates and dogs patrolling the garden. Can't imagine living like that? Nor could we until we were burgled. We thought that we were security conscious but something as simple as unlocked gates meant that thieves got into the back garden, forced open a door and ransacked the house. The police were blunt. 'Always check your fences,' they said. 'They're your first line of protection. Neglect those and you're asking for trouble.'

It is easy to see the importance of physical walls around houses and cities. And it is obvious that real vineyards need a wall or solid hedge to protect the vines from stray animals, thieves or other threats to the crop. But how does this relate to our spiritual 'vineyard' or inner life?

We can think of these walls in several ways. They may represent our physical, emotional, social and spiritual life. They could also be a picture of attitudes or core beliefs that shape the ways we think and act. When any of these areas of our life are weak or unstable, the fruit on the vine is at risk from enemy attack.

Nehemiah 1:1–4;
2:1–10

'Those who survived … are in great trouble … The wall … is broken down …'
(1:3)

For prayer and reflection

Are there unlocked gates or broken fences undermining the security of my vineyard? Am I watchful, aware of the possibility of spiritual attack? Or complacent, thinking 'I'm OK'?

Prison **or protection?**

'… woe to you,
because you load
people down with
burdens …' (v.46)

C ity and castle walls had two functions. The first was to keep legitimate citizens safe from their enemies and the second was to mark out clearly the territory that belonged to them. Performing those functions, the walls provided security and peace. But those same walls could also become a prison. Attacking armies would often besiege a walled city so that the inhabitants couldn't get out. Then they had a choice between starvation and surrender.

When God gave the Law and the commandments to the Jews, they were intended to be boundaries to guide and guard their lives as a nation. But by the time Jesus was preaching and teaching, things were going horribly wrong. The Pharisees and spiritual teachers were putting so many prohibitions and burdens on the people of His day that they became spiritually crushed by all the do's and don'ts. Instead of using the Law in the way that God had intended, the teachers were imprisoning people within a manmade structure.

What about you? Do the walls of your spiritual vineyard form a protective boundary or a threatening barricade? Almost without us noticing, childhood influences or unhelpful teaching can create so many expectations about how we should live as Christians, that faith becomes a prison. Or we may allow Satan to lock us into a stronghold of fear. Fear that we must always get things right if God is to love us; that we must be this or do that if other Christians are to approve of us. Then before we know it, we stop seeing God as the gentle and creative heavenly Gardener, and think of Him as a menacing policeman, narrowing our lives and waiting to catch us out if we put our heads above the parapet.

For prayer and reflection

Father, longing to live in faith and security, I would pray with the psalmist, 'Set me free from my prison that I may praise your name.' (Psa. 142:7)

Reviewing the situation

Are you a planner or a plunger? When faced with a task, some of us want to have it finished yesterday, and so we plunge in, doing the first thing that comes to hand. Others like to pause and consider the situation from all angles before doing anything at all.

Nehemiah was a planner. When he got to Jerusalem he paused and reflected for three days. And then he slipped out at night to assess the task that lay ahead. No fanfare or big promises. He just took one step at a time.

When God draws our attention to something that needs dealing with in our lives, plungers act as if they have an open wound. They want to clean it up, slap on a sticking plaster, and then get back to normal straightaway. The planners, on the other hand, may spend hours thinking, writing lists and praying, but then fall into the trap of not doing anything about the problem. Thought and action are equally important.

As we check the walls of our vineyards for signs of wear and tear, it may seem irrelevant to include the physical, mental and emotional aspects of our lives, as well as the spiritual. But God has made us with needs in all of these areas, and if we are lonely, overworked, under-stimulated mentally or unfit physically, the walls of our vineyard are weakened and Satan can gain a foothold. When Elijah fled from Jezebel, God didn't send an angel to preach a sermon or tell him to get up and get on with his prophetic duties, but to cook him a meal, encourage him to sleep and to point him to others who could help and support him in the task that lay ahead.

Nehemiah 2:11–18

'I went to Jerusalem, and after staying there three days I set out …'
(vv.11–12)

For prayer and reflection

Think about a problem that you've faced recently. Did you plunge or did you plan? What was the outcome?

Be ready to fight for it

'What are those feeble Jews doing? … Can they bring stones back to life …?' (v.2)

The initial work on the walls went ahead at a great pace. They were halfway towards getting the job finished when the opposition really made itself felt. Sanballat and his friends had a vested interest in the project failing. When the exiles were protected from their enemies, the plotters would have no more power over them. And the completion of such a mammoth task would be unarguable proof that God could and would help His people. So they tried to undermine the resolve of the Jews with mockery and threats. Nehemiah refused to be put off. He didn't waste time arguing. He simply prayed, took practical steps to thwart the enemy's plans and encouraged the people to work with all their hearts.

When we decide to repair the weak and broken places in our vineyards, we may make excellent progress initially. But it's very easy to become discouraged halfway through, especially if we look at all that remains to be done or if we get little support from others. When Meryl recommitted her life to God, her husband felt threatened. 'I don't want you to change,' he said indignantly when Meryl tried to live out her new-found faith. 'Why ever would you want to do that?' he asked dismissively when she wanted to go to church. 'I bet you £50 that you'll have given it all up by Christmas,' he said finally. He lost!

Perseverance isn't a popular word these days. 'Do it if it makes you feel good, but otherwise don't bother', we're told. Or maybe we falter because we feel stretched to the limit already and change seems a bridge too far. Mockery is still one of Satan's favourite weapons, but Nehemiah's solution remains effective. God is on our side and He'll help us get the job done.

For prayer and reflection

Consider: God's call will not take us where His hand cannot keep us and give us success.

Be prepared to say no!

It seemed such a reasonable request, and they didn't give up easily. 'Come and meet us, Nehemiah,' they coaxed. 'Let's talk. Disturbing rumours are circulating. We want to help you.' Four times they sent the polite message before they got ugly. But Nehemiah was totally focused on the job in hand and didn't waver.

It is partly a temperament issue. Some people can fix their eyes on a goal and have no inclination to do anything else until it is completed. But many of us are not like that. We have a sneaking suspicion that Thurber was right when he said, 'A woman's place is in the wrong.' So we feel obliged to multi-task, and as we spin the plates of our lives frantically we still feel that whatever we do is not enough.

Many years ago I was at a meeting in which we were all invited to stand and hold out our hands to God, asking Him for whatever gift He wanted to give us to be used in His service. I didn't have the courage to remain in my seat or keep my hands at my sides. But under my breath I was praying, 'Please God don't give me anything else to do. I just can't cope with what I've got.'

When we know that for a while we have to focus on sorting ourselves out, Satan will be quick to impugn our motives. 'You're being selfish. You're not really committed. You could squeeze in that little thing if you really loved the Lord.' It is then that we need to ask God to confirm His word to us and then reply as Nehemiah did.

Once the walls were finished God had wonderful events planned. But first things had to come first.

Nehemiah 6:1–9

'I am carrying on a great project and cannot go down …' (v.3)

'Let us throw off everything that hinders … and let us run with perseverance the race marked out for us … our eyes on Jesus.'
(Heb. 12:1–2)

WEEKEND

A well woman check-up

For reflection: Hebrews 12:1–3,12–13
'… let us throw off everything that hinders …' (v.1)

In a recent survey a huge percentage of women questioned said that they would sacrifice money, promotion, sexual conquests and even a size 10 figure for more … time for themselves. Time to rest, relax, play and, above all, to review where their lives are going.

During the weekend, try to find one hour to think and pray about the 'walls' of your vineyard. Look for the damage or the weak spots. Assess the situation, decide how you want things to be in six months' time and then plan to do just one thing that will begin the restoration process.

- Do you need to lose weight or take more exercise? Organise next week's menus or go for a walk.

- Are you bored and under-stimulated? Borrow or buy that book you've been meaning to read. Exhausted physically? Clear your diary for at least three early nights next week.

- Have you lost touch with friends? Phone one and arrange to meet for coffee. Feel that your family has been neglected? Plan some fun.

- Feeling spiritually low? Read Psalm 86, write your own version and offer it back to God.

A song of joy

Isaiah 27:2–6

'Sing about a fruitful vineyard: I, the LORD, watch over it … so that no-one may harm it.'

For my husband's 60th birthday our children clubbed together and 'bought' him a row of vines in a French vineyard. For one year the vines were registered in his name and he could visit at any time. If he wished he could join in the harvest and, once the wine was ready, it was his at a special price. Not being one for hard labour, Gordon delayed his visit until the wine was ready for collection.

When we got there I was disappointed. The vineyard wasn't the romantic place I'd expected. In late autumn it was just a dry and dusty field with carefully tended boundaries; the vines pruned and trained with rigid precision. But when the farmer started to tell us about the life cycle of 'our' vines it was obvious that to him it was the most exciting and absorbing place on earth. He knew the age of every row of vines and the type of grapes that each would produce. He could tell us the diseases that might attack them and the effect that the weather would have on a vintage. Winter, spring, summer and autumn he had one overriding goal. And that was to ensure the health and productivity of his vines.

Vineyards feature frequently in the Bible. Sometimes they represent God's chosen people and at other times an individual's life. God is often described as the gardener or owner. Like our Monsieur Mazarin He knows His vines intimately and is totally committed to their welfare. As our lives move through the seasons they may seem more exciting or productive at some times than at others. But to God the externals are unimportant. His intention is that we shall be fruitful, and all His dealings with us are focused on that one thing.

For prayer and reflection

Father, I long to produce the very best wine. I will take responsibility for my part. Thank You that I can trust You to do the rest.

Winter or summer He is there

Hosea 6:1–3

'Let us acknowledge the LORD … he will come to us like the winter rains …'
(v.3)

Do you have a favourite season? If you are someone who loves the sun and dreads the short days and long nights of winter, you might wish you lived in the tropics where the weather varies mainly between brilliant sunshine and torrential rain. But every plant has a life-cycle and when Jesus described Himself as the vine and the disciples as the branches, He did so knowing that the vine goes steadily through the pulsating vigour of spring, the burning heat of summer, the fruitfulness of harvest and then the pruning and rest of winter.

In our personal lives it's possible to be in several seasons simultaneously. Work may be at high noon of summer, demanding every bit of our energy, while in our family life the winter chill bites deep as we mourn the death of an elderly parent or struggle to adapt to an 'empty nest'.

We could be rejoicing over a fresh start as we pull a new house or garden into shape while reaping the fruit of hours of work within the church. In life all four seasons may run together. But for these notes we have to focus on one at a time. So we will begin with winter.

Winter months aren't always beautiful outwardly. In the vineyard, canes are battered, leaves tumble to the ground and the soil between the rows may be littered with the debris from the harvest.

In our spiritual lives we may resist the onset of winter, hanging on desperately to a productive season that has ended. But God knows what He is doing as He prunes, turns over the ground and does a work in our hearts to prepare us for the new thing that will surely come.

For prayer and reflection

Consider: There can be no fruit in winter. But without winter there can be no fruit.

Radical action

I don't know if it was winter, but they were dangerous times. With no knowledge of God's Law and no priest to teach it, the land was in turmoil. Then the Holy Spirit touched the life of one man, Azariah. Deeply affected by this experience, he went straight to the king and gave him some pretty robust encouragement. 'Face reality,' he said. 'Be courageous and take firm action to put things right. Then God will bless you.'

Asa took his advice to heart. He utterly destroyed the idols that had filled the vacuum in the people's hearts. He put God back into the centre of national life, with a repaired altar and acceptable sacrifices. Faced with their sinfulness, the people agreed that in future they would give God everything or face death. No exceptions – even for the royal grandmother. And God honoured their obedience and commitment.

Once, I felt that God was telling me to take a sabbatical. I was to give up a number of activities in which I had been involved, and become like a fallow field. Not quite sure what one did with a fallow field I consulted a farmer friend. 'You don't just ignore it,' he said. 'A field that is fallow still has to be ploughed, weeded, fertilised and possibly used for a different crop which will put minerals back into the soil. It is an active resting.' Winter in the spiritual vineyard has similarities to a fallow field. The supports for the branches have to be mended, the vine pruned, and the soil weeded and enriched. Working outside in the cold isn't pleasant but half-hearted cultivation in winter will affect the season to come.

Asa was radical in the steps he took to put the land to rights. How about you?

---

2 Chronicles 15

'But in their distress they turned to the LORD … and sought him, and he was found by them.' (v.4)

For prayer and reflection

Father, help me not to flinch from getting rid of anything that is polluting my life and allow You to prune and plough where necessary.

The **wounds of love**

'... every branch that does bear fruit he prunes so that it will be even more fruitful.' (v.2)

By the beginning of winter the vine sprouts a forest of canes, dotted with a mass of buds containing next season's grapes. But, sadly, there are too many for the vine to support next year. Unpruned, the canes will put such stress on the vine that the fruit will never develop properly and the weight of fruit and foliage may cause the branches to snap off altogether. It must seem like an assault to the vine, but those canes must be pruned. The vital thing is that the gardener knows what to do.

I learned this the hard way. When we were given a loganberry cutting, we were warned that it was very vigorous and would need lots of room. We planted it with care, and soon had plentiful branches and masses of fruit arching along the fence. The plant was rapidly running out of space. I didn't get round to pruning it last winter, and so we came to the spring with a tangle of branches growing in all directions. Unfortunately my gardening expertise is at the 'idiot's guide' level. Faced with a muddle I decided to go for the 'slash and tidy' approach and lived to regret it. We had no fruit this year.

Pruning can be a daunting task. If we belong to the 'if it moves cut it off' school, we may have no fruit for a season or, worse still, a dead plant. If we don't cut enough, we'll just have a reduced problem. Fear of doing damage may stop us doing anything at all.

Thankfully God is the Master Gardener. When He prunes in our lives it may seem harsh or it may cause us pain at the time. But we can rest in the fact that He knows just what He is doing.

For prayer and reflection

As He prunes the dead wood from your life in this winter period, hear God say to you 'Trust Me. I love you more than you will ever know.'

Less **can be more**

Offer a small child a handful of brightly coloured Smarties or one or two large and expensive chocolate truffles, and most of them will grab the small sweets. At that stage they prefer quantity rather than quality. But in the vineyard it is a different story. The skilful vine keeper cuts out the non-essential canes until there are just five left. The sap will then spread evenly along the five branches and the latent fruit in the buds will have all the nourishment they need to develop fully. And with the clutter of extra canes gone, the gardener can see clearly if there are any diseases or pests attacking the plant.

Many of us still have that 'more is more' attitude. We feel that the more we do, the more we are justifying our existence and pleasing God. In any case we feel defined by our activities. 'Everybody knows me as a lay-reader, the church caterer, the youth group leader,' we may say to ourselves. 'If God asks me to lay that down, who would I be? I wouldn't belong in the same way.' And so we spread ourselves so thinly that nothing gets done properly, and our activities produce little except exhaustion. Busyness does not guarantee fruitfulness.

When we submit to God's pruning, we learn that it's fine to say 'no' if God has not called us to begin, or to withdraw (giving others as much notice as we can) if He has shown us that it is time to stop. And we need to do it. God doesn't wrench things from us, or stop us grabbing them back. He just gently calls us to lay them down, saying, 'Trust Me. I take things away only so that you will have room for a deeper relationship with Me.'

Isaiah 55:6–13

"'For my thoughts are not your thoughts, neither are your ways my ways," declares the LORD.' (v.8)

For prayer and reflection

Consider: The fruitful life is not a whirlwind of activity but focused, on the 'one thing' that can never be taken away.

WEEKEND

Take five

For reflection: Acts 14:21–28
'… they sailed back to Antioch, where they had been committed … for the work they had now completed …' (v.26)

I f I try to picture my vine,' said a hectically busy young mum, 'I see Jack's beanstalk, disappearing up to heaven, with branches spreading everywhere. I need to prune, but I wouldn't know where to start. And anyway I'd be sad to give things up.'

How do you feel about reducing your 'branches' to no more than five? These would probably be areas of your life rather than individual activities. Which ones would be key? Why not list or draw them.

What would you do with the things that you had to cut out? We often think of endings as being sad but they needn't be. Paul and Barnabas hadn't preached to every-one, but they had had a clearly defined objective and when they could stamp 'Finished' over that, they returned to their base for a debriefing and celebration.

If God has pointed out something that He wants to prune from your life why not celebrate some endings this weekend? You might want to do it with others or between you and God alone.

Write a list of all the blessings, the lessons you've learned and the people you have appreciated. Then give it to God and be ready to move on.

Tied to the wire

When I visited the French vineyard where 'our' vines were growing, I was surprised to see how short the vines were. I don't know what I was expecting but the reality was a row of thick gnarled trunks, barely reaching my shoulder. The branches that grew from each trunk lay along a series of wires that stretched from one end of the row to the other, supported at intervals by strong stakes. There isn't much living free in a vineyard.

That was in late autumn. Monsieur Mazarin's next task was to cut the old canes from the wire and discard them. Then he would have to tie the chosen five remaining canes to the wire. They wouldn't accept this limitation easily. It would be hard work to bend them into shape and it had to be done gently or they would break. If they could have been asked, I'm sure that they would say that they would rather be free. Stripped of their leaves and with the embryonic grapes still hidden in the buds they didn't need the support then. But it would be essential in the spring if they were not to snap under the weight of their own productivity.

Some of us are 'lone rangers'. We resent having our freedom curbed, or perhaps we have been let down in the past, because the supports we relied on have disappointed us. So we set out to serve God in our own way, feeling safer to trust no one but ourselves. But without God's support system we never develop to our full potential and may even find that the harvest is ruined because we break down with the sheer weight of the fruit.

It is then that He says, 'Trust me and lean hard. I will never let you down.'

---

1 Corinthians 9:24–27

'Everyone who competes in the games goes into strict training.' (v.25)

For prayer and reflection

Father, forgive me for my arrogance in thinking that I can do it best my way. Help me to accept the discipline of being trained by You.

'Celebration **of discipline**'

Hebrews 12:1–12

'… God disciplines us for our good, that we may share in his holiness.' (v.10)

When Richard Foster wrote *Celebration of Discipline*, it became an unlikely bestseller in a pleasure-loving age. People seem to be hungry for a disciplined framework in which to live their lives – in theory. But as the writer to the Hebrews says, 'No discipline seems pleasant at the time, but painful' (v.11). And when the discipline involves moving out of our comfort zones, like the canes on the vine, we would often rather take the easy route.

Foster writes about twelve Christian disciplines. The first four primarily affect our inner life: meditation, prayer, fasting and study. We do these things privately. The next four affect the way we live our lives practically: simplicity, solitude, submission and service. And the final four: confession, worship, guidance and celebration, are experienced most fully with other people.

If you feel that your life is full to bursting it may seem to be the final straw to suggest that you should add anything else to your schedule. But the three groups of disciplines summarise the three basic 'wires' that God wants to train us along. There can be no lasting growth and productivity without an intimate relationship with Him. The outworking of that intimacy will affect the way in which we pace our lives and what we do in His service. And the final group remind us we are part of a body and that other members of our Christian family are vital to our spiritual health and growth. As I struggled to understand what it means to care for your own vineyard in the midst of a hectic life, I found that meditation, simplicity and confession (being accountable to one or two close friends) are great initial starting points. What would help you?

For prayer and reflection

Father, show me where my life particularly needs Your support, and help me to embrace with joy the discipline I need to know You better.

Bursting into life

The road we live on is lined with ornamental cherry trees. When spring comes they lean towards one another, weighed down with pink and white blossom like a glorious bridal arch. The fruit they produce later in the year, though, is more of a nuisance than a blessing since you can't eat it and it squelches under your shoes, coating the soles with a penetrating red dye. But in the spring they are full of promise.

Springtime in our spiritual lives is also a time of joy and anticipation. Every day is a fresh adventure and everything seems possible. But spring is also a time of great danger to the crop. As the sap begins to flow through the vine, so the pests and weeds also stir into life and the rest period of winter is over for the farmer. If the blossom is to be more than a promise of things to come, there is a lot of work ahead.

It is wonderful when God gives us promises that seem to be just for us. They may relate to plans that He has for our lives. They may give us hope for our relationships, or financial, health or other issues that we struggle with day by day. And then we wait. And if that promise does not come to pass according to our time-scale, the pests of discouragement or the weeds of doubt begin to attack us. Perhaps the fruit of that promise is not what we had expected it to be, rather like the ornamental cherries that litter our drive.

Proverbs says, 'Hope deferred makes the heart sick' (13:12) and we may begin to regret that we'd ever had that promise in the first place. This is where the hard labour of spring cultivation begins.

Song of Songs 2:8–13

'See! The winter is past ... the blossoming vines spread their fragrance.' (vv.11–13)

For prayer and reflection

What promises are you holding in your heart today? Do you still believe, like Abraham, that God will do what He promised?

Preparing the soil

**Ephesians
3:14–21**

'… I pray that you,
being rooted and
established in love,
may … know this
love that surpasses
knowledge …'
(vv.17–19)

My home town is built on clay and is famous for its bricks. This is good news for local builders, but doesn't do gardeners any favours. Roses grow well in clay, but if you want other crops, you need to dig in a great deal of compost and manure that will lighten the soil, not just once, but regularly, and that is backbreaking work.

Vines are often grown on hillsides and in that situation stones have to be cleared before they can become established. Jesus wasn't talking about vines in the parable of the sower, but the principle remains true. If you want a good harvest you need a good depth of fertile soil, and an absence of stones and weeds. And that won't happen by itself.

Paul prayed that the Ephesian Christians would be rooted and established in God's love. This is the soil in which the very best fruit is produced, and deep roots enable plants to flourish even in the most testing conditions of heat or drought. But the love goes both ways. God will never stop loving us, but our love can fall to a very low level at times. How do we judge that? If we don't have an emotional tingle when we think about God, how do we know if we love Him?

Jesus had only one measuring rod – obedience. 'If you obey my commands, you will remain in my love,' He told His disciples, just after He had been talking about the vine and the branches (John 15). And that applies to us too. If we want good soil in our vineyard, where we will stand the best chances of seeing the promises come to fruition, we need to obey God, both in the small things and the major issues of our lives.

**For prayer and
reflection**

**What is the quality
of the soil in
your vineyard?
Is there rock of
disobedience
that needs to be
removed? Why not
talk to God about
that now?**

Weeds **and thorns**

Proverbs 24:30–34

'Thorns had come up everywhere, the ground was covered with weeds …' (v.31)

When our children were young, our garden was a summer cricket square, a winter football pitch and an assault course for bicycles, dogs and the neighbourhood children all the year round. Once we had reclaimed it we had a shock. Whenever we wanted to go away, it seemed to be the wrong time for the garden. The flowers needed planting or watering, the weeds took over as soon as our backs were turned, and the runner beans were ready to eat as soon as we left the house. We were faced with the hard fact that if we wanted a productive garden it needed attention all the year round, but particularly in summer.

We think of summer as holiday time. But for the vineyard it is the most demanding time of year. Parasites, called nematodes, can attack the roots of the vine. Weeds and thorns are at their most vigorous and will choke it and leech all the nourishment out of the soil if left unchecked. And birds are quick to enjoy a free lunch, while mildew and other diseases can make the grapes unusable.

There are lots of spiritual similarities to this invading army. The nematodes are like the secret sins that we just haven't bothered to deal with. Unchecked they will eat away at the roots of our life in God. Jesus compared weeds to the 'cares of this world' when He talked about plants that didn't flourish. If you're a worrier you won't need any reminders of how anxiety can choke the life out of anything. What about the birds and diseases? Could they be compared with disappointment with others, or with God; frustration and anger with our circumstances? All of these and many more can prevent the fruit from reaching harvest.

For prayer and reflection

I want to offer You a bumper crop, Lord. Help me not to become weary, but to wage war on anything that would damage or destroy my life in You.

WEEKEND

For this I have Jesus

For reflection: Isaiah 49:13–23
'But Zion said, "The LORD has forsaken me, the LORD has forgotten me."' (v.14)

'Does it get easier?' asked Mary. 'Do twins ever sleep all night?' 'You wait until their teens,' sighed Debbie. 'They're not asleep and they're not in.' Gill forced the words past the lump in her throat, 'If I don't meet someone soon there won't BE any children for me,' she said sadly.

There is never a problem-free season in the vineyard, and sometimes the onslaught of the enemy is terrifying. Rose* saw her entire family, except for her two little daughters, slaughtered in the Rwandan genocide. Now she is a widow among many widows with no money. But she refuses to be defeated. She has adopted two other orphans and simply trusts God to provide for the food and school fees for her family of four. She translates Christian literature into the local language and organises an annual conference for other widows. As she told us her story she wept. But for every problem in her life she has one remedy. 'For this' she said 'I have Jesus.'

If you're struggling at the moment why not list the challenges you face and then write these words beside each one: 'For this, I have Jesus.'

*Not her real name

Cool **clear water**

John 7:37–44

'If anyone is thirsty, let him come to me and drink.' (v.37)

I was due for a hospital test that involved a radiologist putting dye into my vein and then taking a series of X-rays. On the day before, I was allowed only one pint of liquid, and for the six hours before the test I could have nothing at all. I have never been so thirsty in my life! It was then that I really understood the truth that we can survive without most things, but we can't live without water.

In England we rarely get prolonged droughts, but in hot weather plants still need to be watered regularly. And it is no good just dampening the surface. They need a thorough soaking if they are to flourish. In Bible times there would be no escape from painstakingly watering the vineyard by hand. Today in large vineyards there are often underground irrigation systems which turn on automatically every night, but these can still get clogged by leaves or soil, and the vineyard keeper must check the water sources every day.

Water is vital for a flourishing vineyard. At our local swimming pool the drinking fountains are foot-operated and you get one mouthful at a time. Nearby is an ornamental fountain that bubbles away unceasingly. These different fountains remind me of the time when Jesus offered the living water of the Spirit. He promised this would be a spiritual water source that would never run dry. But the Bible tells us that we can quench the Spirit, either deliberately, as if we take our foot off the pedal, or inadvertently, if we allow sin or distractions to clog up the irrigation system. The water is still available to us but it won't flow in our lives. If that happens our vineyard will quickly become a barren waste.

For prayer and reflection

Holy Spirit I welcome You. Forgive me if I have quenched the flow of Living Water. Please flood my life and bring vitality and fruitfulness today and every day.

273

They're **only little things**

Judges 16:1–20

"'I'll go out as before and shake myself free." But he did not know that the LORD had left him.' (v.20)

S amson was special. The son of his parents' old age, he had been dedicated to God as a Nazirite from birth. His spiritual life seems to have been an odd mixture of a man of God and a wilful prodigal. Spoiled by his doting parents and petulant if crossed, if he wanted something he wanted it now. And it seems that he usually got it. He had grown used to flirting with danger, so taunting the Philistines through tricking Delilah was just a game at first. But eventually the compromises came home to roost. He thought he could batter his way out of trouble as he had done before, but Samson had disobeyed once too often, and he finally paid the price. God had withdrawn His hand of blessing.

Most of the host of enemies that can threaten the vineyard harvest are easily recognised. But Solomon highlights a danger that seems outwardly very attractive: the 'little foxes' that destroy the vines (Songs 2:15). Fox cubs at play are very appealing. It seems impossible to believe that they could grow up into avenging furies that can destroy a flock of chickens in a few moonlit minutes. But little foxes grow into large foxes and so do sins of neglect, wilfulness, compromise and selfishness. We may shrug our shoulders because they don't seem very important. Or we may be so busy 'fighting fires' in the heat of our vineyard's summer that we don't notice these little foxes sliding along by the wall, until they have dug themselves in and grown large and menacing. And then a surge of spiritual strength is needed and disaster strikes. We have compromised or flirted with danger once too often.

Samson wanted privilege and power without accepting responsibility for the outcome of his actions. Do you?

For prayer and reflection

The little foxes of the spirit need exterminating without mercy if our hard labour is not to be in vain.

Fruit at last

....

....

'If a man remains in me and I in him, he will bear much fruit; apart from me you can do nothing.' (v.5)

A t the end of the long hot summer, the work in the vineyard begins to slow down. The vines still need a constant flow of water and the weeds and pests must be kept in check. But beyond that the farmer just has to wait for the fruit to ripen and mature, and for that to happen the branches must be supported so that the weight of the fruit that they are carrying doesn't pull them away from the vine.

Jesus was very clear about that. 'I am the vine and you are the branches,' He said. 'Remain in me ... remain in me ... remain in me.' He said it three times, underlining that this was the key factor in fruitfulness. God wants us to be fruitful. The Holy Spirit produces fruit in our lives. But the first essential is to 'remain' in Jesus so that the sap of His life within us flows freely. And for this to happen we need to be His friends.

How are you on the friendship front? As a child were you one of the lively popular group, first to be picked for the team? Or did you suffer agonies of embarrassment hopping from foot to foot and praying that you wouldn't be left till last? Whatever happened then, relax. There are no first or last in Jesus' friendship group. All are chosen; all are equally special and valued. And all have the same potential for fruit-bearing.

'Stay close,' says Jesus. 'Talk to Me and listen to Me. Act on what I tell you to do. Enjoy being loved. You belong and you are being changed into My likeness. Today I will help you to become a little more loving, joyful, peaceful, patient, kind, good, faithful, gentle and self-controlled. A beautiful harvest.'

....

For prayer and reflection

....

Lord, thank You for choosing me. I can't ripen myself. But I trust You to mature the fruit of Your Spirit in me, each day. For Your glory.

275

So **what is the harvest for?**

John 4:27–38

'… open your eyes and look at the fields! They are ripe for harvest.' (v.35)

The Bible talks about two types of harvest. One is the changed life of an individual Christian; but this is not an end in itself. Our fruitfulness is intended to bring God glory. As we become different, the fruit of the Spirit in our lives demonstrates the reality of God to those who don't know Him. After all, how can they know that God loves them if I don't act lovingly in my everyday dealings with my neighbours and friends? How will my family know His gentleness and forgiveness if I am rude and abrasive? Can I expect people at work to understand God's faithfulness if I am sloppy in what I do?

The other illustration that Jesus uses is of those who don't believe, but who are ready to respond to God if they get the opportunity. Here people themselves are the harvest. However, the fruit doesn't jump off the vine by itself. The workers come and pick the fruit so that it can be sold as table grapes, dried for raisins or processed into wine. If it is left on the vine once it is ripe, it will rot. So we need to be skilful harvest hands.

This is where many of us come to a shuddering halt. It isn't too difficult to see how we can demonstrate the qualities of the kingdom in our lives – even if we don't do it as well as we would like to. But when we reach the point of needing to explain what we believe and why, it's a rather different story.

So how can you put what you believe into words? You may not feel that you're a theologian, but a witness is simply someone who tells what they have seen and experienced. And we all do that – every day.

For prayer and reflection

Write down what your life used to be like, how you met God and what changed. Fine-tune it until you can say it in five minutes. You're a witness!

Crowning the year

I f you're a fan of the radio programme, *The Archers*, another farming soap opera, or you live on a farm, you'll know that during lambing and harvest, life gets really busy. Everyone's total focus is to get the grain in while the weather is dry, or the lambs born safely – which is, of course, another type of harvest. Everybody is involved and those without the skills or time to be out in the fields or the lambing sheds do the back-up jobs at home or in the farm office. There are no passengers, because their future prosperity is at stake.

Do you have that sense of urgency when you think of reaping people for the kingdom of God? Many of us give lip service to the importance of telling people that they're loved and can be forgiven. But if it is inconvenient to do it today – well there is always tomorrow!

Evangelist Rob Frost told a sobering story of his first attempts at mission. A group of bikers came to an evangelistic film, and Rob rather wished that they hadn't. Throughout the performance the lads chewed gum, barracked and catcalled and generally created a disturbance. But when the invitation to make a personal commitment to Jesus was given, the leader of the gang was one of the first to walk to the front. He asked God to forgive him and give him a brand-new life. Three hours later he was killed in a road accident and met God face to face. At harvest, your contribution counts, whether it is front line or in a supporting role, and there's no time for messing about. Jesus said, 'As long as it is day, we must do the work of him who sent me. Night is coming, when no-one can work' (John 9:4).

Psalm 65:1–13

'You crown the year with your bounty, and your carts overflow with abundance.' (v.11)

For prayer and reflection

If you were on trial for inviting others into God's kingdom, would there be enough evidence to convict you?

WEEKEND

Come, you thankful people, come

For reflection: Nehemiah 8:9–18
'Do not grieve, for the joy of the LORD is your strength.' (v.10)

When the quality and quantity of the harvest governed whether people had a good life or starved in the coming year, full barns and empty fields were a cause of tremendous joy and celebration. Sadly, now that we can buy almost anything from a supermarket all the year round, the sheer wonder of harvest has largely faded from our lives.

But there is another kind of harvest that you can bring into God's storehouse with great joy. What has God taught you about caring for your vineyard in this past month? Are there completed tasks you can thank Him for? Have you changed and grown a little more like Jesus? Is there more of the fruit of the Spirit evident in your life? Looking further back, what fruit have you harvested in the last year? Is there anyone who now believes, or has taken another step towards God – someone in whose life you've sowed or who you've 'reaped' for the kingdom?

When you have identified your personal harvest you might like to place objects to represent them on a tray, or make a collage. Then offer them to God and celebrate with others.

There **is a choice**

I wonder how these servants viewed their master. Did the one who was given the most money see him as a lavish benefactor? Perhaps the servant who was given less saw him as stern but just – like a Victorian papa. The third servant certainly seems to have believed him to be an unspeakable tyrant. Desperately afraid of not doing well, he did nothing at all.

Whether or not these are accurate guesses, our view of God will certainly shape the way we respond to Him. So if we secretly fear that we can never do enough or be enough to please Him, we will find it very difficult to stop our 'doing' for long enough to hear what He is saying to us. And yet that is so important. What He says will vary from individual to individual. We must avoid the trap of looking to see what our friends have been given to do or where God's plan is taking them.

Do you remember what Peter said as he walked along the beach with Jesus after the resurrection? Jesus had forgiven him for his catastrophic failure and given him a new task. But Peter doesn't focus on that. Instead he points to John and asks, 'What about him?'

Jesus' reply is brief and to the point, 'what is that to you? You must follow me' (John 21:22).

So we have the responsibility of choice. We can listen and then respond to God's invitation to spend time with Him, allowing Him to prune our activities and discipline us as He sees fit. Or we can choose to stumble on, working in another's vineyard instead of taking care of our own.

The one leads to fruitfulness and His 'Well done'. The other ends in burnout and exhaustion. What will you do?

Matthew 25:14–30

'Well done, good and faithful servant ...' (v.23)

For prayer and reflection

Father, thank You for being the Lavish Lover, giving me so much. Help me to care for my vineyard so that it is beautiful and fruitful, and brings You joy.

Psalms
119–134

Wendy Virgo

When Wendy met and married Terry in 1968, God gave them
a passion to see the Church renewed and restored. As they
gradually rediscovered New Testament principles, a beautiful
network of churches began to grow which became known as
New Frontiers. They had five children who are now all married
and serving God in the UK and South Africa, and now also 12
grandchildren. New Frontiers churches can be found in nearly
60 countries, and so Wendy frequently finds herself travelling
with Terry, and ministering to women all over the world.

Psalms

Psalm 119:1–16

'I have hidden your word in my heart …' (v.11)

Today we begin to explore this longest of all the psalms, a gigantic poem celebrating the composer's love and respect for the Word of God. We don't know who wrote it, possibly David, and it is thought to date from the period of the exile in the sixth century BC. It is very carefully constructed in 22 stanzas of 8 verses each, and each stanza is headed by a letter of the Hebrew alphabet. Right through the poem runs the theme of the reliability and truth of God's Word which the psalmist declares is more precious than gold, and gives direction, meaning and guidance for his life.

A number of synonyms are used to describe the Word: law, testimonies, precepts, statutes, commandments, ordinances, word and promise.

Another theme, introduced in today's verses, is that of the heart. The psalmist does not regard God's ways with a detached, objective attitude; no, he is a passionate follower of God and, for him, to know God's Word is to know God. Therefore he will give his best energies to knowing it, studying it and obeying it.

A challenge lies in every stanza to make God's Word central in our lives. He speaks here of hiding the Word in his heart as a means of keeping him from sin (v.11). Studying God's Word is not just an academic exercise; he receives it with an open mind, a tender heart which is continually questioning, 'What do *You* want, God? What are You saying? How shall I handle this situation?'

Perhaps before we go any further, we need to check our attitude to the Word of God. Has reading it become a ritual? Is it a quick snack every now and then? Or do we treat it seriously, finding in it wisdom that will illuminate our pathway through the whole of life?

For prayer and reflection

Lord, as I study this psalm, teach me to take Your ways seriously. Please make this a period of change in my life as I open my heart to Your Word. Amen.

Digging for **treasure**

Sherlock Holmes settled down in his armchair. 'Watson,' he said, 'you see but do not observe. For example, you have frequently seen the stairs which lead up to this room.'

'Frequently,' responded Watson.

'How many are there?'

'How many? I don't know.'

'Quite so! You have seen, but you have not observed. There are seventeen.'*

We can go through life with our eyes open yet missing obvious things. We can be like that as we read the Bible. We think we have read it, but we have not absorbed truth. And yet there are wonderful things there waiting to be discovered, like buried treasure!

How do we find it? The psalmist knew that if he depended on his own intellect he would not get very far. He needed help. Who better to ask than the Author of the Word? The wonderful thing is that the Holy Spirit is waiting for us to ask Him for help. Jesus told His disciples, '[He] will teach you all things and will remind you of everything I have said to you' (John 14:26).

But why should these things be hidden from us? God's gems do not lie scattered about on the surface as it were. We are told that the 'natural man does not discern spiritual things' (1 Cor. 2:14, NASB). Our capacity to tap into the mysteries of God has been blunted; our eyes have been veiled by sin. We exist on a superficial level, and by ourselves cannot stumble on what belongs to God. We need revelation and, in His goodness, God grants it to those who ask for it. He desires relationship with us and delights to conduct us personally on a voyage of discovery as we turn the pages of His Word.

* Adapted from A. Conan Doyle, *A Scandal in Bohemia*

Psalm 119:17–32

'Open my eyes that I may see wonderful things in your law.' (v.18)

For prayer and reflection

Holy Spirit, I would love to go on a voyage of discovery with You! Please open my eyes that I might find treasure in the Word. Amen.

Walking in **freedom!**

Psalm 119:33–48

'I will walk about in freedom, for I have sought out your precepts.' (v.45)

How often do we hear the yearning cry of 'freedom' in songs, movies and speeches? Freedom is the motivation for revolution, assassination, rebellion. The desire to be 'free' from routine can cause us to lie in bed a bit longer, or urge us to get up earlier! The concept of freedom, depending on how we interpret it, can motivate us to work very hard to get more money so that we can do what we want; or it can make us give up work altogether, arguing that we will experience freedom by drifting through a spontaneous, unstructured life! How do you define freedom?

The psalmist here seems almost slavish in his embracing of God's ways, yet he declares that he 'walks about in freedom'. As he follows godly precepts, he finds release from various things that have the power to keep him in bondage. First, his heart is turned away from 'selfish gain' (v.36). He is finding a new set of priorities: 'worthless things' no longer command his affections (v.37).

He admits in verse 39 that he dreads disgrace, but freedom from this fear comes as he delights in God's good laws. He is afraid that he will be taunted and left tongue-tied and looking foolish. But he is learning that he need not worry about this, for God will not 'snatch his word from his mouth', he can trust Him.

So, for the psalmist, freedom means confidence that God will not let him down at crucial moments, freedom from fear of disgrace and freedom from obsession with 'selfish gain'. He is learning that he can trust the promises of God.

Can you 'walk about in freedom'? Are there things God's Word is highlighting that you didn't even realise were locking you up?

For prayer and reflection

Lord, I want to know and trust Your Word so completely that it enables me to walk about in freedom from every anxiety and fear. Amen.

A consistent lifestyle

The psalmist does not have an easy life. In this stanza, he hints at suffering, including attacks on his life, slander and, not surprisingly, insomnia! Verse 54 seems to allude to an unsettled existence of moving from place to place, but he has learnt that the Word of God is his constant companion and guide – 'wherever I lodge'.

All this has caused him to take stock of his life: 'I have considered my ways' (v.59). But he decides not to depart from his practice of obeying God's precepts (v.56).

He has built up a habit of knowing God's Word, considering it and obeying it; this has brought hope and comfort even while suffering unjust treatment and sleepless nights.

It has also helped him maintain good attitudes. He declares, 'I am a friend to all who fear you' (v.63). He knows he has enemies who slander him, taunt him, threaten him. He doesn't hesitate to call them 'arrogant' and 'wicked'. But all who fear God and follow Him he calls his friends.

This is a good principle. Sometimes we can get muddled about who are our friends and who are our enemies. We can begin to think that fellow Christians are our enemies if they do not see eye to eye with us. But let us remember that a fellow Christian is our brother or sister, not our enemy. The enemy of our souls will seek to divide Christians; it is he who is behind conflict, and our indignation should be directed at him, not our brother or sister in Christ.

The psalmist refuses to be contaminated with bitterness. He retains a sweetness and wholesomeness of heart which enables him to say, 'The earth is filled with your love, O LORD' (v.64).

Psalm 119:49–64

'This has been my practice: I obey your precepts.' (v.56)

For prayer and reflection

Lord, thank You that Your Word can help me develop a healthy perspective. Let its influence keep my spirit sweet. Amen.

WEEKEND

The search for meaning

For reflection: Psalm 34:1–10
'Those who look to him are radiant …' (v.5)

I have been reading poetry. Sonorous words roll and flow, evoking powerful images. Beautifully flowing lines by Keats conjure up the full, warm atmosphere of an autumn afternoon. Wordsworth praises the cuckoo, 'darling of the spring'; John Betjeman, enraged by the relentless march of ugly urbanisation, bids 'friendly bombs to fall on Slough'; and Shakespeare compares his love to a summer's day.

I feel glutted by the beauty and power of words skilfully used to cause the mind to see familiar things in a different light or to reflect on a sight or experience. However, one is often left with a sense of yearning emptiness as the poet tries to explore his feelings. I am struck by how often a poem which begins joyously declines into sad thoughts about death, or the inexorable march of time from which there is no escape.

I turn to this psalm. No nostalgia here, no despairing search for true meaning. The psalmist, even in his darkest hours, finds robust truth, steadfast love and enduring hope as he looks to God. He does not search within himself, but looks upward. This is where he gains a true perspective.

Lord, knowing You makes sense of life. You fill the empty spaces of the human heart. We can taste and see that the Lord is good.

Learning **the hard way**

D on't you hate discipline? I do: I hate giving it and receiving it! I remember squirming with humiliation when I was sent to stand in the corner of the classroom as a little girl. I was furious, but knew I deserved it!

Later, I found that training my own children to obey was hard work. For mothers this is a constant challenge. To be effective, discipline must be consistent, and it must be painful to some degree, whatever the method chosen. The aim of training is fundamentally kind: if done properly, it gives the child boundaries and security.

Repeatedly in this section, the psalmist begs God to teach him, but it seems he had not expected that God would answer by putting him in some unpleasant situations. We don't know exactly what they were, but he speaks of being 'afflicted'.

What we do know is his humble response. 'It was good for me to be afflicted' (v.71). Why? '... so that I might learn your decrees.' Learning for him was not a classroom situation.

He readily acknowledges that 'before I was afflicted I went astray' (v.67). His tendency was to wander off the path of God's will, and the faithful shepherd evidently had to use the rod and staff to bring him back into line. 'In faithfulness you have afflicted me,' he exclaims (v.75).

'... the Lord disciplines those he loves ... No discipline seems pleasant at the time, but painful. Later on, however, it produces a harvest of righteousness ... for those who have been trained by it' (Heb. 12:6–11). An undisciplined person is like a bramble that trails aimlessly, snarling up other plants. When it is pruned back, its fruit is sweeter, bigger and more plentiful, and the bush is a better shape.

Psalm 119:65–80

'It was good for me to be afflicted so that I might learn your decrees.' (v.71)

For prayer and reflection

Lord, please give me a teachable heart that responds well to Your training. Help me to recognise when You are disciplining me and to grow because of it. Amen.

Hanging on!

Psalm 119:81–96

'Your word, O LORD, is eternal; it stands firm in the heavens.' (v.89)

Hope deferred makes the heart sick: in the first stanza the psalmist pours out his anguish and frustration, almost despairing of life, waiting for deliverance from his tormentors. Around the world today many of our brothers and sisters are suffering persecution – harassed, marginalised, jailed and tortured for their faith. 'How long must your servant wait?' (v.84).

In the West, conditions for Christians are far easier. Yet this cry ascends to the heavens from them also; from despairing parents whose children are trapped in addictions, from Christians struggling to live righteously in vice-ridden society, and from families on crime-infested estates. What enables them all to endure?

We turn to the unchanging Word of God. In heaven His intentions are declared. High up, displayed for all to see, nailed to the wall, are His will and His decrees. Eager angels carry out His bidding. Jesus taught us to pray, 'Let your will be done on earth as it is in heaven'. His eternal Word directs, inspires, gives hope and purpose. It discloses His will, and our job is to pray it into being here on earth. Seek His will, then pray it out. This gives us authority in prayer, and we can bring about change as we agree with Him. 'The LORD foils the plans of the nations; he thwarts the purposes of the peoples. But the plans of the LORD stand firm for ever ...' (Psa. 33:10–11).

This principle helped me to pray for a backslidden son. Convinced of God's will to restore him, I fought in prayer using this weapon, 'Lord, You said Your will is fixed in heaven. Let it be done now on earth as it is in heaven. Confound the attempts of the enemy to rob my son of his destiny.' One day, God's light penetrated my son's darkness and changed him.

For prayer and reflection

Lord, I believe Your declared will is good and unchanging. Help me to work together with You by praying it into being on earth. Amen.

Heavenly **wisdom**

**Psalm
119:97–112**

'Your word is a
lamp to my feet
and a light for
my path.' (v.105)

This verse must be one of the best known in the Bible, memorised in Sunday school, enshrined in songs and remembered in times of decision-making. I remember reciting it as a seven-year-old, not understanding it then, but grateful for it as my life unfolded.

Decades have passed since then: has it proved true? In all the changing scenes of life, in its joys and pains, its complexities, mundane passages and moments of high drama, has God's Word been a guiding light?

In today's reading the two stanzas show the psalmist's determined dedication to know God's Word. He has systematically applied himself to meditate on it, love it and obey it. The more he has done this, the more he has grown in wisdom and security.

Has burying himself in it become tedious? No – it appears the more he does so, the more delightful he finds it. It is sweet as honey! Verse 106 says he is so committed to following the enlightened path he has found in God's Word that he has sworn not to depart from it.

This shows that the kind of light he finds there is not mere 'convenience guidance'. It is not a quick fix 'open your Bible and put your finger in', or grab a verse out of a promise box. It is not a box of fortune cookies. It is principles for moral choices; it is truth to live by; it is undergirding wisdom, rocklike, trustworthy. No wonder he says 'Your statutes are ... the joy of my heart' (v.111).

Having God's Word to guide you is like having a torch in your hand; it gives enough light for the next step so that you can put your foot down confidently.

Is your heart set on keeping His decrees to the very end? Mine is.

For prayer and reflection

I am so grateful, Lord, that Your Word is so available to me. Help me to honour it, and not take this privilege for granted. Amen.

Time **to act**

**Psalm
119:113–128**

'… I stand in awe
of your laws.'
(v.120)

The psalmist, in submitting to God's way, finds he fears only one person: God. God's Word is not only delightful, strengthening and trustworthy, it is also 'awesome'. Why? The psalmist finds himself suddenly trembling in God's presence. That voice, so dear and familiar by now, is also holy, uncompromising, majestic, utterly right: like the One speaking. In His presence, he is not about to argue, disagree or debate the issue. No, he is facedown, trembling.

This has clear implications. He cannot take it lightly when others dismiss God's Word. 'I hate every wrong path.' In face of flagrant contempt for God's righteous standards in the world today, we might often identify with the psalmist as he cries out, 'It is time for you to act, O Lord; your law is being broken.' So why doesn't He?

I heard of a Chinese pastor who had been beaten, imprisoned and tortured. Fellow cellmates were asking this question: 'Why doesn't your God act to save you?'

His reply was that as soon as our Lord Jesus unsheathes His sword to avenge those who oppress His beloved people, the day of grace is over. While the day of man's arrogance is extended and wickedness continues, the arm of grace is also extended: there is still time to repent and for mercy to abound, even to the oppressor. So apparent delay for the one oppressed is actually the greatest act of mercy for the oppressor and for all mankind. One day there will be a great shout, 'Enough!' and the flashing sword of our warrior King will be unsheathed. In the meantime, let us continue to 'love his commands more than gold'. Pray for courage to obey them in an unrighteous world. Those who endure to the end will be given a crown of life.

**For prayer and
reflection**

**Lord, I feel sad
and frustrated
when I see the
decline on every
side. Help me to
keep loving Your
ways, and also to
show love to those
who are ignorant
of them. Amen.**

Trembling at the Word

**Psalm
119:161–176**

'Rulers persecute me without cause, but my heart trembles at your word.' (v.161)

What makes you tremble? The idea here is not dutiful compliance, mere lip service to dogma, nor legalistic observance of rules. This is the attitude of one whose heart is so engaged that he is awestruck, and nothing, not even persecution or mockery, will keep this person from honouring God's Word.

I remember a time when I was seeking God about an issue which perplexed me. I was listening to a tape while I was doing the ironing, when something the preacher said transfixed me. The word pierced me to the heart and I literally trembled. God was answering my prayer for understanding by putting His finger on something in my own life which needed resolution. Obedience involved humbling myself and acknowledging some wrong attitudes, and it was painful. But God's word was so clear and uncompromising that I dared not disregard it.

Later on, after I had taken action, I could identify with the psalmist here when he exclaims, 'Great peace have they who love your law' (v.165). I came out of a turbulent time into calm waters. Not only was my heart settled, it had a healthy effect on my marriage and all my relationships.

However, it is possible to be deeply affected by the Word, yet distracted from submitting to it. Felix, Roman governor of Caesarea, 'was afraid' when he heard Paul preaching on 'righteousness, self-control, and the judgment to come', but he did not act on it (Acts 24:25).

This wonderful psalm, as we have seen, consistently celebrates the wonder, truth and power of God's Word, and finishes as it begins, with the writer exclaiming, 'your law is my delight.' Let's keep our hearts soft and open as we continue to explore it.

For prayer and reflection

'Let the word of Christ dwell in you richly ...' (Col. 3:16).

'May my cry come before you, O LORD; give me understanding according to your word' (v.169).

WEEKEND

Thankful hearts

For reflection: 1 Thessalonians 5:18
'... give thanks in all circumstances ...'

My friend sighed. 'What can you say to someone who is always negative about everything?' We all know people like that! They are hard work! It's not that one wants to be unsympathetic, but surely there must be something they can be positive about?

Thankfulness has to be cultivated. Sometimes we don't appreciate ordinary things until we are deprived of them. As I write, Ellen MacArthur has just returned victoriously from her 70-day, record-breaking, round the world voyage. She is now probably appreciating a bed on dry land! I didn't know that was something to be thankful for until I saw what she had been trying to sleep on!

What can you be thankful for? It's surprising when you start 'counting your blessings' how the list grows. If you are in the midst of a crisis, or simply tired and fed up, take a few minutes to stop and take stock. Start somewhere, even if it is just thanking God for a magnificent sky. This is not just looking for the proverbial silver lining; it is consciously drawing on the goodness and kindness of a heavenly Father, who is the Author of every good and perfect gift.

Make a list of things you can be thankful for. Then go through it deliberately, praising God for His goodness. End by thanking Him for His 'unspeakable gift' in Jesus.

Homesick

Psalm 120

'Too long have I lived among those who hate peace.' (v.6)

Pilgrims are making their way up to Jerusalem for the feast days. Some, as this psalm suggests, are travelling a considerable distance. The pilgrim is praying for protection as he journeys through hostile territory. As he thinks about Jerusalem, his heart cries out against the misfortune of those dwelling in 'Meshech' in the far North, or the 'tents of Kedar' in the Arab south. These two places perhaps represent two extremes of the Gentile world near and far.

This then was a lament for homesick Israelites scattered among foreign nations longing for home. It voices the distress arising from living amongst contentious people who wound with their tongues. As the cries of distress rise to God, the answer comes that He will take care of vengeance. Their sharp arrows of lies and slander will be dealt with by sharper more potent arrows, ie, their words will be turned against them.

The pilgrim is weary of their quarrelling, anger and clamour. He is for peace, they are for war. How reminiscent of Paul's words in 2 Corinthians 6:14: 'What do righteousness and wickedness have in common? Or what fellowship can light have with darkness?' Followers of Jesus belong to the Prince of Peace. Consequently, we love peace; it is our natural habitat. But while we live in the world, scattered like salt, we must be ambassadors of that kingdom even as we long for our true home.

When we have peace in our own hearts we can become peacemakers. This peace is not stagnation: it is about generating an atmosphere of harmony in the midst of strife because of who we are.

For prayer and reflection

Peace is a fruit of the Spirit; Lord, please grow that peace in me and help me to actively display it in my life. Help me not to give in to agitation. Amen.

Looking up

Psalm 121

'My help comes from the LORD, the Maker of heaven and earth.' (v.2)

I t is a long and winding road. The pilgrim is weary. He has come through dangerous mountain passes where if his foot had slipped he would have tumbled to his death; through burning deserts where he had been forced to seek shade from the relentless sun. Then to escape its heat, he travelled through the coolness of the night only to find that the darkness and eerie moonlight brought its own peculiar menace.

He trudges up the steep track, his eyes on the path in front, his feet rising and falling in rhythm with dozens of others, the stream of pilgrims swelling into an upward swirling river. A shout is heard: they round a bend and look up, their eyes gladdened by the view. Before them is Jerusalem perched high on its hill.

What joy! What relief! Nearly there! The city awaits. This is not just any hill: this symbolises the dwelling place of God! Now the pilgrim reflects, it is this same God who has watched over his journeying, protecting him from bandits, injury, sunstroke and terrors of the night. His heart swells with gratitude; God has been watching over him all along, and will continue to do so.

Have we not gazed in awe on a mountain range and reflected: a mighty hand constructed this magnificent scenery. But the hills do not contain Him, just as Jerusalem did not. We sometimes need to stand in wonder and lift up our eyes to take our minds off our own smallness and focus on the Maker of heaven and earth, majestic, transcendent, wholly other than us; and yet He sees you going out of your front door today, and coming home tonight. When you sleep His eyes are still upon you. This is our Helper.

For prayer and reflection

Lord, thank You for wonderful mountains and hills. But even more, thank You for the wonder that You are tenderly, intimately concerned in the details of my life. Amen.

The **city of God**

T he trials of the long journey are over, eclipsed by the joy of arrival. At last they are actually standing in the streets of the city. Eagerly the pilgrims look about; the streets are narrow, the buildings crowded together. Here people are close, they share their lives. The happy singing crowds surge along, the different tribes mingling together. They have a common purpose: to praise the name of the Lord. This city is also the seat of authority and justice.

Fellowship, worship and righteous authority: these should characterise the people of God. The New Testament shows us that the people of God now extend beyond the tribes of Israel. Jesus is the Door by which we Gentiles can enter His community, the Church. So the church locally and the Church worldwide should also be expressing these beautiful aspects.

Close relationships were a mark of early church life. It has been said that the early Christians lived in the church and went out to the world; we tend to live in the world and make visits into church! Jesus wants His people close in heart so that they can love, strengthen and care for one another.

The church is also meant to be a worshipping community, who worship in spirit and in truth (John 4:23). Jesus is the focal point of our gathering together, to be worshipped not with lips only but with our lives.

The kingdom of God must also be demonstrated through people standing for truth and justice, making a difference amidst the decay and declining standards of our world. One day all these things will come together in the perfection of the New Jerusalem, where people from every tribe and nation will be in close fellowship around the throne, worshipping the One who holds the sceptre.

Psalm 122

'Jerusalem is built like a city that is closely compacted together.' (v.3)

For prayer and reflection

Lord, I pray that Christians might be known for peace, not dissension; worship not ambition; and as those who promote justice. Amen.

Focused gaze

Psalm 123

'… our eyes look to the LORD our God …' (v.2)

A gain the eyes of the pilgrim are lifted up, this time to the One seated on the throne of heaven; not only in adoration, but in trustful expectation. Perhaps the pilgrim has servants and has noticed their eyes as they wait for instructions, or seen how his wife's loyal maid lives to notice the smallest gesture from her mistress, and runs to do her bidding.

But this is not about waiting for instructions; this servant's eyes are dark with longing as she pleads for mercy. Why? Because the mistress is cruel? No: because she has endured 'much contempt' from arrogant people.

Women all over the world endure much contempt day after day. Their labour is used, their bodies are used; little girls are abused, girl babies are abandoned; fat girls are ridiculed, ordinary girls, fearful of not measuring up to perceived standards of beauty, despise themselves. Women are battered physically, mentally, emotionally and, in some countries, literally treated as slaves.

Many do not realise there is One who knows what it is to be treated with the utmost contempt. 'He was despised and rejected by men' (Isa. 53:3). He, above all, empathises. He knows what it is to be weak and helpless, oppressed and afflicted. Then why does He not do something to alleviate so much suffering? Well, He has been pierced, crushed, smitten, bruised. 'He took up our infirmities and carried our sorrows.' He comes alongside to strengthen and encourage those who call upon Him.

Meanwhile, the cry goes up, 'How long O Lord?' The day will come when His sword is unsheathed and His judgment unleashed. Meanwhile, He alone is able to give strength for endurance, and ultimately, just punishment to the unrepentant proud.

For prayer and reflection

Lord, I add my cries for mercy to those of countless thousands enduring contempt. Holy Spirit, shed the Father's love into their hearts, imparting worth and dignity. Amen.

Rescued!

'We have escaped
like a bird out
of the fowler's
snare …' (v.7)

The pilgrim looks back to an historic incident when Israel was threatened with crushing defeat from a seemingly invincible army that was rapidly closing in on them. They were trapped! In such a case, David 'went down to the stronghold' and 'inquired of the LORD' (2 Sam. 5:17,19).

Are you feeling trapped? Perhaps by grief, debt, illness, guilt? Many things can conspire to hem us in. We can panic, or manoeuvre and manipulate, or seek to distract ourselves; but if the Lord is 'not on our side' or rather if we are not on the Lord's side, the 'torrent' will prove too strong for us and 'sweep us away'. The psalmist here reflects with huge relief that there was another way: there was Someone bigger to turn to. 'Our help is in the name of the LORD.'

The Lord invites us, 'Call to me' (Jer. 33:2). Jesus said, 'In this world you will have trouble' (John 16:33); He did not promise us instant relief. A very dear friend of mine recently died. He suffered from a very painful, crippling disease for 27 years. Not only was he 'trapped' in his distorted body; his wife, who lovingly and patiently served him all those years was also 'trapped'. Yet they were two of the most serene and light-hearted people I have known, always thinking of others, and declaring God's unfailing love. They both knew freedom in their spirits, because Jesus had set them free from the ultimate bondage of sin and self. Now he is completely free, even from the imprisonment of his body.

Jesus proclaimed, 'The Spirit of the Lord is on me … He has sent me to proclaim freedom for the prisoners …' (Luke 4:18). Only He can unlock the prison of guilt and despair; and He can come and sustain us in the midst of suffocating circumstances.

For prayer and reflection

Lord, help me to endure hardship, by calling on Your name and receiving the releasing joy of Your presence. Rescue me from the net of frustration, I pray. Amen.

WEEKEND

Rainbows

For reflection: Genesis 9:8–17
'I have set my rainbow in the clouds …' (v.13)

It rains; then the sun shines and a beautiful, vivid, iridescent arch of many colours appears in the sky. This glorious phenomenon evokes pleasure and awe. It is somehow mysterious and yet stunningly simple; we know it is the refraction of light passing through millions of droplets of water in the atmosphere. Yet prosaic scientific analysis cannot rob it of its splendour.

But it also has a reason for being, as well as a scientific cause: it exists to remind us of God's faithfulness. Noah and his family stepped out of the ark into the mud and looked around at the waterlogged landscape steaming in the sun. Then, arching over the desolation, they saw this incredible spectrum of colour. God speaks: 'Never again will there be such total devastation from a flood.' The rainbow is His covenantal sign.

Floods have come and gone, some have caused life to be destroyed, but not all life. An enduring rhythm has been established: seedtime and harvest, summer and winter, cold and heat, day and night. This is God's providential grace to the righteous and unrighteous. Meditate and worship.

Natural disasters shock, damage and inconvenience us. Earth is subject to decay, groaning and waiting for liberation.

Read Romans 8:18–25 during the weekend.

Rooted **in God**

How many women do you know who are 'unshakable'? This psalm says that those who trust in the Lord are unshakable; it is not a natural characteristic, but born out of learning to trust God when everything around is being shaken. It is not stubbornness, stoicism or a phlegmatic temperament: it is an inner peace and strength that is rooted in confidence in God.

What 'shakes' you? Running out of money? Finding out that your husband is unfaithful? Discovering that you are pregnant? Wrecking the car? We live in a real world; these things are happening all the time, and worse, and yes of course they rock us, but they need not destroy us.

My friend has recently become a widow. At Christmas, her family was joyfully celebrating her husband's fiftieth birthday; three weeks later, this wonderful, energetic, loving, hardworking and apparently healthy man, dropped like a stone, and died of a heart attack.

My friend is deeply grieving; but she tells me that when everything seems overwhelming, she turns to Jesus and finds His peace. It seems so perplexing that her husband should be taken. But she is trusting in God. Her roots go down deep into Him.

I believe the part of a seaweed plant which clings to a rock is called the 'standfast'. There may be a tempestuous storm; but although the seaweed is tossed about, it remains attached to the seabed. 'We have this hope as an anchor for the soul, firm and secure' (Heb. 6:19).

The psalmist is 'battered' by the thought that there is wickedness in his land, evidently unpunished. But he also trusts God to bring perfect justice ultimately. Peace lies in trust, not vengeance.

Psalm 125

'Those who trust in the LORD are like Mount Zion, which cannot be shaken but endures for ever.' (v.1)

For prayer and reflection

Lord, I am increasingly aware of my frailty, as weak as a piece of seaweed. But You are a rock beneath me yet surrounding me. I am only strong in You. Amen.

Tears turn **to laughter**

Psalm 126

'The LORD has done great things for us, and we are filled with joy.' (v.3)

There is a poem, written at the end of the First World War by Siegfried Sassoon which begins, 'Suddenly, everyone burst out singing!' The same sense of joy breaking out after a time of severe trial is in this psalm. Scholars seem agreed that the first line should read: 'When the Lord restored the fortunes of Zion ...' which certainly could refer to the return of exiles after a period of captivity, but could also be describing the heady sense of release that occurs after any major disaster when the danger is past.

The sheer delight and exuberance awakes in us a wistful envy: it must be wonderful to be so deliriously happy! Have you known times like that, or is that still a dream? I believe God wants this to be a repeated experience, not just once in a lifetime. Many people experience a breathtaking sense of liberty when they first realise that Jesus has purchased their freedom from sin and death. I also felt a rush of heady joy when I was first filled with the Holy Spirit, and on many subsequent occasions.

However, the psalmist does not forget that there are seasons of grief. We can be like the dry water courses in the Negev, desert lands in the South; but just as they can be suddenly flooded when the spring rains come, so God's presence can surprise us and turn mourning into dancing.

The picture at the end is of a sower 'burying' seed. Many women weep over lost children, broken relationships, backslidden sons. Turn your tears into prayers of faith. You can hardly believe it now, but God promises that there will be a harvest of overwhelming joy. Keep sowing in faith! It's amazing what God can do!

For prayer and reflection

Lord Jesus, thank You that You endured the cross for the joy that was set before You. You kept going in faith, and the harvest is endless! Amen.

Building for life

his psalm is a comment on the futility of expending major time and effort on projects not initiated by God. If you are an older woman, you may be able to look back on a life which is the product of seeking God and living His way. You have made choices based on His Word and have not regretted it. There is fruit for your labour! But you may be a younger woman who is full of ideas, energy and enthusiasm and you work hard to fulfil your dreams. The trouble is, if you have been blessed with children they are demanding and time-consuming. This psalm reminds us that God is very interested in family life, and the way we prioritise.

'Unless the LORD builds the house, its builders labour in vain.' (v.1)

I had five children; I also had lots of great ideas about what I wanted to achieve, and began to feel frustrated that the children seemed a hindrance to my ambitious schemes! It was through meditating on this psalm that God began to show me that I must see my life from His perspective. Children are not a hindrance: they are an inheritance!

One day I was pushing the baby in the pram, with mounds of shopping piled underneath and the other children around me. I felt tired and sorry for myself. A lady passing by asked, 'Are all these children yours?' 'Yes,' I answered. 'Oh you lucky, lucky woman!' she exclaimed.

I realised that I was indeed rich! I had a full quiver! I began to pray that God would help me to shape my 'arrows' so that they could be fired out to do maximum damage to the enemy and advance the kingdom of God.

Perhaps you need to see your children in a different light. In the end, you will not be ashamed when you hear God's 'Well done'.

For prayer and reflection

Help me, Lord, to build well! Help me fill my time productively, to sleep well at night knowing I am doing what You have ordained. Amen.

The promise **of fruitfulness**

Psalm 128

'Your wife will be like a fruitful vine within your house; your sons will be like olive shoots …' (v.3)

You may not be a wife, but there are promises here for all who 'fear the LORD'. Blessings are promised to those who relate to God reverently and obediently. The picture here is of orderly life, peace and prosperity, and continuity in the order of things: a hard-working man, a contented wife, a happy family, who in turn grow up and produce their own children.

Immediately one wants to take issue: we know plenty of good, hard-working people whose lives do not exhibit this sort of peaceful joy! Their lives are dogged by misfortune and trouble!

Blessings are not automatic. The subject of the poem is 'one who fears God'. That can take courage and faith. 'Walking in God's ways' is not always easy; and 'blessings and prosperity' must be seen from God's perspective. Sometimes it involves being content with a little, not a lot.

Moreover, if we would see promises come to pass, we need to lay hold of them and pray them, declaring God's Word in faith. The enemy wants you to have anything but a quiet peaceful life. He will seek to wreck your walk with God, your marriage and your children's peace. The 'fruitful vine' here alludes to the wife being fertile; but we can also take it in the New Testament sense, 'bearing fruit in every good work' (Col. 1:10), one of which is prayer.

When my kids were small, I would look at them around the dining table, imagining them like olive shoots! It helped me to pray for them to grow up as well-nurtured plants, into mature fruit-bearing trees. Sometimes I had to battle in prayer as they went through turbulent times. But God is faithful; I am now seeing my children's children also being trained to walk with God.

For prayer and reflection

Lord, thank You that You have appointed me to bear fruit. Help me to abide in You, the vine, and to bear fruit for Your glory (John 15). Amen.

The price **is paid!**

Often people like to keep records. They write diaries, try to beat world records, list mileage in their cars, they record outgoings and incomings in their bank accounts. In Psalm 130, someone has been reviewing his wrongdoings, ending in a pit of despair. His sins seem overwhelming; does God keep such a list? If so, his position is hopeless!

And yet ... there is hope. The God he worships will forgive. But He is not like some capricious god of the surrounding nations who can never be placated or who, on the other hand, might just turn a blind eye. No, sin has to be punished.

The previous psalm speaks of one suffering serious oppression. The psalmist feels so beaten up that he compares it to having his back scourged until it resembles a ploughed field. This brings prophetic whispers to us of the Suffering Servant of Isaiah 53:5: 'the punishment that brought us peace was upon him, and by his wounds we are healed'; and 'I offered my back to those who beat me' (Isa. 50:6). The psalmist aches to know forgiveness, with the intensity of a weary night watchman looking for the first light of dawn.

Perhaps you are oppressed with a sense of guilt. You have a record of your wrongs: you just can't forgive yourself, or receive forgiveness! You are 'in the depths', in darkness. But there is light waiting to break in! Someone's back has already been beaten for those sins; there is no need of further payment! You have His promise: 'If we confess our sins, he is faithful and just and will forgive us our sins and purify us ...' (1 John 1:9).

Put your name in Psalm 130:7: 'O _____ put your hope in the LORD, for with the LORD is unfailing love and with him is full redemption.'

Psalms 129; 130

'If you, O LORD, kept a record of sins, O Lord, who could stand? But with you there is forgiveness …'
(130:3–4)

For prayer and reflection

Lord, I am unutterably grateful that You have wiped my record clean by paying the price with Your own blood. You declare me 'Not guilty'! Amen.

WEEKEND

Stones

For reflection: Joshua 4
'What do these stones mean?' (v.6)

I live near a beach covered with pebbles of different colours: greys, whites, reds and browns. I like to wander on the beach picking up stones which attract me by their smoothness or strange shape.

In this Bible story, Joshua instructs the people to pick up stones from a riverbed. They could do this because the river was unusually dry; God had stopped the water flowing so that 40,000 armed men could cross. Twelve men, one from each tribe, were appointed to carry a large stone over. As the last one reached the opposite bank, the waters roared back.

Joshua piled the stones up to mark the spot. Later, when their children would ask, 'What are these stones here for?' their parents who had experienced the miraculous event could tell the story.

Wouldn't you think they would never forget? Sadly, we are prone to forget wonderful things God has done for us. The Bible often urges us to recall past miracles: it stimulates faith in a mighty, unchanging God. '… I will remember your miracles of long ago … What god is so great as our God?' (Psa. 77:11,13).

Keep a record in a journal to remind yourself (and the next generation) what great things the Lord has done for you.

A childlike spirit

I loved breastfeeding my babies. There was something immensely satisfying about putting a hungry, crying infant to the breast, its cries instantly subsiding as it sucked away with all its might! Amazing to think that I had the wherewithal to sustain its life and enable it to grow! But a *weaned* child is another stage.

Recently, I enjoyed reading to my two-year-old grandson. He needs more to placate him now than milk. He wants relationship, undivided attention, visual stimulation and the soothing sound of my voice telling a story. But he can only absorb elementary words and pictures; I can't concern him with 'great matters'.

There are many mysteries that we will never understand this side of heaven, and we must not kid ourselves that we have the capacity to understand them, even if God were to reveal them. The psalmist here is realistic about his limitations as a human being. But he is not allowing himself to be frustrated; he has decided to be content with intimate relationship, rather than intellectual knowledge.

Physicists, brain surgeons, rocket scientists, archaeologists, Greek scholars and many other eminent minds have huge ability to delve into areas of knowledge, and we thank God for them. But some areas are far beyond even them; some matters are 'too wonderful' for them because they belong to God alone; matters of life and death, evil and suffering, heaven and hell.

As we walk with God, we are constantly learning, and He graciously unveils some of His secrets. But we will come to the edge, where 'the secret things belong to God', and that is where we must be content simply to rest beside Him trusting Him, as a child trusts her mother, that He knows best.

Psalm 131

'... I have stilled and quietened my soul; like a weaned child with its mother ... is my soul within me.' (v.2)

For prayer and reflection

Lord, I want to creep up to You, sit with You, quiet and still, and just enjoy being with You. Amen.

A dwelling place for God

Psalm 132

....

'This is my resting place for ever and ever; here I will sit enthroned, for I have desired it.' (v.14)

....

For prayer and reflection

....

Dwell in me, Lord! I want Your presence right at the centre of my life. Help me to remember my body is Your temple and use it accordingly. Amen.

This psalm, probably written early in the reign of Solomon, begins with a plea to remember David, who vowed so passionately to build a house for God; yet it was Solomon who built the Temple.

David's first attempt to bring the ark (symbolic of God's presence) into Jerusalem had ended in tragedy because he had neglected to observe God's ordinances for moving it (1 Chron. 13:5–13). It lay for three months in Kiriath-Jearim (Jaar, in v.6) before being brought back in joyful procession, carried by priests (not a stumbling ox-cart).

Solomon, the next anointed king, now prepares to install the ark in its new resting place, calling on God to accept him, perhaps mindful of what happened when David acted presumptuously.

In the second part, God affirms His sworn oath to place one of David's descendants on the throne. He goes on to declare not only His desire to dwell among men, but the blessings He will pour out on them: abundant provision, garments of salvation, joy.

God always desired close relationship with human beings, walking in the garden with Adam and Eve. With their disobedience came the anguish of separation. But God planned to restore that friendship and dwell with men again. The tabernacle in the wilderness was the first expression of this intent; then Solomon's Temple, and later, other temples.

Then came the Incarnation, 'The Word became flesh and made his dwelling among us' (John 1:14). It all culminated with the revelation of the apostles: 'Don't you know that you yourselves are God's temple and that God's Spirit lives in you?' asks Paul (1 Cor. 3:16). The astonishing truth is that He chooses now to tabernacle in His people by His Spirit.

Precious **unity**

Last year, we had a family reunion, when all my children, assorted spouses and grandchildren had a weekend together. I loved it! I also love being in my church. If I have been away for any reason, I relish coming back into the family of God.

Unity is not natural to fallen humans. It comes from above, as this psalm shows, like dew falling, or like anointing oil poured over the priest's head. It comes from the wonderful harmony enjoyed by Father, Son and Holy Spirit.

Jesus told His disciples, 'On that day you will realise that I am in my Father, and you are in me, and I am in you' (John 14:20); an amazing statement of intimate relationship. God is relational; He wants that aspect of Himself mirrored in His people. He loves to see His family enjoying being together.

In 1 Corinthians 12, the Church is described as a body with Jesus as the head; 1 Peter 2:9 also speaks of us as a 'royal priesthood'. So this picture of oil poured on Aaron's head and running down over his robes brings to mind the Holy Spirit being poured out on the Church, bringing oneness of heart.

Psalm 134 carries on this idea of a group of priests, united by their love for the Lord and their oneness of purpose. The Levitical singers were on duty day and night (1 Chron. 9:33), worship being their primary occupation.

To bless God is to acknowledge gratefully all that He is and all He has done for us. The last verse depicts the Maker of heaven and earth pouring down blessing on Zion, the city of God where His people dwell in harmony. As Paul exhorts, let us 'Make every effort to keep the unity of the Spirit through the bond of peace' (Eph. 4:3).

Psalms 133; 134

'How good and pleasant it is when brothers live together in unity!' (v.1)

For prayer and reflection

Lord, I am not always in harmony with my brothers and sisters. Help me to see where I can be more loving, forbearing and forgiving, that the world can see something of You in our unity. Amen.

Grace, mercy and love

Helena Wilkinson

Helena Wilkinson trained in counselling at CWR. She is the author of nine books including the bestseller *Puppet on a String*, her personal account of overcoming anorexia. In 1994 she founded Kainos Trust, a charity for eating disorder sufferers, of which she was Director. In January 2004 the charity merged with Swansea City Mission. Helena is now based at the mission's retreat centre, Nicholaston House, on the Gower Peninsula where she runs courses. She is a freelance writer and international speaker. For further information visit her website www.helenawilkinson.co.uk

Grace, mercy and love

John 1:1–18

'We have seen his glory, the glory of the One and Only … full of grace and truth.' (v.14)

December can be a stressful month with added extras in our daily routine and the accumulation of all that has gone on during the year. As the days become busier and tick by quickly it can be frighteningly possible to lose sight of all that Advent holds. I hope that even if you are experiencing the rush leading up to Christmas, reading this month's Bible notes will not be yet another thing to fit into busy December days. Instead I pray that you will find yourself with time and space to see the glory of God as you look beyond the babe in the manger to Jesus, your Saviour and King.

Our theme for the month is grace, mercy and love. Grace, mercy and love are manifested through Jesus and showered upon us that we might pour them out to others.

What is your experience of grace and I wonder how you would describe it? Grace is a word that we may not use much and so perhaps we have a limited understanding of it.

Whilst running a retreat last year, I asked each person to write down expressions of God's grace. The responses were delightful: God's riches at Christ's expense; a gift of God's blessings through His love; God's tears for us and His joy in us; the unmerited favour of God; God's acceptance of us despite His knowledge of us; God's smile of approval and assurance; the abundance of heaven free of charge; an expression of God's kindness and longsuffering; that which liberates.

Some of their words opened my eyes afresh. If our understanding of grace is limited then I wonder if, as a result, we rob ourselves of some of the riches that God has for us?

For prayer and reflection

This Advent, expand my vision, Lord, I pray. Envelope me in Your grace; let me see Your glory, move me beyond seeing Jesus the babe to embracing Jesus my King. Amen.

Burning bright

WEEK 48 FRI

Isaiah 61

'... to bestow on them a crown of beauty instead of ashes ... gladness instead of mourning ...' (v.3)

When I consider the limitations of my own definition of grace compared to the root meaning, it is the difference between a flickering candle and a roaring fire! Likewise there is no comparison between the grace that God showers on me and that which I attempt to offer others! If only we could understand God's gift to us and freely give to others what He places in us.

I wonder how your definition of grace compares to that of Scripture? Hebrew and Greek words (the languages in which Scripture was originally written) are vastly richer and more complex than the English, with 'grace' being no exception.

One of the Hebrew words for grace, *chen*, indicates the pure, unmerited favour of God. We don't deserve the goodness that God lavishes on us, and yet He still pours it out from a heart of generosity that offers a way out of our selfish human acts. His grace is an invitation to provide, preserve and be merciful.

Another Hebrew word, *chesed*, which is said to be one of the most important Old Testament words, is translated as loyal love or loving-kindness. It emphasises intensity in kindness and love and speaks of God's covenantal relationship and communion with us. It promises preservation, reaches out in forgiveness, shows itself in hope and produces praise.

There's so much more we could say about *chesed*, but the words already mentioned above bring life to me. What about you? What does it mean to you to be in communion with the Creator of heaven and earth who offers you genuine forgiveness for your foolishness? Can you trust Him to create beauty out of ashes and clothe you with a garment of praise instead of mourning?

For prayer and reflection

God of grace! You clothe me with righteousness; You forgive my sins; You offer me hope; You provide what I need; You preserve my life! I praise and thank You! Amen.

WEEKEND

His star! God's glory!

For reflection: Matthew 2:9

'… they went on their way, and the star they had seen in the east went ahead of them until it stopped over the place where the child was.'

The image we often have surrounding the birth of Jesus is a nativity scene: Joseph and Mary in a stable, Jesus in a manger and shepherds and Wise Men, or Magi, looking on. However, it is thought that there was possibly about a two-year gap between the time when the shepherds visited and when the wise men came bearing gifts. Scripture doesn't say how many wise men there were; because there were three gifts we have assumed there were three. There had to be at least two because the word is in the plural, but there could have been many!

The Magi were led to where Jesus was by a star resting above the house. The star is referred to as *His* star – the King of the Jews' star. The root meaning of the Greek word for star is 'radiance' or 'brilliance'. God's radiance led the Wise Men to the place where Jesus was.

What will draw you closer into Jesus' presence this weekend, this month, this Advent?

Grow **with love**

I wonder what aspect of God's grace has the greatest impact on you at this moment in your life? For me, I think it has to be the concept of intensity in kindness and love. Last Christmas I was given a bag with the words 'All Things Grow with Love' on it. It's so true; we grow when we are planted in an environment of love.

Our own attempts at kindness and love can be transient and inconsistent, but God's love, grace and mercy are so different. He is a God who is '... merciful and gracious, Slow to anger and abundant in lovingkindness and truth' (Psa. 86:15, NASB).

God's grace expressed through kindness and love not only has intensity that saturates every part of our being, but it lasts forever. 'Praise the LORD! Oh give thanks to the LORD, for He is good; For His lovingkindness is everlasting' (Psa. 106:1, NASB). In a world where things change so quickly and do not last, it is good to know that God's love for us will not end.

Another aspect of God's grace that has had a profound effect on me recently is His covenantal relationship – His promise never to leave me or forsake me. God's commitment to us as His children is constantly portrayed throughout Scripture. One of my favourite readings is God's promise to Joshua after Moses' death. Joshua was getting the people ready to cross the Jordan River into the promised land. God said: 'As I was with Moses, so I will be with you; I will never leave you nor forsake you' (Josh. 1:5). Because the Lord will never leave him nor forsake him, Joshua is instructed to be strong and courageous (vv.6–7) and not to be terrified or discouraged (v.9).

Psalm 86:1–13

'Among the gods there is none like you, O Lord ...'
(v.8)

For prayer and reflection

There is no one like You, O God, no one whose grace, mercy or love compares to Yours. I long to offer to others just a fraction of what You give me. Change my heart, I pray. Amen.

No expectation! **No obligation!**

**Romans
6:1–11,23**

'… but the gift of God is eternal life in Christ Jesus our Lord.' (v.23)

Are you ever given a card or present at Christmas by someone for whom you've not bought anything? Perhaps you feel awkward and quickly write a card in return or rush around and buy something to wrap up and offer back to free you of the twinge of guilt or of being shunned or judged for not reciprocating the gesture! In our culture we are conditioned to feel that if we are given something we owe something in return. But grace is not like this. Grace is an expression of unconditional giving.

The New Testament Greek word for grace, *charis*, emphasises favour without expectation of payback. The motive is sheer generosity on the part of the giver and results in delight, charm, pleasure and loveliness poured out in full measure. Not only does *charis* express a grace that affects man's sinfulness and forgives the repentant sinner, it also leaves him bounding in joy and thankfulness! It is an expression of favour, acceptance, kindness and gratitude.

For prayer and reflection

Lord, I repent of selfishness. Help me to give to You and others without wanting anything in return and help me to receive without needing to pay back. Amen.

Wouldn't it be wonderful if we could give generously to others without the desire that they give to us in return? I know I still sometimes tend to give with the hope that I'll have something too! Perhaps we do the same with God – give Him our praise and adoration with a bit of a hidden agenda (the unspoken words of 'If I worship You, I know You will bless me' or 'because I worship You I expect my prayers to be answered according to *my* will'). Maybe you're not like that, but I have to admit that at times, albeit often subconsciously, something of this nature has gone on inside me!

I wonder if we need to separate our giving and receiving: to give generously, without expectation, and to receive gratefully without obligation?

In times **of distress**

he words 'grace' and 'mercy' may roll off our tongues as we explain what God is like or acknowledge Him for who He is, but I wonder in what ways we see mercy differently from grace?

'Grace describes God's attitude toward the lawbreaker and the rebel; mercy is His attitude toward those who are in distress'.* It is God's grace that is offered for the forgiveness of sins and His mercy which is offered towards our suffering. As our passage today highlights, we who had no hope have been saved by grace, which is a pure gift from God who is rich in mercy concerning the distress that our sinfulness and separation from Him creates.

One passage of Scripture in which God's mercy is called upon very clearly is Lamentations. The book, most likely written by Jeremiah, is constructed in mournful poetry and speaks of someone with a broken heart. The words comprise candid descriptions of the depressing accounts of the destruction of Jerusalem, the honest confession of sins that contributed to the destruction and the pleading and desperate cries for God's intervention. It's a melancholic book but, throughout, the words are interwoven with the hope of God's mercy. 'The LORD's lovingkindnesses indeed never cease, For His compassions never fail. They are new every morning ...' (Lam. 3:22–23, NASB).

Is there a situation in your life at the moment where it would be helpful to follow the same pattern as Jeremiah? To offer an explicit description of the struggle, an honest confession of your responsibility/sin, to pray without ceasing for an answer and thanksgiving that He is a God of mercy?

*C.F. Hogg and W.E. Vine, *Notes on Galatians*.

Ephesians 2:1–13

'But because of his great love ... God, who is rich in mercy, made us alive with Christ ...' (vv.4–5)

For prayer and reflection

Thank You that in the midst of my brokenness, Lord, Your compassions never fail. When I am encompassed by darkness, show me the dawn of Your mercy, I pray. Amen.

Sharing in our **sufferings**

Hebrews 4

'For we do not have a high priest who is unable to sympathise with our weaknesses …' (v.15)

The heading in the New American Standard Bible for the chapter in the notes yesterday, Lamentations 3, is: 'Jeremiah shares Israel's afflictions'. To me this sums up mercy! Mercy is not feeling sorry for someone because of the pain or struggle being endured and wanting to do something about it; mercy is *sharing* in the *pain* of the affliction and suffering, or even sharing in the suffering itself! It is not feeling *for*, but feeling *with*.

The Lamentations passage creates a picture of moving from calling upon God to have mercy to having mercy on others.

As our reading today reveals, we have a High Priest, Jesus, who can sympathise with our sufferings. The New Testament Greek word for 'sympathise' is a derivative of two other words meaning 'together with' and 'suffer'. Jesus suffers together with us and, in the same way, we are to suffer with, or have mercy upon, others.

During some of the most painful times in my life all I have been able to pray is 'God have mercy'. What am I saying – 'God help me'? Yes! But when I think about the meaning behind mercy what I am, in fact, saying is, 'God feel with me.'

What's also amazing is that because Jesus sympathises with us it opens the door for us to approach the throne of grace with confidence in order to receive mercy (v.16). We pray, 'Have mercy', not to be relieved of the difficult situation in which we find ourselves, but to draw closer to God. What an awesome thought! When you face trials and tribulations, can you hold on to the fact that Jesus feels with you and is gently leading you to God's throne, where you will meet with Him and be transformed even if your circumstances don't change?

For prayer and reflection

Jesus! You know! You understand! You care! Thank You that You feel with me when I am in pain. Help me to receive Your mercy and to show Your compassion to others. Amen.

Called to **love mercy**

Matthew 5:1–12

'Blessed are the merciful, for they will be shown mercy.' (v.7)

Throughout the Gospels Jesus shows mercy and sets us an example of how we are to be towards other people. Two of the well-known accounts of His mercy being evident are the Samaritan woman at the well (John 4) and the woman caught in the act of adultery (John 8). In both these situations I see respect (breaking cultural barriers in speaking to a Samaritan woman) and tenderness (not bringing about shame on the adulterous woman by avoiding looking into her eyes).

It can be such a challenge to do as Jesus did. Don't you long for God's character to rub off on you, and for mercy to triumph over judgment (James 2:13)? As hard as it is, my desire is to do as 'the LORD Almighty says: "Administer true justice; show mercy and compassion to one another"' (Zech. 7:9).

It is easier to do these things for those to whom we are close or who appear loveable, but what about those who have wounded us? We are called to show mercy to them, too, and it is good to remember that showing mercy does not only benefit the one to whom we offer it – it benefits us as well! 'A man reaps what he sows' (Gal. 6:7).

God's love and mercy change us and bear fruit in our lives; '... because of his great love for us, God, who is rich in mercy, made us alive with Christ ...' (Eph. 2:4–10), therefore our loving others and having mercy towards them will, no doubt, bear fruit in their lives.

Isn't it a nice thought that how we are has the potential to bring freedom to another?

For prayer and reflection

I want to be a fruit-bearer in the lives of others, Lord. Help me to love those whom I find it hard to love and to bless those who persecute me. Amen.

WEEKEND

Faith leads to joy

For reflection: Matthew 2:10
'When they saw the star, they were overjoyed.'

The Magi only had to see the star for their faith to rise and for them to be overjoyed with the knowledge that a King had been born. Don't you think they might have been glad that they had seen the star but at the same time held back a little on their excitement until they saw for themselves that it led them to Jesus and they knew for sure they had got it right?

Do you rejoice when God shows you something even if you have not yet seen the result, or do you tend to wait for the evidence first so that you know for sure that's what He's said?

Maybe you rejoice a bit but also hold back, or don't tell others in case you have got it wrong! The Magi expressed exuberant joy and gladness of heart as soon as they saw the star. The Greek word used for overjoyed is *chairô* which is related to *charis* (one of the words for grace) indicating that the joy and rejoicing experienced is a direct result of God's grace. It is also related to a Hebrew word referring to a young sheep or lamb, skipping and frisking for joy.

What can you express gladness of heart for this weekend?

What is **love?**

When I was considering a subject to write on this month I thought of grace and mercy, but I realised that these cannot truly exist outside of love; 1 Corinthians 13 speaks of the excellency of love. It points out that if we have the different gifts but do not have love then our gifts are like a clanging cymbal and profit nothing! Likewise, if we offer 'grace' and 'mercy' without love then our vain attempts aren't worthy of the fullness of the words upon which we have reflected during the past week or two.

But what is love? I wonder how *you* define love? Our concept of love is often based on what we have been taught as children or on an image portrayed through the media and arts. One day someone was praying for me to know for myself that God loved me. I thought that I would *feel* wonderful afterwards. I didn't feel anything! But I had deeper security.

The bottom line is that 'God is love' (1 John 4:16). His very nature is love. And the call on our lives, being made in His image, is to reflect love. 'We love because he first loved us' (1 John 4:19). We are to live love. Erich Fromm once said: 'Love is not primarily a relationship to a specific person; it is an *attitude*, an *orientation of character* which determines the relatedness of a person to the world as a whole, not towards one "object" of love. If a person loves only one other person and is indifferent to the rest of his fellow men, his love is not love but a symbiotic attachment' (*The Art of Loving*). Somewhat thought-provoking do you not think?

To be loved is our deepest need; to offer love (first to God and then to others) is our greatest satisfaction. How satisfied do you feel in life?

Psalm 89:1–20

'I will sing of the LORD's great love for ever …' (v.1)

For prayer and reflection

Father God, may I be someone who lays a foundation of love before I ever attempt to do anything else. I so need to change. Help me please! Amen.

319

Fountain of life

Psalm 89:14, 21–37

'… love and faithfulness go before you.' (v.14)

I n the Old Testament God reveals Himself to the people of Israel as a God of unconditional love. His gift of Himself in the choice and creation of 'My people' is totally unsolicited, undeserved and unmerited. In Deuteronomy 7 it is very clear that God's love for His people was not based on anything they were, anything they had or anything they could do.

God is described as abounding in love (Psa. 86:15), of which He has a limitless supply. His love is constant, unfailing and unshakable (Isa. 54:10). It is unflagging, inexhaustible and incapable of error. It is steadfast (Psa. 62:12, RSV), which means that it is fixed, unchanging and loyal.

God's love endures forever (1 Chron. 16:34); it is eternal (Jer. 31:3). When all else has passed away, God's love will stand strong (1 Cor. 13:8). 'It is as strong as death … burns like a blazing fire … Many waters cannot quench love; rivers cannot wash it away' (Songs 8:6–7). It is the fountain of life (Psa. 36:9), and it is new every morning (Lam. 3:23).

For prayer and reflection

Thank You, Lord, that my life is a work in progress. Keep showing more of the person You want me to become and open my eyes to see the fullness of who You are. Amen.

His love is overwhelming, tender, intimate and powerful. It speaks of acceptance, affection, justice, compassion, truth and faithfulness. It clothes us, embraces us and never disappoints us! It is the refiner's fire that burns with desire for new life – our new life. His love for us is so great that He is continually working on us. Does that fill you with joy or gloom? I like the idea of being worked on! I see it as exciting and wait with eager anticipation to see what God does next. How often do you take time to look back over your life and consider the ways in which God has fashioned you and enabled difficult situations to form who you are today?

Emotional **sustenance**

Do you know God as provider and are you able to see His provision for you in everyday situations?

We consider God's physical or practical provision – He provides us with a home, friends, finances – but what about emotional provision and substance? Do you believe that He can meet your emotional needs? I see the essence of His nature, His love, as that which we require for emotional stability.

God's love is the provider of: *Comfort* (Psa. 119:76) – God calls us to His side. He exhorts and consoles us. He soothes us in times of grief and fear. *Security* (Isa. 54:10) – His love opens the door to freedom from doubt, anxiety and danger. *Support* (Psa. 94:18) – He lends strength to us, holds us in position and prevents us from falling, sinking or slipping. *Guidance* (Psa. 26:3) – He leads and directs in the way we should go. *Affirmation* (Zeph. 3:17) – God's love expresses His delight in us and affirmation of us as He delights in us and rejoices over us. *Protection* (Psa. 5:12) – His love surrounds us and keeps us from harm or injury. The word 'surrounds' comes from the same verb as 'encompass'. We are encompassed or encircled by God's love and there is no safer place to be.

I have often pondered on what it is that keeps us in that safe place and each time I come back to the fact that there are biblical principles to which we are to adhere. 'Lay hold of my words with all your heart; keep my commands and you will live ... Do not forsake wisdom, and she will protect you ... She will set a garland of grace on your head ...' (Prov. 4:4–9). God's love encircles us but we have a choice to stay in that safe place by walking in His ways.

Psalm 119:65–80

'Let your compassion come to me that I may live ...' (v.77)

For prayer and reflection

Lord, God, Your love is the foundation to my security. You are the rock upon which I am to build my life and Your principles are for my good. Teach me Your ways. Amen.

An **act of will**

'For God so loved the world that he gave his one and only Son …' (v.16)

G od expresses His love for us in a number of ways, but the ultimate expression of His love is no doubt through Calvary (1 John 4:10). God allowed His only Son, who was without sin, to take on the sin of the whole world so that we can be justified and reconciled through Jesus' death and resurrection and know His love and forgiveness (Rom. 5:8–10).

Jesus perfectly embodies God's love. The Greek word for such love is *agape*; a self-sacrificial love that seeks the good of all (Rom. 15:2) and manifests itself in servanthood. Jesus did nothing out of selfish ambition or vain conceit, but out of humility (Phil. 2:3), taking on the very nature of a servant (Phil. 2:7). Through this act, it is clear that servanthood and unconditional love are synonymous. It is also clear that Jesus entrusted Himself to God (1 Pet. 2:23), because He was secure in God's love for Him.

When we, fallible human beings, use the word love it tends to be more of a *philea* love which means to be a friend, or an *eros* love which is romantic. Both of these are focused on feelings, unlike *agape*, which is not solely feelings-based but is a sacrificial love that chooses to love. Jesus didn't *feel* like going to the cross. He made a *choice* to go to the cross; it was a decision based on an act of love. God doesn't love us because He *feels* like loving us but because He is Holy and morally perfect, and His nature is love.

Can you make the choice to love not only God who is perfect but those who don't act very lovingly towards you?

....

For prayer and reflection

....

Lord, open my eyes to the times that I have not acted in love. Teach me what it is to love sacrificially; not only to love when I want to but when it actually costs me to do so. Amen.

Blessings **in return**

A s we love God, my experience is that our eyes are opened more to see His blessings. Throughout the Psalms the psalmists offer back to God, in worship, the revelation God gives them of His own character. So, too, as we soak up the very nature of God, His love in us enflames us. The Lord watches over us (Psa. 145:20), rescues us, protects us, answers us, delivers us and honours us (Psa. 91:14–15), comes and makes His home with us (John 14:23) and brings about security (Prov. 8:21).

Ezekiel 34:11–31

'… there will be showers of blessing.' (v.26)

Out of the fullness we receive, we have an overflow, and as a result we are to clothe ourselves with compassion, kindness, humility, gentleness and patience (Col. 3:12); to love not just with words or tongue but with actions and in truth (1 John 3:18).

Loving others involves moving towards them in vulnerability, with an element of self-disclosure, and without self-protection. For God did not give us a spirit of timidity but a spirit of power and love (2 Tim. 1:7). If we remain in God and our love flows out of that fountain of love, we are able to draw close to others, and as we put on the breastplate of love (1 Thess. 5:8) it makes it safe to do so. We do not have to fear that we will be hurt or rejected by them, for there is no fear in love (1 John 4:18). To be rid of that fear we must put our dependency not in the unstable reactions of other people but in God, our solid rock, until in boldness we can say, 'I depend on God alone; I put my hope in him. He alone protects and saves me; he is my defender, and I shall never be defeated' (Psa. 62:6, GNB).

For prayer and reflection

Thank You, Lord, for Your blessings. You make Your home with me so that even in the midst of turmoil and stress I can know Your peace. Amen.

WEEKEND

Worship comes first

For reflection: Matthew 2:11
'On coming to the house, they saw the child with his mother Mary, and they bowed down and worshipped him …'

I t's interesting that when the Magi arrived the first thing they did was worship. When we arrive in such a setting the first thing we tend to do is hand over the presents and then give thanks to God. The New American Standard Bible expresses that the Magi *fell down* and worshipped. In order to fall down they would have had to lay aside their gifts and give their all to worshipping.

In New Testament Greek one word is used for worship, *proskune* – to reverence towards and to kiss. The Anglo-Saxon word is 'worth ship' – to value. There are 560 worship-related scriptures in the Bible. The biggest book in the Bible, Psalms, is a songbook, a worship book. Above all else, God wants worshippers. Worship is not so much what we *do*, but what we *are*. We are not called to *do* worship, but to *be* worshippers.

Is there a call in this for you to change your priorities?

Most excellent way

I remember as a child being fascinated by the 'Love is ...' cartoons, but these were futile compared to Paul's words about love in 1 Corinthians 13. A friend of mine, Jackie, wrote a beautiful meditation on them. I suggest you take time to ponder the words and allow them to sink in.

Love is patient. Patience is waiting, patience will wait, until 'it' happens, whatever 'it' is. Patience is tolerating each other's mistakes and stupidities. It is forbearance, serenity, long suffering and perseverance.

Love is kind. Kindness is about having a heart of compassion, particularly for the unlovely ... giving a hand or a hug when you least feel like it. It is about being considerate, generous, thoughtful and understanding ... being tender-hearted. You cannot be kind and avoid your neighbour; kindness is about being neighbourly.

Love does not envy. Envy is your pain and discontentment about another's success or superiority. Envy compares you with others, with dissatisfaction; it doesn't recognise that you are a limited edition of one. Envy covets another's looks, relationships, status, possessions and even his or her spirituality ... is never content.

Love does not boast. It does not say or think, 'I am better than you', 'I am more spiritual than you', 'I feel superior to you'.

Love is not proud. Pride easily gets offended, is often over-sensitive. Pride says, 'How dare they!' 'How could you!' 'Why me?' Pride only breeds quarrels and discontent.

Love is not rude. It does not abuse, is not abrupt, and is always respectful, even when wronged.

What do you find most personally challenging in these first six 'Love is ...' statements?

---

1 Corinthians 13:1–13

'But the greatest of these is love.' (v.13)

For prayer and reflection

Father, Yours is the most excellent way. You have given us direction in the way You want us to love because You know what is best for us. Help me to love as You describe. Amen.

325

Rich **rewards**

**Hosea 10:12;
14:1–9**

'… reap the fruit of
unfailing love …'
(10:12)

Paul goes on to describe a further nine aspects of love in his letter to the Corinthians. I wonder as we continue with the meditation how the words speak to you?

Love is not self-seeking. It never says, 'Me first', it always thinks more highly of others than itself. *Love is not easily angered.* It always tries to see things from the other's point of view. It always listens well before responding. It doesn't jump to conclusions but is self-controlled and calm. *Love keeps no record of wrongs.* It is unconditional. It does not harbour resentments to throw up when convenient. It does not become bitter but always forgives.

Love does not delight in evil but rejoices with the truth. It hates sin but celebrates honesty. It speaks the truth, risking rejection and receives the truth even when it hurts. *Love always protects.* It never exposes or humiliates. *Love always trusts.* It always gives another chance. *Love always hopes.* It always looks for the good and believes for the good. *Love always perseveres.* It does things time and time again and never gives up. *Love never fails.*

I read today's passage around the same time as reading 1 Corinthians and it spoke to me of the importance of sowing righteousness by loving in the way in which Paul describes, and in so doing we will reap the fruit of such love and will break up our unploughed ground. What ground in your life is unploughed? We often cry out to God asking that He would change us or heal us, but more recently I have been aware of how He changes me as I live according to His ways. Loving others and conducting my life according to how Paul describes love not only blesses those around but sets me free!

For prayer and reflection

I want to reap the fruit of unfailing love. I want to taste its sweetness in my mouth and offer its goodness to those around. May it happen, Lord! Amen.

Time **to be free**

O ver the past couple of days we have looked at those wonderful words in 1 Corinthians 13. Sir Walter Scott once said: 'Love rules the court, the camp, the grove and men below and heaven above; for love is heaven and heaven is love.' Love is the centre point from which all in our life must be directed. 'Love feels no burden, thinks nothing of trouble, attempts what is above its strength, pleads no excuse of impossibility; for it thinks all things lawful for itself, and all things possible' (Thomas à Kempis).

'One word frees us of all the pain and weight of life. That one word is love' (Sophocles). I think that love frees us because God is love and when we operate in love, His life is breathed into us. The love of which the Bible speaks is not static – it is active, alive and brings about change.

Jesus' love speaks of having time for people, of unconditional acceptance, regard and empathy. Can you see how His love demonstrated the following through these accounts? *Restoration*: Zacchaeus, a wealthy tax collector, is brought to the place of paying back and giving away (Luke 19:1–10). *Transformation*: Bartimaeus not only received his sight but turned to follow Jesus (Luke 18:35–43). *Liberation*: the Samaritan woman is offered living water welling up to eternal life in exchange for her thirsty adulterous life (John 4:4–28). *Hope*: a mourning widow sees her only son brought back to life (Luke 7:11–15). *Satisfaction*: the feeding of the 5,000, which provided not only physical nourishment but also spiritual encouragement (John 6:5–14).

In what way has God's love recently changed you? Does your love for others release change in them?

Isaiah 40:25–31

'... those who hope in the LORD will renew their strength.' (v.31)

For prayer and reflection

Your love brings freedom, O God. Liberate me in the areas where I am bound. Set me free to worship You and to be the person You made me. Amen.

Cherished **and chosen**

Psalm 33

'... he who forms the hearts of all, who considers everything they do.' (v.15)

I find it liberating to contemplate God's love for people whatever our background or mistakes. This is highlighted through Jesus' interactions during His time on earth as we saw yesterday. We are dearly loved by God, so greatly loved in fact that it was out of the overflow of His love that we even came into being! Cardinal Hume once summed up this thought by saying: 'We love people because they are there, but with God it is the other way round: because he loves them they are there.'

'God picked us out for Himself as His own – in Christ before the foundation of the world; that we should be holy and blameless in His sight ... He foreordained us (planned in love for us) to be adopted as His own children through Christ Jesus, in accordance with the purpose of His will – because it pleased Him' (Eph. 1:4–5, AMP). 'We are a chosen people, a royal priesthood, a holy nation, a people belonging to God' (1 Pet. 2:9). 'How great is the love that the Father has lavished on us, that we should be called children of God!' (1 John 3:1).

For prayer and reflection

What incredible love the Father has for us, and so what is it that keeps us in the place of not feeling loved? Could it be that in our making a choice to love God we discover His love for us? Does it begin with us seeking after God with all our heart rather than just telling ourselves that He loves us? 'Then you will seek Me, inquire for, and require Me (as a vital necessity) and find Me when you search for Me with all your heart. I will be found by you, says the Lord, and I will bring you back from captivity' (Jer. 29:13–14, AMP).

Thank You, Father, that I am here because You chose me. Place within me the desire to seek after You with all my heart, not part of my heart but *all my heart*. Amen.

Sheltered **and secure**

'… under his wings you will find refuge …' (v.4)

If we do not seek after God with all our heart and in so doing discover the depth of His love for us, it can be easy to deviate into seeking happiness in the form of conditional love. Such love demands and fails, and as a result we can then easily hold in our minds a picture of God's love as being conditional, having strings attached and bound to result in rejection or disappointment at some stage.

Without the certainty of God's unconditional love for us and our expression of our love for Him, we can end up manoeuvring our world in order to feel safe, and in so doing fail to relate to God and others in a way that brings satisfaction. When we seek after God with all our heart and spend time in His presence, in relationship with Him, His love flows in abundance, and we cannot fail but love in return. Love is made complete/perfect (1 John 4:17); meaning that those who abide in God, are possessed of the very character of God. This in itself enables us to love ourselves, others and God.

In what ways have you endeavoured to create safety outside God's love? Has it really resulted in a lasting sense of feeling safe?

My experience is that it is God's love for us that makes it possible for us to have a positive and loving attitude towards ourselves. Without God's love for us perhaps self-love could be vulnerable to egocentricity and narcissism.

God's love and acceptance of us as we are, despite our failings, lays the foundation for us to love and accept ourselves, which in turn is the prerequisite to loving others. 'If I do not love myself, I can only use others; I cannot love them' (John Powell, *Unconditional Love*).

For prayer and reflection

You are my safe place, O God. Under the shelter of Your wings is where I find security. There is no better place to be. Amen.

WEEKEND

The greatest gift

For reflection: Matthew 2:11

'Then they opened their treasures and presented him with gifts of gold and of incense and of myrrh.'

After they had worshipped, the Wise Men presented the gifts they had brought to honour the birth of Jesus – gold, incense (frankincense) and myrrh. All three speak symbolically of who Jesus is.

Gold is a sign of royalty and kingship, emphasising that the baby is indeed a king, and no ordinary king either – the Messianic King. But how did Gentile, Babylonian astrologers know anything about the birth of a Jewish king? Was it because they studied the stars or because prophecies of Daniel were written in the city of Babylon, part of them in their language – Aramaic?

The second gift, frankincense, represents sweet aroma, prayers and intercession, but it is also the symbol of deity. It was part of the special scent burned on the Altar of Incense within the Holy Place. The smoke from the incense came into the very presence of God in the Holy of Holies. This gift emphasises that Jesus is God.

The third gift, myrrh, is symbolic of suffering and bitterness, and the resin is associated with death and embalming. The gift was prophetic of Jesus dying to pay the price for our sins.

Spend time reflecting on the symbolism of these gifts.

Journey to **wholeness**

e started by focusing on grace and mercy, and then we looked at love. To conclude I would like us to place these in the context of wholeness. Grace, mercy and love all form part of what I see as five steps which, among other things, help us to move towards wholeness.

1. Clothing ourselves with the Lord Jesus Christ.
2. Allowing intimacy to lead to forgiveness.
3. Renewing our minds.
4. Blessing others and receiving blessing.
5. Embracing suffering.

Our verse for today tells us to 'clothe ourselves with the Lord Jesus Christ'. What do these words mean to you? To me they speak of my choosing, on a daily basis, to dress myself in the nature of Jesus, rather than waiting for God to bestow these things upon me! How would you clothe yourself with Christ? I think I would start by spending time in His presence, simply worshipping Him.

To spend time in the presence of God is to spend time bathing in His love. Peter Gillquist in his book *Love is Now* says, 'God's love not only makes possible the complete cleansing of our lives allowing us a fresh, new confidence before Him, but He also declares us free and unshackled from the law. Through Christ we have been ... placed upon what Isaiah the prophet called the "highway of holiness". It is a spacious, scenic, and, unfortunately, seldom-travelled road to freedom.'

If you have time, read Isaiah 35. The whole chapter portrays the wonder of new life: vibrant, colourful, scented blossom bursting forth out of parched, dry and dead land, the outcome of clothing ourselves with Jesus Christ. Life-quenching water is ours, where previously we were thirsty and fainting.

Romans 12:9–21; 13:14

'Rather, clothe yourselves with the Lord Jesus Christ ...' (13:14)

For prayer and reflection

Thank You, God, that You haven't finished with me yet! You are the potter and I am the clay. Go on moulding me and making me into who You want me to be.

Intimacy **and forgiveness**

1 John 1:5–10;
2:1–14

'If we confess our sins, he is faithful and just and will forgive us our sins …' (1:9)

When we love someone deeply and his or her character is one of compassion, goodness, kindness, grace and mercy, we long to spend time with that person and doing so is a pleasure because it has a positive effect on us. It is the same with God. My experience is that in the place of intimacy with God I am changed: one of the ways I am changed is that I become more loving and forgiving.

It is out of God's great love that He extends His forgiveness to us. Let us become forgiving people too. Are there people you need to forgive? Have you remembered to include yourself? If you are struggling to forgive, have you tried going back to the place of praising God for who He is and soaking up His grace, mercy and love extended to you?

Which do you find most difficult: believing that if you confess your sin God is faithful and just to forgive you; forgiving those who have wounded you; or forgiving yourself?

For prayer and reflection

Your forgiveness is like a breath of fresh air to me; a new beginning. Thank You, Lord. I praise You that You withhold no good thing from me. Amen.

Whilst we find that we are more prone to want to forgive when we are clothed with the character of Jesus there is still a choice to be made both to forgive and not to do those things that hinder our intimacy with God. The NASB says '... make no provision for the flesh in regard to its lusts', and when we look more deeply at these words we gain insight into the steps we can take. 'Make no provision' means to think ahead, understand, reflect and work on our carnal mind. Lusts refer to the desires that result from the condition of the diseased soul.

Are you thinking ahead about what might cause you to stumble and cost you your peace?

Un-muddling our minds

Continuing from yesterday with the importance of working on our carnal mind, Paul in his letter to the Romans makes it clear that the Word of God contains power, the power of God's love to transform our lives by the renewing of our minds (Rom. 12:2), but first we need to let the Word dwell in us richly (Col. 3:16). Do you tend simply to read the Word of God or do you ask God to implant and root truth into your mind (James 1:21, AMP)?

One of the greatest breakthroughs I have had in changing my thinking came through reading a book by Liberty Savard called *Shattering Your Strongholds*. In it she talks about the principle of binding ourselves to Jesus and loosing ourselves from that which has held us captive. Amongst other things I began to bind my mind to the mind of Christ and to loose my mind from negative thoughts and painful past experiences. How do you deal with your negative thoughts?

Whatever way we deal with negative thinking, we need God's love poured out into our hearts through the Holy Spirit (Rom. 5:5). The words 'poured out' suggest that His love is free-flowing. The New English Bible says 'God's love has flooded our innermost heart.' The tense of the verb is perfect, 'which implies a settled state consequent upon a completed action'. As J.I. Packer points out in his book *Knowing God*, 'The thought is that the knowledge of the love of God, having flooded our hearts, fills them now, just as a valley once flooded remains full of water'.

Don't you long for the valley to be full and remain that way? I do! Is there anything you need to do today to allow the valley to fill?

Colossians 3:1–17

'Set your mind on things above ...' (v.2)

For prayer and reflection

Father, flood my innermost heart with Your love. Cleanse my mind and bind it to the mind of Christ, that I may dwell on things above and not on earthly things. Amen.

Songs **of blessing**

Zephaniah 3:9–19

'... he will quiet you with his love, he will rejoice over you with singing.' (v.17)

Clothing ourselves with the Lord Jesus Christ, and His characteristics of, amongst other things, grace, mercy and love, and allowing the overflow of His love in us to be evident in terms of forgiveness and the renewal of our minds, results in a blessing. God's love is like a river which flows and will keep flowing until it hits something which blocks it. One of the greatest blockages is our attempt at self-preservation. Are you in that place of being able to say to God 'I surrender' or is self-preservation and the need to hide your vulnerability still strong in your life?

I have used self-preservation strongly over the years but know that letting go of my own attempts at keeping pain out do not carry the blessing that is found in trusting God with my pain. It is incredibly powerful when in that place of vulnerability you let down your guard, allow the river of God's love to flow and listen for His still small voice which at times is spoken and at times sung. In our verse for the day Zephaniah says of God, '... he will rejoice over you with singing'. Psalm 32:7 says, 'You are my hiding place; you will protect me from trouble and surround me with songs of deliverance.' He is protecting us, surrounding us, delivering us in His song. As you surrender to Jesus, what is He singing over you?

For prayer and reflection

Singing is associated with joy. Isaiah 51:3 says, '... he will make her deserts like Eden, her wastelands like the garden of the LORD. Joy and gladness will be found in her, thanksgiving and the sound of singing'. And Isaiah 51:11 says, '... They will enter Zion with singing; everlasting joy will crown their heads.' Can you receive that for yourself today?

I desire new songs. I want to sing a new song in praise of You, my God, and I want to hear Your songs over me. Amen.

Embrace suffering

WEEK 52 FRI

t the beginning of the week I mentioned that grace, mercy and love all form part of what I see as five steps which, amongst other things, help us to move towards wholeness. The last of these five steps is embracing suffering. Suffering is uncomfortable and we live in an age that is focused on getting rid of our pain, and yet today's passage tells us to exult in our tribulations and, strangely, Jesus came as the suffering servant.

We have seen over the past few days how we must clothe ourselves with Christ's love, but as the Amplified Bible tells us, this should be to such an extent that it 'compels us' (2 Cor. 5:14); that is it 'controls, urges and impels' all we do. We need to clothe ourselves with Jesus' love to such an extent that we are urged to embrace suffering when it comes and impelled to persevere, see character change and walk in hope.

When I look back over the past few years I see that my life has carried great suffering, but I also see that it is in these times that I have come face to face with the reality of God's grace, mercy and love.

Would I have preferred to have had a life free of that amount of pain, misunderstanding, illness, loss and mistakes? Of course! Therefore, would I have preferred not to have known the depths of God's grace, mercy and love in that pain? Of course not! The pain was worth the reward of tasting God's goodness. Which would you rather have: as much of a pain-free life as possible or as much of God's grace, mercy and love at any cost?

Romans 5:1–11

'... suffering produces perseverance; perseverance, character; and character, hope.' (v.3–4)

For prayer and reflection

Lord, I want Your grace, mercy and love more than anything and as hard as it is, I am prepared to pay the cost because I know You only want the best for me. Amen.

Courses and seminars

Publishing and new media

Conference facilities

Transforming lives

CWR's vision is to enable people to experience personal transformation through applying God's Word to their lives and relationships.

Our Bible-based training and resources help people around the world to:
· Grow in their walk with God
· Understand and apply Scripture to their lives
· Resource themselves and their church
· Develop pastoral care and counselling skills
· Train for leadership
· Strengthen relationships, marriage and family life and much more.

CWR Applying God's Word
to everyday life and relationships

CWR, Waverley Abbey House,
Waverley Lane, Farnham,
Surrey GU9 8EP, UK

Telephone: +44 (0)1252 784700
Email: info@cwr.org.uk
Website: www.cwr.org.uk

Registered Charity No 294387
Registration No 1990308

Our insightful writers provide daily Bible-reading notes and other resources for all ages, and our experienced course designers and presenters have gained an international reputation for excellence and effectiveness.

CWR's Training and Conference Centre in Surrey, England, provides excellent facilities in an idyllic setting – ideal for both learning and spiritual refreshment.